The Legendary Past

Michael Oakeshott on
Imagination and Political Identity

Natalie Riendeau

ia

imprint-academic.com

Published in the UK by
Imprint Academic, PO Box 200, Exeter EX5 5YX, UK

Distributed in the USA by
Ingram Book Company,
One Ingram Blvd., La Vergne, TN 37086, USA

ISBN 978-1845407605

A CIP catalogue record for this book is available from the
British Library and US Library of Congress

The index for this volume was produced by Indexing Specialist (UK) Ltd.

For my family, friends,
and teachers

Contents

Abbreviations

CPJ   *The Concept of a Philosophical Jurisprudence*

EM   *Experience and its Modes*

HC   *On Human Conduct*

HCA   *Hobbes on Civil Association*

LHPT   *Lectures in the History of Political Thought*

MPME   *Morality and Politics in Modern Europe*

OH   *On History and Other Essays*

PFPS   *The Politics of Faith and the Politics of Scepticism*

RP   *Rationalism in Politics and Other Essays*

RPML   *Religion, Politics and the Moral Life*

VMES   *The Vocabulary of a Modern European State*

VL   *The Voice of Liberal Learning*

WH   *What is History? and Other Essays*

.

Introduction

Humans, Michael Oakeshott declares, inhabit a 'mysterious and menacing universe'.[1] While this might sound like a dramatic declaration (an example of Oakeshott's colourful use of language), a hyperbole the meaning of which may be easily dismissed or deemed to be only of relatively minor importance to his thought, such a conclusion would, in fact, be mistaken. The idea that humans are able to find their way in a menacing and mysterious universe, more than this, that they are successful in making themselves at home in such a world, an achievement that paves the way for 'human living-together', to use Hannah Arendt's expression, and consequently the political, is key to Oakeshott's political thought.[2] Humans, he observes, know who they are, where they are in the world and how they came to be there. In other words, they have an identity, a sense of self-consciousness as well as of self-understanding, as do their societies.[3] Oakeshott contends that it is human imagination, by means of an 'epic story of the past', which endows humans and their societies with identity, self-consciousness and self-understanding, thereby ensuring the successful accomplishment of the 'primordial activity of making ourselves at home in the world'.[4] [5] Imagination creates a world of sense and meaning for humans to inhabit.

This kind of reflection on the human need to inhabit a world of sense, a world created by the human imagination, is perhaps not commonly associated with Oakeshott. The key role played by imagination in Oakeshott's thought is largely overlooked or ignored by commentators. Yet, imagination is a fundamental element of his reflection on the political since it is intimately linked to the problem of human living-together and of identity, two themes which characterize his thought. When examining the question of human living-together,

---

[1]   WH: 347.
[2]   H. Arendt, 1993: 141.
[3]   WH: 345–372.
[4]   WH: 348.
[5]   RP: 180.

commentators typically focus on Oakeshott's writings on the civil association and the civil condition. In *On Human Conduct*, Oakeshott defines the civil association as a rule-articulated association. Within the context of the civil condition, all that is required to sustain human living-together is the continued recognition of the authority of the rules of association as rules.[6] The idea that a common good or a common purpose might ensure social cohesion is rejected by Oakeshott as this sort of endeavour belongs to enterprise association and impedes individual freedom. Civil association allows individuals to pursue their own projects so long as this is done within the context of the recognized rules of the association.[7] Nothing more is required to sustain an association of individuals. As for political activity, it is the modification of the rules in order that they conform to current social realities. That is, individuals who live together over time develop a political tradition of behaviour, or practice, and, when well versed in their tradition, are able to identify the changes it intimates in order to ensure its coherency and, thus, its continued existence.[8] Oakeshott contends that such an understanding of civil association and of the civil condition cannot be founded.[9] In this sense, the conception of the political he defends is devoid of foundations. This leads observers to conclude that Oakeshott's political thought is antifoundationalist.

I do not dispute the fact that civil association and politics understood as a traditional manner of behaviour are fundamental to Oakeshott's conception of the political. However, this is only a partial view of Oakeshott's thought on the political, one that overlooks the fundamental question of identity. Although little attention is paid in the secondary literature to the matter of identity, it is of central importance to Oakeshott, and, in particular, to his conception of conservatism. A political society cannot function without an identity and sense of self-consciousness. This is simply inconceivable for him. Rules and judicial procedure cannot endow a society with its identity and ensure its continued existence. Simply put, human living-together requires more than the continued recognition of the authority of rules by *cives*. This is where imagination, political imagination to be precise, comes into play. In what follows, I show that it is by means of what Oakeshott terms legends of political life that the political imagination endows a society with its identity and sense of self-consciousness. What is more, legends of political life ensure that a society's identity and sense of self-

---

6   *HC*: 128.
7   *HC*: 313–317.
8   *HC*: 162–173.
9   *HC*: 173–177.

consciousness do not become corrupted by change. Political legends, then, satisfy certain basic human needs: they situate us in time and space; they tell us who we are, where we are in the world, how we came to be here and they project us into the future. In short, what legends of political life provide is stability. It is these creations of the political imagination that stabilize a political society. Given legends' stabilizing function in relation to society, I claim that they in fact serve as weak foundations for the political. Thus, although civil association, tradition and practice may be devoid of foundations, a society's identity and sense of self-consciousness are founded. Legends of political life are a very specific kind of foundation. They may be said to be a type of constructed foundational narrative. For this reason, I argue that Oakeshott is a weak foundationalist in the constructivist tradition established by Hannah Arendt, who is well known for her theoretical work on foundational narratives. In other words, I do not make the claim that foundations understood as '"prior" claims about unquestionable or sacred or natural premises' are to be found in Oakeshott's political thought.[10] Rather, by foundations I mean stabilizing constructs for the political. It is in this sense that political legends should be understood to found the identitary element of human living-together.

I posit that Oakeshott's concept of legends of political life is composed of three constitutive elements: reflection upon the political, the practical past and poetry. Perhaps the best known legend of political life, and the most successful in Oakeshott's opinion, is the one created by the poets of Ancient Rome and which tells the story of the foundation of Rome. No other legend of political life, Oakeshott contends, has surpassed the Roman legend in its ability to endow a people with an identity, a sense of self-consciousness and of self-understanding. The Roman political legend is a text-book example of how together poetry, the practical past and foundational reflection upon the political work to stabilize a society. The story of the foundation of Rome by Romulus is an event recalled to mind from the practical past, the story of which, constructed or created by Roman poets, endows Roman political society with its identity and heightened sense of political self-consciousness. As the case of Rome highlights, the practical past is emblematic and not historical. As such, the practical past transforms the lives, utterances, achievements and sufferings of mankind into emblematic actions and pronouncements. These emblems are not evoked in a procedure of critical historical enquiry, but are recalled to mind as unproblematic images. Their purpose is not to inform us about the historical past. Rather, they are valued for their present usefulness.

---

10 J. Seery, 1999: 471.

As the example of Rome demonstrates, their usefulness lies in their capacity to stabilize the practical present. To this end, the practical past constitutes a vocabulary of practical discourse composed of symbolic characters. This practical discourse contains emblems of all the virtues, vices and predicaments known to mankind.[11] Political societies have recourse to this vocabulary of symbolic characters in order to secure their identity. Romans, Oakeshott contends, astutely secured their identity by recalling the emblematic action of the foundation of Rome by Romulus. Moreover, the kind of reflection upon the political the Roman legend of political life affords allowed Roman society to understand its political experience in the idiom of general ideas. The Roman political legend founds Roman society in so far as it endows it with its heightened sense of political self-consciousness and its identity. However, the foundational role of political legends does not end here. The Romans augmented their legend by binding all political change back to the story of the foundation of Rome, thereby augmenting the original foundation. The Roman legend, therefore, created and recreated the values of Roman society, thereby guarding it against the corruption of its consciousness.[12]

It is in this sense that I posit that Oakeshott's weak foundationalism is a form of 'contingent foundations' since it unites permanence and change. While poetry and the practical past together endow a society with its identity, it is poetry which guards it against the corruption of its consciousness. For this reason, I claim that Oakeshott's conservatism is deeply poetic and, furthermore, that it is profoundly influenced by the Roman practice of preservation and augmentation of the legend of political life. In sum, then, legends of political life are poetic constructs which recount the story of an event from the practical past and which afford for a foundational kind of reflection upon the political. It is my position that legends of political life, such as Oakeshott conceives of them, serve as constructed foundations for the political and sustain human living-together by endowing a society with and, thereafter, guarding its identity.

Thus, my aim is to establish the importance of imagination for Oakeshott's political thought. It is imagination which resolves what Oakeshott terms the human predicament, by which he understands the primordial human need to make ourselves at home in the world. Imagination, by means of a constructed foundational narrative, achieves this by founding a political society's identity and ensuring its

---

11 For Oakeshott's discussion of the pratical past, see *OH*: 10–48.
12 For Oakeshott's discussion of the Roman political experience, see *LHPT*: 176–251.

continued existence. It follows, then, that when the fundamental role played by imagination in regards to identity is acknowledged, it informs us that far from being devoid of foundations, Oakeshott's political thought belongs to the Arendtian constructivist tradition of foundations. In other words, establishing the importance of imagination for Oakeshott's political thought demonstrates and confirms his weak foundationalism.

Summary of the Chapters

The book comprises five chapters. The aim of Chapter 1 is to situate Oakeshott within the contemporary debates on foundations. I begin with an overview of the debates surrounding the question of foundation in modernity and then focus upon the contributions made by Richard Rorty, Judith Butler and Hannah Arendt, all three of whom attempt to stake out a middling position between permanence and contingency, as I argue Oakeshott does.[13] In this respect, I pay particularly close attention to Arendt and the ideas she develops concerning constructed foundational narratives in relation to Ancient Rome and the early United States.[14] Both of these political societies were able to tie permanence and change together by means of constructed narratives centred upon the remembered past event of foundation. The Roman and American identities are thus founded, but may also be augmented in so far as change may occur so long as all political change is tied back to the original foundation. Therefore, foundations for Arendt are contingent in that they found a political society, but also allow for its augmentation. It is this sort of contingent foundation which I claim constitutes Oakeshott's weak foundationalism. Furthermore, like Arendt, the single most important source of inspiration for Oakeshott's conception of foundational narratives is the political experience of the Ancient Romans. Both claim that the Romans were by far the most masterful creators of foundational narratives. Hence, while Oakeshott may not be a foundationalist in what John Seery terms the Edenic tradition, which conceives of foundations as prior claims about unquestionable premises, Oakeshott's use of imagination, specifically of legends of political life, situate him within what Seery defines as the Arendtian constructivist tradition, a form of weak foundationalism which unites permanence and change.

In Chapter 2, I set out to determine what precisely legends of political life are and how they function. I do this with reference to the modes of experience and philosophy. I begin with philosophy. I ask

---

13 See Rorty 1988, Butler 1991 and Arendt 1963 and 1993.
14 See Arendt 1963.

whether legends of political life are a form of philosophical reflection upon the political. I show that legends are not philosophy; rather, they are weak foundational reflection upon the political, similar to Oakeshott's characterization of political doctrines. While legends and doctrines engage in the same sort of political reflection, legends are not, for that reason, political doctrines. For Oakeshott, political doctrines, in that they transform a political tradition of behaviour, or a political practice, into an ideology or abstract system of ideals and rights, pose a danger in so far as they make it less easy for societies to change.[15] This is not the case with political legends, which allow societies to represent their political experience to themselves and, thus, enable them to gain self-knowledge and to be self-critical without turning that experience into a fixed ideology or doctrine. What is fixed is a political society's identity which may always be augmented since the legend of political life may be augmented as opposed to doctrines, ideologies and systems of ideals which are fixed and finished. Therefore, I posit that legends are a legitimate manner for a society to understand its political experience in the idiom of general ideas. The chapter concludes with a discussion of the relationship between legends and history. Although legends tell the story of a past event, I establish that, for Oakeshott, they are not in fact historical narratives. Rather, they belong to the practical past the purpose of which it is to stabilize an otherwise problematic present by endowing a society with its identity, its sense of self-consciousness as well as with its sense of self-understanding and of self-knowledge. The chapter ends by highlighting the importance of the practical past for Oakeshott's thought. The second chapter, then, analyses two of the three constitutive elements found in legends. The third, poetry, is broached in Chapter 3 in the context of a discussion concerning the poetic character of human activity and is further developed in Chapter 4.

The purpose of Chapter 3 is to justify my claim that Oakeshott's conception of the political is foundationalist. I demonstrate that Oakeshott defends a mixed form of politics understood as a mixture of permanence and contingency. Oakeshott exposes this conception of the political in full in *The Politics of Faith and the Politics of Scepticism*. There, he argues that faith (permanence, foundation) and scepticism (contingency) are the two poles which define the boundaries of modern political activity. Political activity cannot be sustained at either end of the political spectrum as these extreme conceptions of the political are self-destructive. In other words, faith and scepticism need each other.

---

15   *WH*: 154.

In the absence of this partnership, the political cannot survive.[16] Politics, then, is necessarily a mixture of faith and scepticism, that is, of permanence and contingency and, as such, implies some kind of foundations for the political. Oakeshott calls this exploration of the middling ground between faith and scepticism the politics of the mean in action. Thus, faith is a legitimate part of politics. Yet, the politics of the mean in action is not the only mixed form of the political he identifies in *The Politics of Faith and the Politics of Scepticism*. In addition, he also discusses the modern alliance between scepticism and natural rights (faith). Whereas Oakeshott defends the politics of the mean in action, he rejects the 'mésalliance' between scepticism and natural rights outright.[17] Why is the one form of mixed politics acceptable to him and the other deemed to be illegitimate? The answer may be found in the first 'Tower of Babel' essay, which forms part of the collection *Rationalism in Politics*, where Oakeshott identifies two forms of morality: the morality of a habit of behaviour (contingency) and the morality of the reflective application of a moral criterion (faith, Rationalism). He considers two mixed forms of morality: one dominated by the habit of behaviour and the other by the reflective application of a moral criterion. He concludes that only the mixed form of morality dominated by a habit of behaviour, that is, by contingency, is sustainable.[18] The same reasoning may be applied to the mixed forms of politics. Only the politics of the mean in action is deemed by Oakeshott to be a legitimate form of politics because contingency dominates the mixture, whereas the alliance between the politics of scepticism and natural rights is dominated by faith, in other words, by an overly reflective manner of behaviour. Thus, I argue that since faith (permanence) is a constitutive element of Oakeshott's conception of the political, there is necessarily a foundational element present as well. However, it is a very specific sort of foundation, one that must conform to the criterion established by Oakeshott which is that contingency must dominate the mixture. Hence, the concept of 'contingent foundations' I borrow from, but define differently than, Judith Butler.[19] I argue that legends of political life are just such a type of foundation. Finally, the chapter ends by broaching the matter of poetry. While discussing the forms of morality in 'Tower of Babel', Oakeshott asserts that an overly reflective manner of behaviour essentially denies 'the poetic

---

16   *PFPS*: 106–124.

17   *PFPS*: 82–83.

18   *RP*: 467–480.

19   Butler 1991.

character of all human activity'.[20] Poetry is here understood as a contingent manner of behaviour. I contend that it is poetry which allows
for the reconciliation of permanence and contingency in human
activity. By this I mean that poetry is at once contingent and, as I show
in Chapter 4, it is also permanent and foundational in that it guards a
society's identity against the corruption brought on by change.

The objective of Chapter 4 is to establish that poetry is also a constitutive element of legends of political life. Legends are poetic constructs; that is, they are the creations of poetry. It is poetry, Oakeshott
asserts, which makes society live.[21] This means that poetry, by the intermediary of legends, serves a fundamental purpose in relation to the
political and society. As I show, it is poetry which guards a society
against the corruption of its consciousness by making it conscious of
itself and by creating and recreating its values. Legends, and
Oakeshott's use of poetry in this context, constitute a kind of foundation for the political. Put another way, society needs common
references in order to sustain its identity and it is poetry, through its
creations, legends, which provides society with them. It will be
objected, however, that the role I claim for poetry in relation to society
by the intermediary of legends respects neither Oakeshott's conception
of poetry nor the absolute independence he posits for the modes of
experience. It will be argued that Oakeshott defends a theory of art for
art's sake. That is, art is not a sign or a symbol. This is not to say that it
holds no meaning, only that its meaning is internal to itself rather than
in external references. For this reason, art transmits no message, be it
political or other.[22] In addition, it will be pointed out that, for
Oakeshott, the modes of poetry and practice simply cannot interact as I
claim they do given that the modes of experience are independent of
one another. This argument does represent a serious challenge to my
position. However, in answer, I point out that in spite of Oakeshott's
staunch position, the relationship between practice and poetry is ambiguous in his thought. He himself observes that poetry's emancipation
from the mode of practice has been long and difficult, and, significantly, that it has only been uncertainly achieved in modernity. The
reason for this, I argue, is that humans need the meaning and messages
as well as the signs and symbols legends carry and transmit since they
allow persons, as well as societies, to understand themselves and the
world around them. Poetry emancipates itself with difficulty from the
authority of practice because the political in particular needs the

---

[20] *RP*: 479.
[21] *RPML*: 94.
[22] See Campbell Corey 2006.

foundational stability legends provide. Legends, then, I contend, are a mixture of poetry and practice. They are poetic constructs which endow a society with its identity and guard it from corruption. Thus, legends are a weak foundation for the political.

In order to better understand how legends of political life work contingently to found the political, and, more particularly, a political society's identity, in Chapter 5 I explore the Roman and English legends. The chapter begins with an in depth look at what Oakeshott considers to be the most successful legend of political life: the one generated by the political experience of Ancient Rome. I make the case that the Roman legend of political life serves as the model and ideal for Oakeshott's own concept of foundational narratives. He asserts that no other people in history has constructed a legend, an 'imaginative construction', which surpasses the Roman political legend's ability to endow a people with identity and a sense of self-consciousness.[23] However, what Oakeshott's study of the Roman political legend reveals is that a society's relationship to its legend is more complex than this, it goes beyond endowment of identity. The Roman legend tells the story of the foundation of Rome by Romulus, the event which represents the foundation of Roman freedom. Oakeshott contends that the Romans explored the intimations of the original foundation of freedom in order to increase its meaning. Furthermore, all political change was tied to the original foundation, thereby preserving Roman identity. Thus, political authority came to be understood as the preservation and the augmentation of the foundation, that is, of the Roman political legend.[24] What the example of Rome demonstrates is that political societies perpetually return to their legends to explore their intimations, preserve their meanings and augment them. This, I posit, is the understanding of contingent foundations to be found in Oakeshott's political thought. A political legend which endows a society with its identity and which is at once preserved and augmented.

Since Oakeshott models his concept of legends of political life upon the political experience of Ancient Rome, it may perhaps be contended that they do not fulfil the same role in modernity because they are simply not modern. This, however, would be a mistake. In the second part of the chapter, I show that legends of political life are thoroughly modern and that they construct modern political societies' respective identities just as the Roman legend did for Ancient Rome. Oakeshott, perhaps not surprisingly, gives as an example of modern political legend-making the English legend of political life, which, he claims,

23   *LHPT:* 176–178.
24   *LHPT:* 176–251.

began to be constructed in the seventeenth century.[25] I explore the English legend in order to show that it is consistent with the criteria of legends of political life established by Oakeshott.

In order to highlight the fundamental, contributory role played by legends of political life in relation to a political society's identity, chapters 4 and 5 also treat the importance of identity for Oakeshott's thought. Identity, be it a person's or a society's, is central to Oakeshott's conservatism as well as to his critique of Rationalism. A society's identity is continually threatened by change. The key for a society to conserve its identity is twofold. First, a society must be able to guard its identity; and second, it must find a way to assimilate change without becoming unrecognizable to itself. The discussion of poetry in Chapter 4 shows that only poetry (and least of all politics) is able to guard society's identity against the corruption of its consciousness by creating and recreating its values and ensuring its self-knowledge. For this reason, I contend in that chapter that Oakeshott's conservatism is deeply poetic. As concerns the manner by which change may be assimilated without corrupting a society's identity, I make the case that Oakeshott finds this in the Roman political experience. By exploring the intimations of the original foundation and binding all change back to it, the Romans were able to at once preserve and augment their political identity without losing the sense of who they were. I claim that Oakeshott incorporates this element of the Roman political experience into his conception of the conservative disposition. The idea of exploring a society's intimations and implementing the changes it suggests, thereby augmenting the political practice, is at the core of Oakeshott's understanding of a traditional manner of political behaviour. Therefore, in Chapter 5, I also make the argument that Oakeshott's conservatism is shaped by the Roman political experience. Finally, in the last section of that chapter, I broach the question of identity in relation to modern Europe. Modern Europe's consciousness, Oakeshott contends, is threatened of corruption by Rationalism. This, I argue, is the position he defends in the essay 'Rationalism in Politics'. Since only poetry can guard a society's or civilization's identity from corruption, I contend that Oakeshott's critique of Rationalism is in fact best understood as a poetic attempt, a poetic plea, to save modern Europe from the perils of Rationalism before it is rendered unrecognizable to itself. In this sense, 'Rationalism in Politics' may be interpreted as a work of poetry.

In sum, my aim is to rehabilitate and give its rightful place to imagination in Oakeshott's political thought.

---

[25] *LHPT*:46.

Chapter One

The Problem of
Foundations in
Political Modernity

Introduction

Michael Oakeshott is a philosopher of the human imagination. This statement may at first seem odd or peculiar since we are not accustomed to think of him in these terms. More commonly, he is thought of as a philosopher of tradition and practice, of the civil association, of history and as a formidable critic of Rationalism. Yet, imagination occupies a non-negligible place in his political thought. Nevertheless, imagination and the role it plays in Oakeshott's reflection upon the political are largely neglected by commentators with the notable exception of Noël O'Sullivan who underscores the role played by imagination in Oakeshott's thought in 'disclosing the full texture and complexity of human experience'.[1] This is perhaps due to the fact that imagination and the political imaginary are not deemed to be serious fields of study or are considered philosophically insignificant or unimportant. To this end, O'Sullivan emphasizes that imagination has 'generally been excluded from philosophical attention in modern Western intellectual life'.[2] Yet, I would argue that Oakeshott's conception of the political cannot be understood without taking into account the fundamental role played by imagination. When studying the question of human living-together in Oakeshott's thought, commentators typically focus on the civil association and the civil condition. This is coherent within the context of modernity and modern political thought where the modern state is often theorized in judicial and procedural terms. Moreover, it is all the more understandable since Oakeshott himself claims that civil association is a rule-articulated

---

[1] N. O'Sullivan 2002: 73.
[2] *Ibid.*

association and that the language of civil intercourse is a language of rules.[3] In civil association, human living-together is understood as the recognition of the authority of rules as rules by *cives*. While Oakeshott's theorization of civil association and of the civil condition is certainly central to his reflection upon the political, it is, however, but only one part of his thought on human living-together. For Oakeshott, there is more to the political than the recognition of rules. (He makes this plain in regards to tradition, although it may be argued that the recognition of rules may develop into a political practice.) Fundamental to human living-together is identity which is intimately linked to political imagination. More specifically, politics requires what Oakeshott terms legends of political life which, I claim, found a political society's identity. However, as Terry Nardin and Luke O'Sullivan point out, 'the notion that a society requires such a myth if it is to have the cohesion necessary for civil association [...] is one that he never really worked out in detail; it is the source of some unresolved tensions in his thought'.[4]

My purpose, then, is to show that legends of political life serve as weak foundations for the political. In Chapter 3, I show that Oakeshott's conception of politics as a mixture of contingency and permanence implies foundations. I argue that a contingent form of foundations grounds this mixed form of politics and that political legends are just such a type of weak foundations. Contrary to the majority of commentators, then, I contend that there is a foundational element to Oakeshott's political thought and that legends serve this purpose. In order to support my claim, I make the case that Oakeshott conceives of legends of political life as poetic constructs which stabilize a problematic present by recalling to mind an event from the practical past. To this end, I posit that political legends are composed of three constitutive elements. The first is poetry which endows a political society with its identity and sense of self-consciousness and guards it against the corruption of its consciousness by creating and recreating its values (this is the subject of Chapter 4). The second is the practical past which, for its part, stabilizes a problematic present by ensuring that humans know who they are, where they are in the world and how they came to be there. Thirdly, legends are a foundational kind of reflection upon the political, one which, like political doctrines, allows for the intellectual organization of political ideas (the practical past and political reflection are treated in Chapter 2). Together, then, poetry, the practical past and foundational reflection upon the political are the con-

---

3   *HC*: 124.
4   T. Nardin and L. O'Sullivan 2006: 15.

stitutive elements of legends of political life, a weak foundation for the political. For Oakeshott, by far the most successful legend of political life is the one generated by the political experience of Ancient Rome. In Chapter 5, I explore how the Roman political experience influenced and shaped Oakeshott's conception of political legends and weak foundationalism. Moreover, since it is a legend's poetic character which allows for a society's identity to be radically guarded, I posit in Chapter 4 that Oakeshott's conservatism is deeply poetic. Furthermore, in Chapter 5, I claim that since Oakeshott is profoundly concerned with modern Europe's consciousness, which he believes is threatened of being corrupted by Rationalism, the essay 'Rationalism in Politics', most notably, is best interpreted as a poetic attempt to guard its identity.

The present chapter begins with a discussion of the contemporary debates surrounding the questions of foundations. I examine the approaches to the question taken by Richard Rorty, Judith Butler and Hannah Arendt, all of whom attempt to stake out a middle ground between permanence and contingency. In order to make sense of the debates, I refer to the distinction John E. Seery makes between Edenic and constructed foundations. While agreeing with commentators that Oakeshott is not an Edenic foundationalist, I nevertheless make the claim that he is a weak foundationalist in the Arendtian constructivist tradition. As the discussion will show, both Arendt's and Oakeshott's respective conceptions of constructed foundations are deeply influenced by the political experience of Ancient Rome.

The Problem of Foundations in Political Modernity

The problem of foundations in modernity, simply put, is as follows: is it possible, necessary or even desirable to seek the compatibility of, on the one hand, an absolute such as God or Nature to justify the Law, and the requirement, which characterizes modernity, of submitting everything to the methodical doubt, on the other.[5] Contemporary political philosophers have responded to the problem with a variety of projects and analyses. I examine the ideas put forward by Rorty, Butler and Arendt. I have chosen these authors because all three, like Oakeshott, defend an historical position. Moreover, all three attempt to stake out a middling position between permanence and contingency. To put it in Arendtian terms, like the Romans, their aim is to tie together permanence and change. I claim in Chapter 3 that this is precisely the median position that Oakeshott conceptualizes with the idea of 'the politics of the mean in action', a mixture of the politics of scepticism and of the politics of faith which, I contend, necessarily implies some type of foundational

---

[5]   G. Labelle 1998: 673.

element. Furthermore, Rorty has written on Oakeshott regarding the matter of foundations and finds merit in his conception of a foundationless politics. However, I argue that while Oakeshott's conception of the political is devoid of a certain sort of *a priori* foundations, it cannot do without stabilizing constructs. To this end, the emphasis Rorty places on human 'making' and 'poetic achievement' in an historical world devoid of philosophical foundations echoes Oakeshott's own concern with 'creation' and 'recreation' as well as the poetic dimension of all human activity. In order to better understand the conceptions of foundations defended by Rorty, Butler and Arendt, I adopt the theoretical framework proposed by Seery and argue that the various arguments and positions in regards to the question of foundations fall into one of two traditions or categories: Edenic and construction. Rorty and Butler are representatives of the Edenic tradition, while Arendt is the leading figure of the constructivist tradition. I then proceed to ask how Oakeshott's position on the question of foundations should be categorized. While agreeing with commentators that Oakeshott clearly does not belong to the Edenic tradition; nevertheless, I claim that this does not mean that Oakeshott's political thought is devoid of foundations. On the contrary, I contend that it may be argued that he defends an Arendtian constructivist conception of political foundations.

Richard Rorty, Judith Butler and
Hannah Arendt on Foundations

To echo Arendt, the problem of foundations in political modernity is the problem of the absolute. Do we need an absolute to found the political? How can we manage to justify and legitimate 'all positive, man-made laws' without an absolute such as God, nature or reason and so forth?[6] This problem, or tension, which is inherent to political modernity raises a certain number of additional questions regarding foundations. Chief among them: are foundations necessary for the political in modernity? Are foundations even desirable or do they lead, as certain thinkers hold, to exclusion and oppression? Do foundations become irresistible and thus incontestable?[7] Contemporary thinkers have responded to the problem in a number of ways and offer a variety of analyses which reflect the wide-ranging and diverse character of the debate. However, in an effort to make sense of the debate, theorists are generally identified as 'foundationalist' or 'antifoundationalist'.

Among the most notable contributions to the debate is the pragmatist position defended by Richard Rorty. As such, he is typically

---

[6]   H. Arendt 1963: 160.
[7]   J. Butler 1991.

identified as an antifoundationalist thinker. His conception of the relationship between philosophy and politics is deemed to be pragmatic in that he holds that contemporary liberal democracy does not need philosophical foundations or presuppositions. This is due to the fact that the Enlightenment idea of 'reason', which holds that there is a relation between the 'ahistorical essence of the human soul and moral truth that ensures that free and open discussion will produce "one right answer" to moral as well as to scientific questions', has been discredited by contemporary thinkers.[8] They have abandoned the Enlightenment assumption that religion, myth and tradition can be opposed to something ahistorical such as the nature of the human subject—which, since the seventeenth century, is the topic of philosophical enquiry which has gradually come to replace 'God' as the European culture became secularized.[9] [10] In short, human beings are 'historical all the way through'.[11] The absence of philosophical foundations is not problematic for contemporary liberal democracy, Rorty argues. On the contrary, by means of a discussion of the thought of John Rawls, he attempts to show how the absence of philosophical foundations is beneficial to, and liberates, politics. He posits that in contemporary liberal democracy, justice has become the first virtue. It follows that liberal democracy can be indifferent to philosophical disagreements about ahistorical human nature, the nature of selfhood, the motive of moral behaviour and the meaning of human life.[12] Such topics of philosophical enquiry are simply irrelevant to politics. In sum, Rorty contends that the 'Enlightenment attempt to free oneself from tradition and history, to appeal to "Nature" or "Reason", was self-deceptive'.[13] Rorty's conception of liberal democracy is thoroughly historicist and antiuniversalist.[14] The principal consequence of this for liberal democracy is that 'social policy needs no more authority than successful accommodation among individuals, individuals who find themselves heir to the same historical traditions and faced with the same problems'.[15] Hence, Rorty claims that Rawls retains the Socratic commitment to the free exchange of views, but rejects the Platonic commitment to the possibility of universal agreement and consequently to universal and ahistorical 'truth'.[16] Rorty con-

---

8   R. Rorty 1988: 258.
9   *Ibid.*
10   *Ibid.*: 264.
11   *Ibid.*: 258.
12   *Ibid.*: 261.
13   *Ibid.*: 262.
14   *Ibid.*
15   *Ibid.*: 264.
16   *Ibid.*: 269–270.

tends that 'truth' in the Platonic sense is simply not relevant to democratic politics and, in instances where politics and philosophy conflict, democracy takes precedence over philosophy. In other words, philosophy is not relevant to politics.[17]

Finally, two additional points made by Rorty should be noticed here. First, he claims that contemporary thinkers such as Rawls, and he himself should be included here, are attempting to stake out a middle ground between relativism and a 'theory of the moral subject'.[18] That is, between an ahistorical essence and relativism. In Chapter 3, I make the case that Oakeshott is also engaged in this philosophical enterprise which seeks to identify a middle ground between permanence and contingency. The second point is that a politics devoid of philosophical foundations is able to perceive moral progress as a 'history of making rather than of finding, of poetic achievement by "radically situated" individuals and communities, rather than as the gradual unveiling, through the use of "reason", of "principles" or "rights" or "values"'.[19] As I will show, Oakeshott, similarly to Rorty, argues that poetry plays a vital role in relation to human activity. Although he rejects abstract principles, rights and values as foundations for the political, he attributes a foundational role to poetry since it is legends of political life, poetic constructs, which found a political society's identity.

Another important contributor to the contemporary debates on foundations is Judith Butler, who is highly critical of the role played by foundations in theory. She argues that foundations 'function as the unquestioned and the unquestionable within any theory'.[20] This, coupled with the fact that foundations are constituted through exclusions, and, further, that 'any totalizing concept of the universal will shut down rather than authorize the unanticipated and unanticipatable claims that will be made under the sign of "the universal"', makes foundations a highly problematic theoretical tool with dramatic consequences for the political.[21] In other words, from Butler's 'historically constrained perspective', foundations exclude and, thus, need to be problematically thematized in order to grasp what the 'theoretical move that establishes foundations *authorizes*'.[22] [23] Butler is adamant that she does not want to do away with foundations since the absence of foundations and antifoundationalism belong together to different ver-

---

[17]   *Ibid.*: 270.
[18]   *Ibid.*: 266.
[19]   *Ibid.*: 267.
[20]   J. Butler 1991: 153.
[21]   *Ibid.*: 154.
[22]   *Ibid.*
[23]   *Ibid.*: 153, original emphasis.

sions of foundationalism.[24] Rather, she is attempting to stake out a middle ground between universalism and contingency. Put another way, she contends that the theoretical move that establishes foundations authorizes an element of contingency. In this sense, she maintains that 'I am not doing away with the category, but trying to relieve the category of its foundationalist weight in order to render it a site of permanent political contest'.[25] That is, Butler attempts to devise a conception of 'contingent foundations'. For her, this is of the utmost importance because a social theory committed to democratic contestation 'needs to find a way to bring into question the foundations it is compelled to lay down'.[26] What Butler understands by 'contingent foundations' is akin to the critique of the subject, which, she insists, is not a negation or a repudiation of the subject. Rather, it is 'a way of interrogating its construction as a pregiven or foundationalist premise.[27] The subject, thus deconstructed, is not negated or dismissed, according to Butler. Rather, once a term like 'the subject' has been 'called into question' and 'opened up' it becomes available for a 'reusage or redeployment that previously has not been authorized'.[28] Butler conceives of foundations as 'ungrounded ground'; that is, as terms that must remain open and thereby contestable.[29] For her, contingent foundations thus understood allows for the term to be released 'into a future of multiple significations'.[30] Foundations become a 'site where unanticipated meanings might come to bear'.[31] In sum, Butler attempts to move beyond the foundationalist/antifoundationalist debate by theorizing 'contingent foundations'. Foundations exist to be put into question, and, thus, wherever there is a foundation 'there will also be a foundering, a contestation'.[32]

For Hannah Arendt, 'the most elementary predicament of all modern political bodies' is their 'profound instability' which is the 'result of some elementary lack of authority'.[33] Put another way, political modernity is confronted with the predicament of how to found authority. This problem finds its expression in the problem of an absolute. The need for an absolute appeared with Christianity when the 'Word

---

[24] *Ibid.*
[25] *Ibid.*: 154.
[26] *Ibid.*
[27] *Ibid.*: 155.
[28] *Ibid.*: 159.
[29] *Ibid.*: 160.
[30] *Ibid.*
[31] *Ibid.*
[32] *Ibid.*: 161.
[33] H. Arendt 1963: 158.

became flesh', that is, with 'the incarnation of a divine absolute on earth'.[34] Secular, positive, posited, man-made laws were understood as the mundane expression of a divinely ordained law and consequently required the sanction of the Church.[35] Secularization, or the emancipation of the secular realm from the tutelage of the Church, 'inevitably posed the problem of how to found and constitute a new authority'.[36] Arendt argues that the first and most conspicuous consequence of secularization was the rise of European absolutism which understood the will of an absolute sovereign to be the source of both power and law. The absolute monarch claimed rulership by virtue of divine rights.[37] However, the substitute of the institution of kingship for 'the lost religious sanction of secular authority' did not prove to be a satisfactory solution since an absolute sovereignty lacked a transcendent and transmundane source and therefore could only degenerate into tyranny and despotism.[38] Absolute monarchy having failed as a solution to the problem of an absolute, it was followed by the solution of the absolute sovereignty of the nation.[39]

However, the inheritance of absolutism is only part of the problem as concerns the need for an absolute to found authority in modernity. Arendt argues that of greater importance and significance was the fact that the meaning of the word 'law' had changed dramatically since the last centuries of the Roman Empire. She asserts that in spite of the tremendous influence of the Roman concept, laws came to be understood as commandments.[40] That is, they were 'construed in accordance with the voice of God'.[41] For this reason, laws understood as commandments could only be binding with a higher, religious sanction. In this sense, Arendt states that 'only to the extent that we understand by law a commandment to which men owe obedience regardless of their consent and mutual agreements, does the law require a transcendent source of authority for its validity, that is, an origin which must be beyond human power'.[42] The model for Western civilization's conception of the law was Hebrew in origin and represented the divine Commandments of the Decalogue.[43] Throughout the centuries, the

---

34   *Ibid.*: 195.
35   *Ibid.*: 189.
36   *Ibid.*: 159.
37   *Ibid.*: 195.
38   *Ibid.*: 158.
39   *Ibid.*: 195.
40   *Ibid.*: 190.
41   *Ibid.*
42   *Ibid.*
43   *Ibid.*

place of divinity was held by the Hebrew God, Christ, the vicars of Christ, kings and finally by natural law.

The problem of an absolute, then, is a thoroughly modern problem. Arendt observes that neither the Greeks nor the Romans were ever perplexed by the problem of the need for an absolute. This is due to the fact that neither Greek nor Roman law was of divine origin, nor did their concept of legislation need divine inspiration. Moreover, Roman law never required a transcendent source of authority.[44] Arendt has a great regard for the Roman political experience in particular. As we will see, the Roman concepts of authority, religion, tradition and freedom as well as the coincidence of foundation, preservation and augmentation are the sources of her conception of foundational narratives. Moreover, she claims that the American Founding Fathers turned to the Roman political experience in order to establish an innovative 'new-old way' of founding the political for modernity. I will discuss Arendt's ideas regarding foundation at some length in order to justify my claim that Oakeshott is a weak foundationalist in the Arendtian constructivist tradition. I will pay close attention to her discussion of the foundation of Rome as the Roman political experience is essential to Oakeshott's understanding of legends of political life.

Arendt wrote extensively about the Roman political experience in *Between Past and Future* (1961) and *On Revolution* (1963). Her concern is with the foundation of Rome and the concepts developed to conceptualize the event: authority, religion, tradition and freedom. In his appreciative review of *Between Past and Future*, Oakeshott notes that in order to understand political experience 'Dr. Arendt draws upon the evidence of the popular meanings of words and upon the writers who most closely reflect common ways of thinking: the historians, the orators and the poets'.[45]

Arendt speaks of the 'Roman trinity' of authority, religion and tradition. By this she means that the three words are profoundly interconnected and that the one necessarily involves the others.[46] To these three words may be added the word freedom. Arendt explains that the word and the concept of authority are Roman in origin.[47] Authority and tradition played 'a decisive role in the political life of the Roman republic'.[48] Consequently, the Romans in their 'indefatigable search for tradition and authority' derived the idea of authority from the political

---

44   *Ibid.*: 186–187.
45   *WH*: 317.
46   H. Arendt 1993: 93, 125.
47   *Ibid.*: 104.
48   *Ibid.*: 120.

realm.[49] Specifically, authority emerged out of the Roman experience of foundation, Arendt claims.[50] She asserts that at the heart of Roman politics 'stands the conviction of the sacredness of foundation'.[51] What makes foundation sacred, following Arendt, is that once a political community has been founded it remains binding for all future generations.[52] For the Romans, to be engaged in politics meant 'first and foremost to preserve the founding of the city of Rome'.[53] The foundation of Rome, that is, the foundation of a new body politic, became to the Romans 'the central, decisive, unrepeatable beginning of their whole history, a unique event'.[54] The foundation of a new body politic is an unrepeatable beginning, a unique event. For the Romans, the foundation of Rome acquired an aura of sacredness since it remained binding for successive generations. The idea of sacredness suggests that the foundation of Rome was in one sense a religious event and that preserving the foundation was not only a political, but also a religious duty. This is precisely what Arendt argues. She asserts that the founding of Rome as well as the sanctity of the house and hearth formed 'the deeply political content of Roman religion'.[55] The word religion for the Romans literally meant *re-ligare*, that is, to be tied back or obligated to the original foundation.[56] In other words, to be religious meant to be tied to the past or bound back to the beginning, more specifically to the 'enormous, almost superhuman and hence always legendary effort to lay the foundations, to build the cornerstone, to found for eternity'.[57] In *On Revolution*, Arendt affirms that the idea of being tied back or bound back to the foundation of Rome corresponded to the Roman understanding of *pietas*, that is, piety. She writes that 'to remain tied back to the beginning of the ancestors in pious remembrance and conservation meant to have Roman *pietas*'.[58] She therefore concludes that religion and politics were quasi-identical activities for the Romans since both were concerned with the conservation of the original foundation.[59]

It was in this particular political and religious context that the word and concept of authority appeared. Arendt traces the origin of the

---

49 *Ibid.*
50 *Ibid.*: 141.
51 *Ibid.*: 120.
52 *Ibid.*
53 *Ibid.*
54 *Ibid.*: 121.
55 *Ibid.*
56 *Ibid.*
57 *Ibid.*
58 H. Arendt 1963: 202.
59 H. Arendt 1993: 121.

Roman word *auctoritas* back to the verb *augere* which means to 'augment' or to 'increase'.[60] What authority augmented was the foundation
which had been laid down by the ancestors.[61] Arendt argues that those
in authority constantly augmented or increased the original foundation
and that the uninterrupted continuity of the augmentation and of its
inherent authority could only be maintained by means of tradition, by
which the Romans understood 'the handing down, through an
unbroken line of successors, of the principle established in the
beginning'.[62] For Arendt, then, to be in authority in Rome meant to
remain in this unbroken line of successors.[63] The authority of the living
was always derivative and depended upon the authority of the
founders.[64] The Roman concept of authority, therefore, has its roots in
the past, more specifically, in the foundation of Rome. Authority
derives its binding force from that remembered sacred event. Every act
was tied back to the sacred beginning and, thus, the whole weight of
the past was added to every moment.[65] It follows that 'precedents, the
deeds of the ancestors and the usage that grew out of them, were
always binding'.[66] In this sense, Arendt asserts, 'anything that
happened was transformed into an example, and the *auctoritas maiorum*
became identical with authoritative models for actual behaviour, with
the moral political standard as such'.[67]

In order to better understand what it meant for the Romans to be in
authority, Arendt distinguishes between the word *auctores* and the
word *artifices*. The latter word referred to the actual builders and
makers and it signified the exact opposite of *auctores* when the root of
that word, *auctor*, meant the same thing as the English word 'author'.
An author, following the Roman understanding, was not a builder;
rather, he was the one who inspired the whole enterprise. Consequently, it is the spirit of the author much more than the spirit of the
builder which was represented in the building itself.[68] In short, while
the *artifex* only made the building, the *auctor* is 'the actual "author" of
the building, namely its founder; with it he has become an "aug-
menter" of the city'.[69]

---

60   H. Arendt 1993: 121–122; H. Arendt 1963: 202.
61   H. Arendt 1993: 122; H. Arendt 1963: 202.
62   H. Arendt 1963: 202.
63   *Ibid.*
64   H. Arendt 1993: 122.
65   *Ibid.*: 123.
66   *Ibid.*
67   *Ibid.*
68   *Ibid.*: 122.
69   *Ibid.*

For Arendt, then, the highest human value for the Romans was the foundation of new states and, subsequently, the conservation and augmentation of the foundation which was understood to be sacred since it was binding for all future generations.[70] It is from this sacred, unrepeatable beginning that the interconnected concepts of religion, authority and tradition sprang. All three played an indispensable role in the conservation and augmentation of the original Roman foundation. To be religious in Rome meant to be tied back or bound to the foundation of the city of Rome. To be in authority meant to conserve and augment, by means of advice, the foundation Romans were religiously bound to. For Arendt, the concept of authority, in which permanence and change were tied together, was one of the most important contributions the Roman political experience made to philosophic Western thought.[71] The fact that change could only mean the increase and enlargement of the old endowed Roman political structures with durability, continuity and permanence.[72] In this respect, Arendt speaks of 'the miracle of permanence'.[73] Continuity and permanence implied being bound to the past and, if religion tied Romans to the past, it was tradition which preserved it. Pursuing the religious theme, Arendt asserts that the past was sanctified through tradition. Tradition preserved the past by handing down from one generation to the next the 'testimony of the ancestors, who first had witnessed and created the sacred founding and then augmented it by their authority throughout the centuries'.[74] It was by means of tradition that the ancestors augmented the foundation by their authority. Therefore, for authority to be inviolable tradition had to be uninterrupted.[75] Consequently, authority and tradition were inseparable for the Romans. More importantly, in Rome, to act without authority and tradition, that is, without the 'accepted, time-honored standards and models, without the help of the wisdom of the founding fathers, was inconceivable'.[76] For Arendt, the coincidence or the 'trinity' of authority, tradition and religion formed the backbone of Roman history.[77]

The Roman concept of freedom also springs from the act of foundation. Arendt claims that freedom for the Romans was not 'an attribute

---

[70]   H. Arendt 1963: 202.
[71]   *Ibid.*
[72]   H. Arendt 1963: 202; H. Arendt 1993: 127.
[73]   H. Arendt 1993: 127.
[74]   *Ibid.*: 124.
[75]   *Ibid.*
[76]   *Ibid.*
[77]   H. Arendt 1963: 202.

of the will but an accessory of doing and acting'.[78] In other words, freedom was experienced in the process of acting. She identifies two verbs in the Latin language which signify 'to act'. The first is the verb *agere* which means 'to set something in motion'.[79] The second is the verb *gerere* which means 'the enduring and supporting continuation of past acts whose results are the *res gestae*, the deeds and events we call historical'.[80] Arendt argues that, for the Romans, action occurred when something new came into the world.[81] That is, action begins in a beginning. Since freedom for the Romans meant to act, freedom and the idea of beginning were consequently interconnected.[82] More specifically, freedom sprang from the unrepeatable beginning, that is, the act of foundation. Arendt writes that 'Roman freedom was a legacy bequeathed by the founders of Rome to the Roman people; their freedom was tied to the beginning their forefathers had established by founding the city'.[83] Part of the Roman understanding of freedom, then, was connected to the idea of beginning. The Roman concept of freedom sprang from the foundation of Rome, and along with being closely connected to the idea of a beginning, it also meant to care for the affairs of the city as well as ensuring the permanence of the foundation by augmenting it.

In sum, the Romans, Arendt contends, were successful in laying foundations for the political, thus ensuring human living-together. By tying every new event, act or decision back to the new beginning, the foundation could at once be preserved and augmented. Permanence and change were tied together. Put another way, the Romans created a foundational narrative which they preserved and cared for in order to bequeath a world fit to live in to future generations. That is, the Romans built a world of sense fit for human life and living-together. This political narrative, constructed on the glorified Roman past, informed Romans of how their society came about, how it evolved, what its values were, and, significantly, was simultaneously the origin as well as the guaranty of their freedom. Arendt argues that the fact that Roman historians 'always felt bound to the beginning of Roman history, because this beginning contained the authentic element of Roman freedom and thus made their history political' underscores the importance of the past sacred event for the Roman political experi-

---

78 H. Arendt 1993: 165.
79 *Ibid.*
80 *Ibid.*
81 *Ibid.*: 166.
82 *Ibid.*
83 *Ibid.*

ence.[84] Every act and event which composes the Roman foundational narrative was related to the 'always legendary effort to lay the foundations, to build the cornerstone, to found for eternity'.[85] It is a story from the past which founds the political not only for the present, but for eternity. Finally, of fundamental importance to Arendt is the fact that the Roman concept of authority was derived from the practice of augmenting the original foundation.

As Oakeshott points out in his review of *Between Past and Future*, Arendt claims that it is this understanding of authority which has been lost in the modern world.[86] The importance of the permanence and the durability authority gave to the human world cannot be underestimated, Arendt argues, since humans are 'mortals – the most unstable and futile beings we know of'.[87] The loss of the concept of authority, such as it was understood in antiquity by the Romans, is 'tantamount to the loss of the groundwork of the world'.[88] Nevertheless, she does not completely despair since the loss of authority does not necessarily entail the loss of 'the human capacity for building, preserving, and caring for a world that can survive us and remain a place fit to live in for those who come after us'.[89] A case in point, according to Arendt, is the Founding Fathers of the American republic, whom she counts among the most successful of builders in history. The foundation of the United States of America following the American Revolution, Arendt contends, is the most successful example of the human capacity for building, preserving and caring for a world in modernity. The American foundation was successful, Arendt asserts, because the Founding Fathers took the foundation of Rome as their model and in so doing resolved the problem of an absolute. In a similar sense, Oakeshott affirms that 'it is not a matter of chance that American politics is shot through with expressions that come from Roman politics; the founding fathers had clearly before them the republican constitution of Rome'.[90] For Arendt, like Rome, what saved the American Revolution was 'the act of foundation itself'.[91] The Founding Fathers felt compelled to turn to the Romans, Arendt claims, because it became evident to them that a dimension of their experience had not been handed down by Western tradition. Thus, it was because they needed models and examples in

---

84   *Ibid.*
85   *Ibid.*: 121.
86   *WH*: 316–317; H. Arendt 1993: 91.
87   H. Arendt 1993: 95.
88   *Ibid.*
89   *Ibid.*
90   *LHPT*: 222–223.
91   H. Arendt 1963: 196.

order to make sense of their own experience that they turned to what was for them 'the great model and precedent [...] the Roman republic and the grandeur of its history'.[92] For Arendt, the two key ideas the American Founding Fathers adopted from the Roman political experience was the Roman concept of authority as well as that of the sacredness of a founding past event.

Arendt claims that the 'most important single notion' the men of the American Revolution adopted from the Romans was their concept of authority understood as the coincidence of foundation, augmentation and conservation.[93] The Roman concept of authority solved the problem of how to ensure the perpetuity of the Union and of how to bestow permanence upon a foundation since it showed how the act of foundation 'inevitably develops its own stability and permanence'.[94] That is, authority is a 'kind of necessary "augmentation" by virtue of which all innovations and changes remain tied back to the foundation which, at the same time, they augment and increase'.[95] Consequently, by virtue of the fact that the Constitution is amended and augmented, thereby increasing and augmenting the original foundation, it develops its own authority, stability and permanence. Put another way, 'the very authority of the American Constitution resides in its inherent capacity to be amended and augmented'.[96] Permanence and change are tied together and consequently the American foundation may be qualified of being a contingent foundation.

Arendt maintains that the Americans had been right to derive the stability and authority of the republic from its beginning.[97] For her, it was 'the authority which the act of foundation carried within itself [...] that assured stability for the new republic'.[98] It was the act of foundation itself which would become the source of authority in the new body politic. This implies that it is futile to search for an absolute to break the circle in which all beginnings are caught because 'this "absolute" lies in the very act of beginning itself'.[99] The problem the Founding Fathers faced was that they could only conceive of a beginning, that is, the act of foundation or constitution, as an event that had occurred in the distant past.[100] Arendt argues that this problem was solved by the Ameri-

---

92 *Ibid.*: 197.
93 *Ibid.*: 203, 202–203.
94 *Ibid.*: 203.
95 *Ibid.*
96 *Ibid.*
97 *Ibid.*: 199.
98 *Ibid.*: 200.
99 *Ibid.*: 205.
100 *Ibid.*: 199.

cans' 'extraordinary capacity to look upon yesterday with the eyes of centuries to come'.[101] What in effect ensured the success of the foundation, and guarded it against the onslaught of time, was the American practice of 'Constitution worship' which began the moment the Constitution began to operate.[102] Americans' attitude toward the founding document was religious in the Roman sense of '*religare*', of being bound to a beginning. In other words, American piety consisted in being bound to the Constitution or beginning in the same sense as Roman *pietas* consisted in being bound to the beginning of Roman history.[103] Oakeshott also remarks upon the relationship the American people maintain with their constitution. He states that 'some peoples have looked back to an "original constitution" and believed it to be their destiny to remain faithful to it. There is something of this feeling in modern America'.[104] However, Oakeshott differentiates between the Roman and American experience by emphasizing that the Romans 'had no such "constitution". What they looked back to, and were "bound" to, in *pietas* and *fides*, was the event of "foundation" and the "founding father", Romulus'.[105]

It is Arendt's position that the act of remembrance of the event of foundation shrouds the outcome of the foundation, the actual Constitution, 'in an atmosphere of reverent awe which has shielded both event and document against the onslaught of time and changed circumstances'.[106] For Arendt, the authority of the American republic will be safe and intact 'as long as the act itself, the beginning as such, is remembered'.[107] It is in this sense that the practice of Constitution worship ensured the success of the American Revolution. It is the act of remembrance which safeguards the authority of the republic and ensures its perpetuity. Remembrance, therefore, arguably implies a narrative centred on the act of foundation, on the beginning. The fact that the Constitution has come to be worshipped and is shrouded in reverent awe demonstrates that such a narrative has been well established in the United States since the moment of its foundation. For Arendt, then, the foundation of the American republic, which found in the Roman spirit the source of its inspiration, is proof that it is possible in modernity to build, preserve and care for a world that will survive mere mortals. Thus, by adopting the Roman concept of authority in

---

[101] *Ibid.*
[102] *Ibid.*
[103] *Ibid.*
[104] *LHPT*: 218.
[105] *Ibid.*
[106] H. Arendt 1963: 205.
[107] *Ibid.*

which foundation, augmentation and conservation coincide, and combining it with remembrance, the American republic succeeded in bestowing 'upon the affairs of men that measure of stability without which they would be unable to build a world for their posterity, destined and designed to outlast their own mortal lives'.[108] Oakeshott echoes Arendt's argument that the beginning and the act of foundation are of fundamental importance for the American republic, just as they were for the Romans. To this end, he asserts that:

> 'Freedom' was something that a Roman felt himself to have inherited from the way in which the Roman state came into existence—something, perhaps, a little like the feeling that modern Americans have that freedom is something they have inherited from the way in which the United States came into being.[109]

Foundations: The Edenic and Constructivist Traditions

The preceding discussion reveals that the question of foundations is complex and that contemporary thinkers have explored numerous avenues in order to find a solution to what Arendt calls 'the problem of the absolute'. In spite of their differences, the conceptions of foundations put forward by Rorty, Butler and Arendt share one common characteristic: they all strive, in their own ways, to stake out a middling position between the absolute and pure contingency. They attempt to theorize how to found the contingent. This is perhaps the most promising approach to resolving the problem of the absolute. (I will argue in Chapter 3 that a mixed form of the political may also be identified in Oakeshott's thought.) Nevertheless, numerous differences still separate contemporary thinkers in relation to foundations. Following Seery, the 'running academic debate between "foundationalism" and "anti-foundationalism"' leads to a great deal of confusion and muddled thinking.[110] In an effort to overcome the confusion surrounding contemporary debates on foundations, Seery in his essay 'Castles in the Air: An Essay on Political Foundations' proposes a framework to help make sense of foundations. As the preceding discussion revealed, the term 'foundation' can mean different things and be used in different ways by theorists. Rorty and Butler refer to a stricter, more orthodox understanding of 'philosophical' foundations, while Arendt talks about foundational narratives the purpose of which it is to found a body politic and ensure its stability and preservation. Seery's starting point is just such an observation: the term foundation itself is muddled. It

---

[108] *Ibid.*: 182.
[109] *LHPT*: 248.
[110] J. Seery 1999: 466.

carries different meanings and understandings. In order to remedy the
problem, Seery proposes a dichotomy whereby foundations may be
categorized as belonging to either of two traditions: the 'Edenic'
tradition or the 'constructivist' tradition.[111] In short, Seery distinguishes
between foundations that are pre-given and foundations that are
erected. The Edenic tradition, where foundations are pre-given, is the
most prominent tradition in the West owing to its Biblical beginnings.[112] It posits 'separate spatial realms in which human activity takes
place'.[113] These separate realms can be traversed only by an 'extraordinary, eventful temporal movement or transformative act'.[114] This
movement or act allows for the complete relocation from one realm to
the other. The temporally prior realm is always depicted as 'pristine,
harmonious, united [and] sacred'.[115] In sum, it is a garden-like state of
nature.[116] To this realm is opposed the realm of civil or political society
which is depicted as 'sinful, secular, denatured [and] compromised'.[117]
Due to its distance from grace, civil society is the realm of 'conflict,
strife, diversity and incompletion'.[118] Although the language of Edenic
theorists has become secularized in modernity, nevertheless, Seery
maintains that they continue to observe and respect the strict distinction between the natural and civil realms.[119] It is for this reason that
he categorizes both Rorty and Butler as belonging to the Edenic
tradition of foundations. He argues that for them 'a "foundation" is
always located in a naturalized, sacred realm'.[120] Foundations, or
grounding claims, for these thinkers are '"prior" claims about unquestionable or sacred or natural premises'.[121] In this sense, foundations are
deemed to be pre-given.

In the constructivist tradition, on the other hand, foundations are
understood to be erected or built. That is, they are man-made. Seery
contends that the constructivist tradition of foundations is 'forward
looking [...] instead [of] backward scrutinizing'.[122] It approaches
foundations in terms of architecture and city planning rather than in

---

[111] *Ibid.*: 470.
[112] *Ibid.*
[113] *Ibid.*
[114] *Ibid.*
[115] *Ibid.*
[116] *Ibid.*
[117] *Ibid.*
[118] *Ibid.*
[119] *Ibid.*: 471.
[120] *Ibid.*
[121] *Ibid.*
[122] *Ibid.*: 472.

terms of metaphysics and selfhood.[123] Constructivist theorists will be found 'building cities in words or imagining elaborate poetic under-worlds' as opposed to their Edenic counterparts who are preoccupied with prior grounding claims about unquestionable, sacred or natural premises.[124] In this sense, Seery contends that Edenic theorists tend to write 'didactic treatises' about human nature, natural rights and human identity before they talk about politics as such; hence, their preference for the 'philosophical ponderous' treatises of Aristotle, Aquinas, Hume and Locke.[125] Constructivist theorists, for their part, favour the 'poetic-ally creative accounts' of Homer, Plato, Virgil, Dante and More which inspire and guide the building and imagining of cities and their under-worlds.[126] Fundamental to this conception of foundations is the idea that poets, and not Gods, are the architects of political foundations.[127] Thus, the constructivist tradition views foundations to be the result of human enterprise and the purpose they serve is to 'lend stability to building projects'.[128]

Seery's two examples of constructivist theorists are the fifteenth-century writer Christine de Pizan and Arendt. Although I will focus on his discussion of Arendt, it is important to note that Seery finds in Christine de Pizan 'that shift, from spiritual odyssey to political endeavor' which, he claims, represents the 'crucial distinction between the Edenic versus constructivist traditions'.[129] As concerns Arendt, Seery begins by emphasizing the essential point Arendt makes about politics, that is, that 'political action steps into the liminal period of the present but that moving occupancy assumes meaning, a thread of continuity, only by drawing upon the past and by anticipating the future'.[130] It is this lesson, that past, present and future are interrelated and make sense of the political present, that Arendt states again and again as regards founding and foundations, Seery maintains.[131] Seery asserts that, for Arendt, foundations 'attempt to solve the problem of human beginnings, the question of how an unconnected, new event — how a new "We the people" — can break into the continuous sequence of historical time'.[132] He reminds us that Arendt explains that because

---

[123] *Ibid.*
[124] *Ibid.*
[125] *Ibid.*: 473.
[126] *Ibid.*
[127] *Ibid.*: 476.
[128] *Ibid.*: 473.
[129] *Ibid.*: 476.
[130] *Ibid.*: 477.
[131] *Ibid.*
[132] *Ibid.*: 478.

such beginnings are usually shrouded in mystery the purported connection between past and present, between dead ancestors and live bodies, must therefore always be speculative.[133] Foundations, thus understood, rely on the faculty of imagination, and not historical memory, Seery claims.[134] Relying on this faculty of imagination, foundations engender foundation legends which present the arbitrariness of a new beginning against the background of ongoing historical time.[135] To this end, foundation legends recall a beginning at which a 'We' is supposedly first experienced and articulated.[136]

Seery underscores that 'the central figure Arendt always mentions in discussing political foundings is Virgil'.[137] For Arendt, Seery argues, the genius of Virgilian politics lay in the foundational idea that the alleged beginning was never absolutely new, but was rather re-establishment, which preserved a thread of continuity between a new human community and an older one.[138] Seery reminds us that it is Arendt's contention that the American Founding Fathers learned how to found the political and authority without reference to a transcendent God from the Ancient Romans, more specifically from Virgil.[139] Therefore, the single most important source of inspiration for thinkers of the constructivist tradition is Rome. This is clearly true for Arendt and I will argue in Chapter 5 that it is also true for Oakeshott. In sum, then, for Seery, Arendt believes that humans as mortals need stabilizing constructs and that these constructs take the form of foundational narratives.[140] These narratives are the source of permanence and stability for Arendt because, in their use of imagination, they make sense of an arbitrary new beginning which breaks into continuous historical time.

The dichotomy Seery establishes between the Edenic and the constructivist traditions shows that there are different kinds of foundations. When we talk about political foundations, we often times refer to entirely different conceptions and understandings of a foundation and of its role in relation to the political. The term can mean either prior grounding claims about unquestionable, sacred or natural premises, or it can refer to stabilizing constructs. Commentators who study the question of foundations in Oakeshott's political thought focus on the Edenic understanding of foundations. That is, when they question

---

133   *Ibid.*
134   *Ibid.*
135   *Ibid.*: 479.
136   *Ibid.*
137   *Ibid.*: 477.
138   *Ibid.*: 480.
139   *Ibid.*: 477–483.
140   *Ibid.*: 483.

whether his theorization of the political presupposes foundations, they mean foundations in the Edenic sense. When it is asserted that Oakeshott's conception of the political is devoid of foundations, what is meant is that his thought is devoid of Edenic foundations. Attention is focused exclusively on this understanding of foundations. However, given the importance of the influence of the Roman political experience on his thought, is it satisfactory to simply consider the Edenic tradition of foundations in relation to Oakeshott to the exclusion of the Arendtian constructivist tradition? If we consider that for Arendt and Seery the primary source of inspiration for the constructivist tradition is the Roman foundation and experience of politics, which, as David Boucher points out, is also one of the most important sources of inspiration for Oakeshott's conception of conservatism, it seems appropriate to explore whether he belongs to the constructivist tradition of foundations.[141] Thus, although Oakeshott may not defend an Edenic conception of foundations, this does not mean that his political thought is entirely free of foundations. On the contrary, I make the case that following the Roman experience and Arendt, Oakeshott provides some type of stabilizing construct for the political. And, like Arendt, this built world of sense and meaning is centred upon a remembered past event.

Before pursuing my argument that Oakeshott is a weak foundationalist in the constructivist tradition, it may be helpful to develop the understanding of the concept further. Firstly, although I use the terms 'construction' and 'constructivism' to define Oakeshott's conception of political imagination, I use them in a very different way from the one involved in Kantian constructivism. My concern here is not with a constructive procedure by which persons construct moral or political principles or doctrines as it is in Kantian constructivism.[142] Rather, my concern is with solidarity amongst strangers, that is, the bond which unites members of political societies, and, notably, modern political societies following what Oakeshott refers to as the dissolution of communal ties.[143] My position is that such solidarity is constructed in that human imagination constructs a common political imaginary with which members of a political society identify. In this, I follow Benedict Anderson and argue that this is also Oakeshott's position. By this, I mean that legends of political life comprise the common imaginary allowing for solidarity amongst strangers and that, as such, they constitute weak foundations for the political.

---

[141] D. Boucher 2005a: 85.
[142] L. Krasnoff 1999: 387.
[143] *LHPT*: 416.

Anderson defines the modern nation as 'an imagined political community'.[144] That is, it is the modern construction of a solidarity amongst strangers. What specifically is constructed is a new imaginary, one that is able to replace the religious, metaphysical imaginary as well as the old communal solidarities. This 'imagined community', or 'new imaginary', is therefore situated between the universal and the particular. As such, it is a 'concrete universal' which ensures solidarity amongst strangers since all members of a political community identify with the same imaginary.[145] Anderson claims that the modern concept of time, conceived of as 'homogeneous, empty time', what he also terms 'the conception of simultaneity', and print-capitalism made possible the emergence of common political imaginaries.[146] Anderson asserts that this understanding of time makes it possible to 'think' the nation in that it allows for 'the idea of a sociological organism moving calendrically through homogeneous, empty time' to emerge.[147] In this sense, the nation, Anderson maintains, 'also is conceived as a solid community moving steadily down (or up) history'.[148] While Anderson states that the novel and the newspaper, both of which first appeared in eighteenth-century Europe, in providing the technical means for 're-presenting' the nation are the forms of imagining which best exemplify why the modern conception of time is so important for the creation of the imagined community of the nation, I will focus on his discussion of narratives of identity which also contribute to the shared political imaginary.[149]

When discussing what he terms the biography of nations or narratives of identity, Anderson emphasizes the point that nations are aware 'of being imbedded in secular, serial time, with all its implications of continuity'.[150] However, as Anderson argues, ruptures of the late eighteenth century lead nations to 'forget' the experience of this continuity, thus giving rise to the need for narratives of identity.[151] Anderson holds that because nations have no clearly identifiable births and thus have no Originator, their biographies 'can not be written evangelically, "down time", through a long procreative chain of begettings'.[152] For this reason, he explains that the only option 'is to fashion it "up time" —

---

[144] B. Anderson 1996: 6.

[145] J.Y. Thériault 2002: 329.

[146] B. Anderson 1996: 24, 37–46.

[147] *Ibid*.: 24, 26.

[148] *Ibid*.: 26.

[149] *Ibid*.: 24–25.

[150] *Ibid*.: 205.

[151] *Ibid*.

[152] *Ibid*.

towards Peking Man, Java Man, King Arthur, wherever the lamp of archaeology casts its fitful gleam'.[153] Moreover, Anderson underlines that this manner of fashioning narratives of identity is 'a curious inversion of conventional genealogy' in that these narratives start from an originary present.[154] For example, World War II begets World War I.[155]

Hence, these narratives of identity which start from an originary present and are fashioned up time are constructs which, along with other forms of imagining, comprise nations' common imaginary. Anderson is careful not to qualify these narratives of 'historical'. As we will see, this is also the case for Oakeshott. Like Anderson, he posits that legends originate in what he terms the practical present and are not historical in nature, but, rather, belong to the practical past. This will be discussed in detail in Chapter 2. In sum, then, for Anderson, a modern nation's solidarity is constructed by means of imagination, and, notably, through narratives of identity. This is how I conceive of constructivism for the purpose of my argument which is to show that, for Oakeshott, a political society's sense of self-consciousness and identity, which ensure human living-together, are constructed by human imagination.

Although Oakeshott's concept of legends of political life does not solely apply to the modern state (in this sense, he lends significant importance to the legend-making skills of the ancient Romans); nevertheless, in order to more fully understand the constructivist element in his thought, it is important to situate him within the context of modern thought on the state. In *Lectures in the History of Political Thought*, Oakeshott states that the least tangible of the themes of modern European political thought are the questions of the character of a state and the ties which bind members of a state to one another.[156] The question of ties or bonds is fundamental because the modern state, following the dissolution of the communal ties which composed the structure of life in a medieval community, generated the unattached individual.[157] My concern here is to grasp his thought on the ties which unite members of a state and to situate legends of political life within that understanding.

Oakeshott identifies three interpretations of the 'collectivity of a "state"' in modern European thought.[158] The first interpretation understands the modern state to be a 'natural' community where members

---

153 *Ibid.*
154 *Ibid.*
155 *Ibid.*
156 *LHPT*: 425.
157 *LHPT*: 416.
158 *LHPT*: 421.

are joined to one another by 'natural' bonds, for example by common blood.[159] The state here appears as a 'natural' society with a 'natural solidarity'.[160] It is of the order of nature and necessity. In the second interpretation, the modern state is understood as an 'artificial' association of human beings where members, by agreement or choice, are united by artificial bonds in the pursuit of a common purpose or enterprise.[161] The artificial bonds which unite its members are the 'specifically chosen purpose and the specific arrangements agreed upon for its pursuit'.[162] Oakeshott cites Thomas Hobbes as a representative of this interpretation. More specifically, the civil association for Hobbes is 'an "artificial" association of human beings united in an agreed pursuit of "peace" among themselves'.[163] Finally, the third interpretation understands the modern state to be an 'historical' association of human beings where the bond which unites its members is 'forged by time and circumstance'.[164] According to Oakeshott, the historical understanding of the modern state is an attempt to overcome 'the intellectual disposition which assumes that everything in the world must be either "natural" or "artificial"'.[165] Following this interpretation, a state is understood as a collection of human beings 'whom chance has brought together, and who have acquired a sentiment of solidarity from having enjoyed, over the years, a common and continuous "historical" experience'.[166] For Oakeshott, it is the memory of shared experiences, including of historical events, which go to make the state understood in historical terms and which bind its members to one another.[167] That is, it is what Oakeshott terms 'the total of contingent circumstances', by which he means a common language, a literature, common laws, folktales, legends and songs that together constitute the collectivity of a state understood as an historical association.[168] Oakeshott points out that none of these things is either 'natural' or 'artificial'.[169] For instance, a language is not 'natural' to a 'people', yet it was not invented or designed with the intended purpose of uniting a collection of human

---

159 *LHPT*: 413, 421.
160 *LHPT*: 420.
161 *LHPT*: 413, 414.
162 *LHPT*: 421.
163 *LHPT*: 419.
164 *LHPT*: 421.
165 *Ibid.*
166 *LHPT*: 422.
167 *Ibid.*
168 *Ibid.*
169 *Ibid.*

beings.[170] Language, like the other undesigned, circumstantial and contingent ties which constitute the collectivity of a state understood as an historical association, is the product of history and, therefore, of human choices.[171] In sum, then, the modern state understood as an historical association is neither natural nor artificial, neither necessary nor designed.[172] For Oakeshott, then, the 'ties which unite its members, all of them the products of time and circumstance, are as strong as they have managed to become'.[173] Moreover, as Luke O'Sullivan notes, for Oakeshott, the historical understanding of the state reveals 'a political character, a tendency to do things a certain way'.[174] He adds that such an historic character, or we may also say identity, oscillates 'within more or less clearly defined limits'.[175] Thus, the historical understanding of the state offers a median position between the state conceived of as natural and particular on the one hand, and artificial and abstract on the other.

As will be discussed in Chapter 3, of the three interpretations of the state Oakeshott identifies in modern European thought, it is the interpretation of the state understood as an historical association with its strong emphasis on the common experience of living together which corresponds most closely to his conception of the political as a tradition of behaviour. Nardin and O'Sullivan also arrive at this conclusion in their introduction to the *Lectures in the History of Political Thought*.[176] Thus, it follows that the ties that bind members of a state to one another are historical in character. As for legends of political life, in so far as they are the ties which unite members of a state, I claim that they are historical constructs and not artificial constructs.

While artifice does characterize legends of political life, they are not, however, genuinely artificial. That is to say, although legends are the creation of poetry, they are not works of art such as Hobbes understands the civil association to be. Following Oakeshott's interpretation of Hobbes's thought in 'Introduction to *Leviathan*', Hobbes conceives of the civil association as an artefact.[177] When considering Hobbes's distinction between art and nature, Oakeshott argues that, for him, the cause of a human work of art is the will of a man.[178] Willing is therefore

---

170 *Ibid.*
171 *Ibid.*
172 *LHPT*: 421.
173 *LHPT*: 422.
174 L. O'Sullivan 2004: 15.
175 *Ibid.*
176 T. Nardin and L. O'Sullivan 2006: 23.
177 *RP*: 246.
178 *RP*: 247.

a creative activity.[179] Moreover, Oakeshott asserts that, for Hobbes, the will of a man creates not only when it is single and alone, but also in concert with other wills. Thus, the civil association, the product of an agreement between wills, is a work of art.[180] As Arendt argues in *The Human Condition* when discussing Hobbes's *Leviathan*, 'seventeenth-century attempts to formulate new political philosophies or, rather, to invent the means and instruments with which to "make an artificial animal" [...] called a Commonwealth, or State' are closely connected to the later impulses of history to move away from nature.[181] Quoting Oakeshott's 'Introduction to *Leviathan*', which she qualifies as excellent, Arendt emphasizes that, for Hobbes, the civil association, a human creation, is the 'most human of human "works of art"'.[182] Thus, the rules and standards by which to build and judge this creation do not lie outside of men.[183] While sharing certain similarities in this respect, arti-fice and history are nevertheless distinct. If we refer to Oakeshott's interpretation of artifice and history, legends of political life, although the product of human ties, are not artificial ties in that, contrary to genuine artefacts, they are 'not designed and made to serve any specific and premeditated purpose'.[184] In this sense, I argue that legends of political life are contingent foundations for the political in that they found a political identity and sense of self-consciousness which can be augmented to fully reflect the common experience of living together. In other words, they translate a shared common experience into the idiom of general ideas. Finally, legends of political life are more substantial ties than the 'fragile and changeable' bond which unites members of an artificial association.[185] The idea put forward by Oakeshott that the bond of artificial association is fragile and not sufficiently substantial echoes my argument that 'the recognition of the rules as rules' is insufficient to sustain solidarity amongst strangers.

For these reasons, legends of political life are historical ties uniting members of a state understood as an historical association. It is import-ant, however, to use the term 'historical' with caution. It should be noted that Oakeshott uses scare quotes when referring to the historical interpretation of the state in modern European thought. As I argue in Chapter 2, this is because, for Oakeshott, the category of the past is large and that what this interpretation of the state invokes is not his-

---

179 *Ibid.*
180 *Ibid.*
181 H. Arendt 1998: 299.
182 *Ibid.*
183 *Ibid.*
184 *LHPT*: 421.
185 *LHPT*: 423.

tory, but rather the practical past. It is my position that this also holds true for legends of political life. Legends, the creation of poets, recall an event from the practical past in order to stabilize an otherwise problematic present.

In sum, this is how I understand the constructed element I argue is present in Oakeshott's thought. Legends of political life, understood as the memory of shared experiences, are less substantial than natural bonds, but are more substantial than artificial bonds. As will be explored further in Chapter 3, this is characteristic of Oakeshott's practice of inhabiting the middle ground between extremes. In this quest to escape from the dilemma between art and nature he follows Edmund Burke. For Burke, Oakeshott argues, the state understood as history is both natural and artificial.[186] In this sense, 'a product of human history is, like a work of art, the product of human choices; but it is not the product of an express design. And, also, it is like "nature" in having the durability and the unavoidable character we associate with "nature"'.[187] My aim, then, is to show that, for Oakeshott, the bonds that unite members of a state comprise legends of political thought, products of imagination, time and circumstance, which make sense of 'the long enjoyment of a common experience of living together'.[188]

Oakeshott's Concept of 'Legends of Political Life'

Oakeshott is generally categorized as an 'antifoundationalist' political theorist by commentators. This is both logical and coherent since it is congruent with the dichotomy between Rationalism, permanence and perfection, on the one hand, and tradition, practice, contingency, on the other, which is central to his thought. His critique of Rationalism and of systems of *a priori* abstract ideals is reflected in his antifoundationalist stance. This position is confirmed by most commentators (see Auspitz 1976; Campbell Corey 2006; Coats, Jr. 2003 and 2005; Haddock 2005; Mapel 1990; Parekh 1979; Rayner 1985; Vincent 2004). However, what commentators, and Oakeshott himself, focus on explicitly and exclusively is what Seery terms Edenic foundations understood as prior claims about unquestionable, sacred or natural premises.[189] Clearly, Oakeshott rejects foundations understood in Edenic terms—although it may be said that his very rejection of them places him squarely within the Edenic tradition. Yet, as I will argue in Chapter 3, the mixed form of the political Oakeshott defends in *The Politics of Faith and the Politics of*

---

[186] *LHPT*: 424.
[187] *Ibid.*
[188] *LHPT*: 425.
[189] J. Seery 1999: 471.

Scepticism as well as the mixed form of the moral life he deems to be legitimate in 'The Tower of Babel' implies some sort of foundations for the political. Since Oakeshott only recognizes the legitimacy of mixed forms of the political and of morality where contingency dominates, foundations must therefore be contingent. In other words, contingent foundations cannot be 'rationalist' or overly reflective. Rights which emerged contingently cannot subsequently be founded as natural rights by means of a bill of rights, which for Oakeshott is precisely what the American Founding Fathers are guilty of when founding the American republic.[190] A tradition of political behaviour or a political practice cannot legitimately be turned into an abstract system of ideals or rights. This is precisely what the Romans astutely (or, perhaps more accurately, inadvertently) managed to avoid. They never transformed their political experience into an ideology or an abstract system of ideals. Yet, they did nevertheless translate their political way of life into the idiom of general ideas.[191] Oakeshott contends that they did so by means of a legend of politics. That is, they represented their political experience to themselves in terms of a legend constructed by poets. To this end, he asserts that:

> The manner in which the Romans governed and were governed during the thousand years of their political experience was never turned into a coherent system of abstract ideas. Instead, its intellectual organization was that of a legend in which the events and the fortunes of this remark-able people was endowed with a universal significance by being made to compose a work of art—a drama, or a story, whose moral was always being made explicit in events.[192]

The Roman political experience generated a legend of itself in which the Romans 'expressed their beliefs about themselves as a community and about what they were doing in the world'.[193] What is more, this legend also generated political sentiments, beliefs and ideas which, Oakeshott claims, gave it 'a remarkably comprehensive intellectual organization'.[194] In sum, the Roman legend of politics founded Roman identity. This, I posit, is the key to the question of contingent foundations in Oakeshott's political thought. The idea that political experience may be translated into the idiom of general ideas by means of a legend of politics and not a political doctrine is crucial for Oakeshott and it explains in part why he so greatly admired the Romans. The import-

---

[190] *PFPS*: 82–83; *WH*: 235–243.
[191] *LHPT*: 207.
[192] *LHPT*: 208.
[193] *LHPT*: 207.
[194] *Ibid.*

ance of legend and myth cannot be underestimated for it allows his thought to move beyond the dichotomy between permanence and perfection and tradition, practice and contingency. The idea of contingently founding the political by means of the poetic and legends concurs with the second type of foundations identified by Seery: poetic, constructivist foundations. The tradition of constructivist foundations, described by Seery as 'stabilizing constructs', has been largely influenced by Roman political thought, in particular by Virgil.[195]

These are all questions which will be explored in the following chapters. In Chapter 2 and Chapter 4, I examine the idea of legends and make the case that these constructs serve as contingent foundations since they found a political society's identity. These chapters focus on the nature of legends. In order to determine what legends are, I relate them to Oakeshott's modes of experience as well as to philosophy. I argue that legends do not belong to philosophy or history, but that its status as poetry is more difficult to establish given poetry's ambiguous relation to practice in Oakeshott's thought. Throughout the discussion I will argue that legends are contingent foundations which serve as stabilizing constructs for the political in that they found a political society's identity. But first, I will address the secondary literature devoted to Oakeshott's concept of myth and legend.

Interpretations of the Concepts of 'Myth' and 'Legend' in Oakeshott's Political Thought

As Bruce Frohnen remarks, discussion of Oakeshott's view of myth is 'curiously rare', and as for a systematic discussion of the idea of legend, it is inexistent. What discussion there is centres on '*Leviathan*: A Myth' and the two essays entitled 'Tower of Babel'.[196] As Luke O'Sullivan points out, this is all the more curious given that, for Oakeshott, myth is the basis of the state's authority.[197] More specifically, a myth of the state founds authority on some culturally acceptable source.[198] The most thorough and in depth study of the role played by myth in Oakeshott's thought is provided by Frohnen (1990). In his insightful study, Frohnen argues that at the heart of Oakeshott's work lies an 'explicit moral dimension and overtly moral prescription' which is typically overlooked by commentators.[199] This is due to the fact that Oakeshott does not formulate his moral prescription in philosophical terms. In this

---

[195] J. Seery 1999: 483 and 473, 479–480, 485.
[196] B. Frohnen 1990: 790, footnote 2.
[197] L. O'Sullivan 2008: 26.
[198] *Ibid.*: 29.
[199] B. Frohnen 1990: 791.

sense, Frohnen asserts that 'Oakeshott does not provide a sustained reasoned philosophical argument setting forth what it is that makes for a good and moral life'.[200] Oakeshott cannot provide such a philosophical argument as it would not respect the strict division he establishes between philosophy and practice. Simply put, such an argument would not be philosophical but rather ideological. For this reason, Frohnen contends that Oakeshott 'gives us myths — actually versions of what he sees as our one fundamental myth'.[201] Myth is the means by which Oakeshott formulates and expresses his idea of what constitutes a good and moral life.

For Frohnen, in interpreting *Leviathan* unorthodoxly as a myth, Oakeshott advances the argument that Hobbes recognizes that humans need non-rational arguments in order to sustain human living-together. While 'properly instituted laws obligate — are just — because this is what reason dictates', this type of argument is not sufficient to convince humans to 'act in accordance with this rational precept'.[202] In order to convince humans to recognize and respect just laws, Oakeshott's Hobbes, Frohnen maintains, must 'address what is definitely not rational in man'.[203] Frohnen claims that, like Hobbes, Oakeshott is also keenly aware that in spite of the fact that he himself believes that reason provides 'sufficient grounds for following philosophical precepts in politics', humans 'being creatures of passion, are not generally convinced by arguments appealing solely to their reason'.[204] However, the fact that humans are creatures of passion not generally convinced by purely rational arguments is not the only reason explaining the need for non-rational argument. The need for such a type of argument is also partly due to the limited nature of human reason. Frohnen argues that for Oakeshott reason does not institute practice. Rather:

> The origins of existing practices lie outside the reach of rational cognition; they must be accepted and practiced unquestioningly because the activity determines its own coherence. Reason follows action and is subservient to it. History bequeaths to us habits, both intellectual and practical, which form our present character and actions.[205]

What history bequeaths is a civilization. Frohnen maintains that for Oakeshott it is not heroic to attempt to act or reason in contradiction to a civilization's inherited habits, but rather it is unreasonable to do so

---

200 *Ibid.*: 792.
201 *Ibid.*
202 *Ibid.*: 794.
203 *Ibid.*
204 *Ibid.*: 795.
205 *Ibid.*: 799

since such an attempt is 'to attempt to contradict the very nature of things'.[206] That is, it is an attempt to contradict civilization. To act rationally for Oakeshott means to act in accordance with and within the context of the inherited civilization. Since reason is a limited faculty it must be supplemented by habit and unquestioning acceptance if humans are to make sense of the world and act rationally.[207] In other words, given that reason is so limited it is 'only effective in the context of, within the horizons set by, the myth of civilization'.[208] In '*Leviathan*: A Myth', Oakeshott claims that myth is the substance of civilization. It is therefore impossible to dispense with illusions, that is, with myths.[209] Oakeshott contends that *Leviathan* is a retelling of the myth of Western civilization, which he understands to be the myth of medieval Christianity. This myth, which remains the myth of European peoples, tells the story of 'mankind's fall "from happiness and peace" through the sin of Pride'.[210] Frohnen argues that Oakeshott, following Hobbes, also seeks to tame human pride by retelling the myth of civilization. He writes that it is with 'the making of something noble from and the prevention of catastrophe with proper pride, that Oakeshott is most concerned in his own retellings of this most important of human myths'.[211] Oakeshott's concern in the two essays entitled 'Tower of Babel' is with the absence of this proper pride.[212] In the essay which forms part of the collection *Rationalism in Politics*, Frohnen, quoting Oakeshott, reminds us that he tells us that the myth of civilization centres on the pursuit of perfection, an impious and yet unavoidable activity in human life. As such, it involves the penalties of impiety: the anger of the gods and social isolation.[213] While it may be suitable for individuals to pursue perfection, for a society 'the pride involved in attempting this shortcut to heaven, this pursuit of an inherently unrealizable perfection' is disastrous.[214] This is because society requires moral and political peace and the message of Oakeshott's story is that 'the search for perfection results in a "chaos of conflicting ideals" which society cannot survive'.[215] Frohnen interprets the pursuit of perfection as a prideful shortcut to heaven. It is a shortcut from the 'poetic' nature of human activity

---

206 *Ibid.*: 800.
207 *Ibid.*
208 *Ibid.*
209 *Ibid.*: 799.
210 *Ibid.*: 802.
211 *Ibid.*
212 *Ibid.*
213 *Ibid.*
214 *Ibid.*: 803.
215 *Ibid.*

in which 'human action is necessarily nonreflective and habitual since we only know what we intend by our acts when we have acted'.[216] Frohnen also lends great importance to Oakeshott's contention that rationalist morality is the 'denial of the poetic character of all human activity'.[217] The loss of the poetic character of morality, that is, the loss of the 'habituated (affectionate, non-reflective) morality of the early Christians, the pursuit of moral ideals has characterized and confused moral activity in our civilization'.[218] The purpose of the myth of the Tower of Babel, Frohnen maintains, is to awaken us to and disclose this self-deception.[219] While this self-deception concerns the mistaken idea that ideals can prescribe behaviour, it also goes much further than this, Frohnen argues.[220] He asserts that 'at the heart of this self-deception lies a curious blend of slavish concern with material benefits and hubristic pride in the powers of human reason'.[221] It is Frohnen's contention that it is this 'blend of sensuality and improper pride which is the very essence of Oakeshott's chosen myth'.[222] Oakeshott retells this myth in the concluding essay of *On History*, also entitled 'Tower of Babel'. For Frohnen, Oakeshott's story is the retelling of the Hobbesian myth of pride and sensuality. Its intention is to 'show the fearsome consequences of both of man's great polar sins'.[223] More than this, however, Oakeshott's purpose is to teach humans a lesson and Frohnen claims that 'it is only through our acceptance of the meaning (and not only merely the logic) of Oakeshott's Hobbesian myth that Oakeshott's lesson may be learned'.[224] Frohnen argues that the aim of Oakeshott's Hobbesian myth is to teach humans 'the forbearance which is the fundamental basis of civil association'.[225] To this end, the myth aims to convince humans of the 'superiority of a prudent, moderate pride' and consequently to tame their passions.[226] Given that Oakeshott's moral argument takes the form of a myth, Frohnen argues that his '(poetic) concern is with a moral teaching'.[227] His teaching, Frohnen maintains:

---

[216] *Ibid.*
[217] *RP*: 479.
[218] B. Frohnen 1990: 803.
[219] *Ibid.*
[220] *Ibid.*
[221] *Ibid.*
[222] *Ibid.*
[223] *Ibid.*: 805.
[224] *Ibid.*: 806.
[225] *Ibid.*
[226] *Ibid.*
[227] *Ibid.*

seeks to convince us, not merely that it is unreasonable to act so as to disturb the peace of civil association, but that it is *better* not to do so; one which would have us emulate epicurean character and pride for the sake of the life as well as the peace it provides [...] Acceptance of the given myth, for Oakeshott, allows the man of proper pride to avoid the sin of God-displacing pride and to pursue his own ends without worry or doubt, molesting none and even achieving virtue in the social interactions in which he chooses to engage.[228]

In other words, myth is the means by which Oakeshott transmits his moral prescription, that is, it is not founded 'on any argument from objective moral truth'.[229] Frohnen believes that Oakeshott addresses human passion because most humans are incapable of recognizing that this myth is necessary if civilization is to survive. Consequently, Frohnen claims that for Oakeshott 'reason tells us both that there is no objective truth and that illusions must be accepted as if they were true'.[230] Otherwise, Frohnen argues that Oakeshott believes that the improper myth of 'limitless satisfactions' will come to embody civilization.[231] In sum, to question the 'mythical foundations of civilization is both dangerous and immoral'.[232]

The focus of Ian Tregenza's work is Oakeshott and Hobbes. He broaches the question of myth when considering Oakeshott's unorthodox reading of *Leviathan*, specifically as it relates to the critique of Rationalism. Tregenza believes that Oakeshott's intention in the essay '*Leviathan*: A Myth' is to distance Hobbes's conception of reason from Rationalism. For Tregenza, this involves 'downplaying the rationalistic elements and emphasizing the non-rationalistic [...] elements of Hobbes's thought'.[233] It is to this end that Oakeshott makes use of the idea of myth in his reading of Hobbes. Tregenza writes that in a 'radical departure from the received wisdom on Hobbes, Oakeshott makes the startling claim that *Leviathan* is a work of myth not science. It represents a profound retelling of the myth of European civilization. The substance of civilization itself is mythical'.[234] *Leviathan* is a work of myth and not science because 'it displays an awareness of the fact that civilization is above all a work of imagination'.[235] Myth is the substance of civilization which is therefore the product of imagination. The

---

[228] *Ibid.*
[229] *Ibid.*
[230] *Ibid.*
[231] *Ibid.*
[232] *Ibid.*: 790.
[233] I. Tregenza, 2002: 350.
[234] *Ibid.*: 354
[235] *Ibid.*

scientist is unable to grasp this understanding of civilization. He believes that it is 'something more substantial than imagination'.[236] Only the artist is aware of his dreaming powers. It is in this sense that Hobbes is understood by Oakeshott to be an artist and *Leviathan* to be a work of literature 'in the deepest sense of the term'.[237] Tregenza argues that for Oakeshott 'occasionally a work of gigantic imaginative achievement comes along which penetrates to the heart of this dream and retells it giving it a new vitality. *Leviathan*, according to Oakeshott, is a work of this scope'.[238] *Leviathan* is a retelling of the myth of civilization. Hobbes was not the first to retell this myth. We are reminded that Augustine, in combating the heresy of pelegianism (of which Rationalism constitutes a new form, according to Oakeshott), revitalized the narrative myth of European civilization.[239] In this sense, Tregenza maintains that Oakeshott 'sees here continuity, not rupture, between Hobbes's and Augustine's respective versions of the myth'.[240] To emphasize his point, Tregenza quotes Oakeshott to show that for him the importance of *Leviathan* lies in the fact that 'it is the first great achievement in the long-projected attempt of European thought to re-embody, in a new myth the Augustinian epic of the Fall and Salvation of mankind'.[241] However, Tregenza observes that Hobbes's myth is not the only retelling of an old myth. He points out that Bacon's *New Atlantis* is the retelling of the competing pelagian myth. He contends that there are 'two competing myths of civilization, written at a similar moment in history, with two corresponding accounts of, what Oakeshott calls, "the human predicament" and the contribution that the political order makes to its resolution'.[242] Tregenza, then, beginning from Oakeshott's argument that myth is the substance of civilization pursues this idea to its logical conclusion and puts forward the idea that for Oakeshott political modernity is characterized by the tension between these two competing myths of civilization.

For his part, it is Thomas W. Smith's interest in Oakeshott's philosophy of history which leads him to consider Oakeshott's interpretation of Hobbes's *Leviathan*, not only within the context of his reflection on history, but also in relation to his thought more generally. Smith states that Oakeshott considers *Leviathan* to be a political myth, that is, 'an artful contrivance, an example of what Oakeshott terms the "message-

---

[236] *Ibid.*

[237] *Ibid.*

[238] *Ibid.*

[239] *Ibid.*: 355

[240] *Ibid.*

[241] Oakeshott quoted by I. Tregenza 2002: 356.

[242] *Ibid.*: 356.

bearing survivals" of legend, saga and myth'.[243] As we will see in the section on history, Oakeshott distinguishes legend, saga and myth from legitimate history. However, this does not mean that myth, and consequently *Leviathan,* are illegitimate or inferior in any way. On the contrary, Smith maintains that for Oakeshott *Leviathan* is a 'political masterpiece because it is a masterly political myth, an accomplishment in the history of political thought [...] shared only with *The Republic*'.[244] *Leviathan* achieves the fusion of 'history ("the ordered register of past experiences"), and prudence ("the power to anticipate experience by means of the recollection of what has gone before", the "end and crown" of experience)'.[245] Smith emphasizes the importance of this fusion for Oakeshott who, in his 'Introduction' to *Leviathan*, points out that this allows Hobbes to say that 'of our conceptions of the past, we make a future'.[246] What Hobbes tells us, and as we will see later on, is that myth allows us to make or build a future, thereby allowing us to know who we are and to feel at home in the world. For Smith, Oakeshott's reading of *Leviathan* 'illumines Hobbes and unifies his philosophy. In *Leviathan* Oakeshott sees "the transposition of an abstract argument into the world of the imagination"'.[247]

In their respective discussions of the role played by imagination and myth in Oakeshott's thought all three commentators focus almost exclusively on the essay '*Leviathan*: A Myth' and the two 'Tower of Babel' essays. Although it should be noted that given his interest for Oakeshott's philosophy of history Smith examines the distinction he draws between myth and legitimate history. Consequently, it has been well-observed that for Oakeshott myth is the substance of civilization. While the essay '*Leviathan*: A Myth' and its discussion of the role of the artist and of literature is of vital importance to the understanding of myth in Oakeshott's thought (I examine it in detail in Chapter 4 which treats the idiom of poetry), I argue that Oakeshott's conception of myth and legend, that is, of a constructed foundational narrative, is richer and more complex than is indicated by the discussion in that essay. '*Leviathan*: A Myth' is only one of the constitutive elements which compose legends. I take a different approach to the question of myth and legend as my concern with this narrative form is different from that of the other commentators. As the example of Rome suggests, Oakeshott conceives of an important role for legends of political life. They, in

---

[243] T.W. Smith 1996: 611.

[244] *Ibid.*: 612.

[245] *Ibid.*

[246] Hobbes quoted by Oakeshott and cited by T.W. Smith 1996: 612.

[247] Oakeshott quoted by T.W. Smith 1996: 613.

effect, found a political society's identity. My purpose is to explore how
they work as a foundational narrative for the political. In order to
determine what legends of political life are, I relate them to modes of
experience and philosophy. I make the case that legends involve a
certain kind of reflection upon the political, a concern with the past and
constitute a form of poetry. The aim is to understand how all these
elements interact with one another and work together to compose
legends. The political experience of the ancient Romans suggests a
certain number of questions which will guide my reflection: What is the
relation between legend and a society's identity, sense of self-
consciousness and knowledge of itself? How do legends allow humans
to feel at home in the world? And finally, how do they work as
contingent foundations for the political?

Conclusion

Oakeshott's answer to the problem of foundations in political
modernity is more complex than may at first appear and is far less
straightforward than the interpretations defended by commentators.
The problem of the compatibility between an absolute such as God or
Nature deemed necessary to legitimate and justify positive, man-made
laws, on the one hand, and the requirement to submit everything to the
methodical doubt, on the other, which characterizes political
modernity, is a problem which Oakeshott takes seriously and which he
seeks to resolve in a creative, original and practical manner. Foundations understood as prior claims about unquestionable or sacred or
natural premises are not to be found in Oakeshott's political thought. I
agree with commentators on this point. Oakeshott's political thought is
devoid of pre-given foundations or what Seery terms Edenic foundations. I discuss this in detail in Chapter 3. However, Oakeshott's
answer is not to say that the political is altogether devoid of foundations. It is only possible to arrive at such a conclusion if the fundamental and essential role played by imagination in Oakeshott's political
thought is ignored. Oakeshott's conception of the political, more
particularly of a political society's identity, requires foundations.
Political imagination is Oakeshott's creative and original answer to the
problem of foundations in political modernity. Following Anderson, I
argue that the modern nation-state is an imagined political community,
a constructed solidarity amongst strangers who identify with a
common political imaginary. In other words, they share a common
political identity since political imagination founds a political society's
identity, thereby ensuring human living-together. I make the case that,
for Oakeshott, legends of political life play this foundational role. The
shared political imaginary is conceived of by Oakeshott as a con-

structed narrative, a poetic creation, centred upon a remembered past event. Such a constructed narrative is also a manner for a society to reflect upon the political and translate its political experience into the idiom of general ideas. For this reason, I claim that Oakeshott, far from being antifoundationalist, belongs to the Arendtian constructivist tradition of foundations. However, Oakeshott's constructed foundationalism differs from Arendt's in so far as his conception of political legends does not necessarily refer to an arbitrary new beginning, but, rather, following his understanding of the modern state as an historical association, legends of political life make sense of a tradition of political behaviour. In other words, political legends constitute the ties that bind otherwise unattached individuals who have a memory of shared experiences.

Furthermore, I claim that Oakeshott concurs with Seery that it is poets and not Gods who are the architects of political foundations. In other words, a political society's identity is erected or built and not pre-given. As we will see in Chapter 5, the fundamental role attributed to poets reveals the importance of the Roman political experience for Oakeshott's conception of political legends. He holds that the Romans showed the greatest genius for politics. In particular, their poets, and not their gods, were the creators of a legend of political life which has never been surpassed in its ability to endow a society with its sense of identity. He makes clear that the Roman political legend was the work of poets and, thus, that they were responsible for the imaginary construct which founded their society's identity. I argue in Chapter 5 that the Roman political legend inspires Oakeshott's own concept of foundational narratives. The importance Oakeshott attributes to the Roman political experience is consistent with Seery's claim that the single most important source of inspiration for thinkers of the constructivist tradition is Rome. Moreover, the fact that legends of political life are in essence contingent foundations places Oakeshott squarely in the Arendtian constructivist tradition since one of Arendt's main concerns is to find a way for permanence and change to be tied together, something which the Romans achieved. I show in the third and fourth chapters that it is poetry which unites permanence and contingency and, thus, gives rise to contingent foundations in Oakeshott's political thought. Political imagination, then, by means of legends of political life, founds a political society's identity and ensures human living-together since all of its members identify with the same imaginary. In sum, for Oakeshott, imagination is indispensable to the political.

Chapter Two

Legends of Political Life: Constructed Foundations for the Political

Introduction

Oakeshott, like all political philosophers, is deeply concerned about human living-together. The question is central to his political thought. When we think about Oakeshott and the question of human living-together, we are perhaps most accustomed to do so in terms of the modes of association: civil and enterprise. The problem he explores in *On Human Conduct* is how to ensure human living-together while ensuring individual freedom. He concludes that civil association is the mode of association which, in moral terms, best respects the modern individual's moral disposition. This reflection upon the civil condition is a fundamental part of Oakeshott's work and it is indispensable if we want to understand his thought on human living-together. However, Oakeshott's thought in relation to human living-together does not end with this type of procedural, judicial and analytical reflection upon the modern European state. Imagination plays a central role in Oakeshott's thought in relation to human living-together. I make the case that the political imagination, by means of legends of political life, founds a political society's identity. Put another way, imagination ensures solidarity amongst strangers since all members of a political society identify with the same constructed political imaginary. As we will see in the present chapter, legends of political life allow humans to make themselves at home in the world, to know who and where they are in space and time and to project themselves into the future. In sum, political legends are stabilizing constructs for the political.

The purpose of the present chapter, as well as of chapters 3 and 4, is to determine political legends' constitutive elements. Oakeshott's philosophy cannot be understood without first understanding his theory of experience and of modes. This theory structures his entire thought.

Every aspect of the world and of human life is understood in terms of the modes of experience and of philosophy. In other words, humans apprehend the world through the modes of experience. Although there is no limit to the number of modes by which we can experience the world, Oakeshott identifies four: science, history, practice and poetry. I posit that since Oakeshott's political thought cannot be understood without understanding the modes of experience that this is also true for legends of political life. In order to determine political legends' constitutive elements, I relate them to the modes of history and poetry as well as to philosophy. In the present chapter, I examine two of their constitutive elements. I ask if legends of political life are philosophical and if they are historical. In chapters 3 and 4 I relate legends of political life to poetry. Political legends are incontestably a type of reflection upon the political since they allow political societies to translate their experience into the idiom of general ideas. I argue, however, that they do not consist in philosophical reflection, but, rather, political legends are a foundational type of reflection upon the political in that it is reflection which 'fixes' a political society's identity. In this sense, reflection here is not 'perpetually en voyage', but is firmly anchored. I then treat the mode of history. I show that, for Oakeshott, legends of political life are not occurrences of the historical past, but of the practical past, a fundamental element of his weak foundationalism. Political legends are constructed upon a remembered event, recalled from the practical past, the recounting of which stabilizes the practical present. Although Oakeshott distinguishes the practical past from the historical past, it is not for that matter an illegitimate or inferior type of past. On the contrary, it is an indispensable ingredient of civilized life. Oakeshott is adamant that legends of political life and the practical past are indispensable to political societies since it is these constructs which endow them with their sense of identity and ensure that they have knowledge of themselves, thereby ensuring human living-together. The aim of the present chapter, then, is to show that foundational reflection upon the political and the practical past are two of the constitutive elements of legends of political life. I begin the chapter with an overview of Oakeshott's theory of experience and its modes.

The Modes of Experience

In order to understand how Oakeshott conceives of legends, or myths as he also designates these narratives, it is necessary to first outline his theory of modes and experience. He first elaborates his theory in 1933's *Experience and its Modes*. There, he sets out his version of idealism. Noël O'Sullivan argues that the central theme of *Experience and its Modes* is

Oakeshott's 'rejection of all claims to absolute knowledge'.[1] In other words, Oakeshott's main argument is that 'all human knowledge is inescapably *conditional*'.[2] As we will see, and as O'Sullivan explains, this is what Oakeshott means when he speaks of the 'modality' of experience.[3] It is his position that 'we always look at the world from a particular standpoint'.[4] Experience, Oakeshott posits, forms a single, homogeneous whole.[5] Following in the idealist tradition, Oakeshott asserts that experience is thought because there is 'no experiencing which is not thinking, nothing experienced which is not thought, and consequently no experience which is not a world of ideas'.[6] For him, experience is thought and involves judgment since humans perceive only that which they recognize. That is, humans recognize only that which has meaning or significance for them and for there to be meaning or significance there must necessarily be judgment.[7] Judgment involves thought and, consequently for Oakeshott, all experience is thought. Experience, he argues, begins and ends with judgment.[8] Put another way, to be conscious of something is 'to recognize it; and recognition involves us at once in judgment, in inference, in reflection, in thought'.[9] Therefore, experience is thought and thus constitutes a world of ideas.[10]

By the term 'world', Oakeshott means a 'complex, integral whole or system'.[11] What is given in experience is just such a world of ideas.[12] However, what is given is never satisfactory. It is incapable of maintaining itself as a world.[13] Thus, for Oakeshott, 'the given in experience is given always in order to be transformed'.[14] In experience a given world of ideas is transformed into a 'world of ideas which is more of a world'.[15] By this, Oakeshott means that the unity of a world of ideas is enhanced. That is, 'a given world or unity of ideas is reorganized into a

---

1   N. O'Sullivan 2002: 71.
2   *Ibid.*, original emphasis.
3   *Ibid.*
4   *Ibid.*
5   *EM*: 26–27.
6   *Ibid.*
7   *EM*: 16.
8   *EM*: 20.
9   *EM*: 14.
10   *EM*: 27.
11   *EM*: 28.
12   *Ibid.*
13   *EM*: 28–29.
14   *EM*: 29.
15   *EM*: 30.

closer unity'.[16] What is thus achieved is a world of ideas that is complete and can maintain itself.[17] Experience remains incomplete until the world of ideas is fully coherent. That is, until it becomes impossible to 'suggest or oblige another way of conceiving it'.[18]

The transformation of a given world of ideas into an achieved world which is more of a world requires a critical attitude towards what is given in order to discover the unity it implies. In other words, the world that is achieved in experience is 'contained seminally or implicitly in what is given'.[19] In sum, for Oakeshott, a given world of ideas is 'always amplified by the elucidation of its implications'.[20] It is important to note that while Oakeshott argues that the given world is transformed, he uses the term 'amplification' to designate the act of transformation. This means that the given world of ideas is not completely transformed or changed. Rather, Oakeshott asserts that in experience 'the given is simultaneously conserved and transformed'.[21] Moreover, Oakeshott adamantly refutes the idea that the transformation and amplification of a given world is done in such a manner that it corresponds to a fixed idea.[22] In experience, 'coherence is the sole criterion'.[23] By coherence, Oakeshott means that the only absolute in experience is 'a complete and unified world of ideas'.[24] Thus, when experience corresponds with the criterion of coherence, it in fact corresponds with itself. For Oakeshott, what is elucidated is 'the implications of a given world of ideas under the guidance of the criterion of coherence'.[25] What Oakeshott also exposes here is a certain conception of knowledge particular to experience and understood as 'the achievement of the coherence of a given world or system of ideas by the pursuit of the implications of that world'.[26]

The criterion of coherence in experience also relates to truth. Oakeshott argues that truth belongs to what is achieved in experience. By this he means that truth is a result and what is true is so because it is a result.[27] This implies that the criterion of truth is the coherence of an

---

16 *Ibid.*
17 *EM*: 29.
18 *EM*: 34.
19 *EM*: 31.
20 *EM*: 33.
21 *EM*: 37
22 *EM*: 33.
23 *EM*: 37.
24 *EM*: 40.
25 *EM*: 43.
26 *EM*: 41.
27 *EM*: 48.

achieved world of experience. In other words, for Oakeshott, a world of
ideas is true 'when it is coherent and because it is coherent'.[28] Consequently, the implication of Oakeshott's understanding of truth is that
there is no external means by which it can be established since truth is
the truth of a given world of ideas.[29]

Finally, Oakeshott asserts that reality is experience and, since
experience is a world of ideas, reality is, subsequently, also a world of
ideas. That is, reality is 'what is achieved and is satisfactory in experience'.[30] What is achieved and is satisfactory in experience is a coherent
world of ideas. Thus, reality is a coherent world of ideas and it is 'real
because it is coherent'.[31] However, Oakeshott stresses that reality is not
a world of mere ideas, which are abstractions, but of concrete ideas or
things. By thing, Oakeshott means 'whatever behaves (and can sustain
such behaviour) as a single whole or unity'.[32] It is a unity and, consequently, a totality. Reality, then, is a fully coherent world of concrete
ideas. It knows no degrees since it is perfect and complete.[33]

Modifications may be distinguished within experience. They occur
when 'at any point short of complete coherence there is an arrest, a
modification of the full character of experience'.[34] More precisely, a
mode of experience is the whole of experience perceived from a limited
standpoint. Put another way, it is a limited view of the totality of
experience and, as such, it is necessarily abstract.[35] Alternatively,
Oakeshott also refers to modes of experience as arrests in experience.
He contends that at the point of the arrest a separate world of ideas is
constructed, thus constituting a mode of experience.[36] Modes consequently are specific worlds of ideas. They are abstract because they
are only partial experience. In this respect, they are inherently defective
because they are the whole from a limited standpoint. While, as
mentioned previously, Oakeshott asserts that the number of potential
modes of experience is unlimited, in *Experience and its Modes* he identifies three specific modes: history, science and practice. In the 1959
essay 'The Voice of Poetry in the Conversation of Mankind' he aug-
ments his theory of modes by distinguishing a fourth mode of experience, that of poetry. Because it is an abstract, homogeneous world of

---

28   *Ibid.*
29   *Ibid.*
30   *EM*: 57–58.
31   *EM*: 58.
32   *EM*: 62.
33   *EM*: 67.
34   *EM*: 71.
35   *EM*: 71, 73.
36   *EM*: 73–74.

ideas, for Oakeshott, each mode of experience is 'wholly and absolutely independent of any other'.[37] It therefore follows that there is no direct relationship between the modes of experience. Oakeshott argues that it cannot be otherwise because 'each abstract world of ideas is a specific organization of the whole of experience, exclusive of every other organization'.[38] Consequently, it is impossible to pass in argument from one mode of experience to another.[39] As for the relation of modes to the whole of experience or a fully coherent world, since abstract worlds of ideas are arrests in experience they do not belong to reality. They are the 'organization of the whole of experience from a partial and defective point of view'.[40] The whole of experience is not made up of these separate, abstract, homogeneous worlds of ideas. Rather, the whole of experience is implied in the modes and it cannot be dependent of them since it is logically prior to them.[41]

If history, science and practice (which includes the modulation of politics) are modes of experience; that is, the whole of experience perceived from a partial or limited standpoint, Oakeshott defines philosophy as 'experience without reservation or presupposition'.[42] It is experience which is self-conscious, self-critical and which is pursued for its own sake.[43] Philosophical experience is 'wherever in experience the concrete purpose is pursued without hindrance or distraction'.[44] It remains unsatisfied with anything short of a completely coherent world of ideas. In this sense, philosophy's task is to consider the character of every world of experience from 'the standpoint of its capacity to provide what is satisfactory in experience'.[45] Its task then is to recognize abstraction and to overcome it.[46]

It is important to observe the connection between the idealist criterion of coherence Oakeshott elaborates in *Experience and its Modes* and his understanding of a tradition of political behaviour in the essay 'Political Education'. The link between the idealist philosophy of *Experience and its Modes* and the conception of politics in *Rationalism in Politics* is clear. In 'Political Education', Oakeshott conceives of politics as a tradition of behaviour. Such a tradition emerges amongst a

---

37 *EM*: 75.
38 *EM*: 75–76.
39 *EM*: 76.
40 *EM*: 78–79.
41 *EM*: 79.
42 *EM*: 82.
43 *Ibid.*
44 *EM*: 81–82.
45 *EM*: 83
46 *EM*: 84.

collection of people, who, over time, come to recognize themselves as constituting a community in that each member recognizes and respects the arrangements of the community and the manner of attending to them. In other words, such a collection of people form a single community since they recognize the authority of rules (arrangements) and the political procedure to amend the rules.[47] The criterion of coherence applies to the tradition and its arrangements. A tradition is coherent in so far as its arrangements reflect current social practice and reality. A political society's arrangements are never fully coherent. There is always an element of incoherency present within a tradition of political behaviour. The aim of political activity is to attend to a community's arrangements in order to make them and the tradition as coherent as possible. For Oakeshott, this is achieved by exploring and pursuing what the arrangements intimate. In so far as arrangements are incoherent, that is, they do not correspond to current social practice and values, they call for amendment and intimate change.[48] In other words, a community's arrangements 'intimate a sympathy for what does not fully appear'.[49] Political activity consists in exposing a sympathy and demonstrating that it ought to be recognized and that the change it suggests should be implemented. An 'ought' is therefore transformed into an 'is'. In sum, politics is 'the pursuit of the intimations' of a tradition of political behaviour. The purpose of the pursuit is to ensure the augmentation of a political tradition's coherency.[50] Moreover, for Oakeshott, the criterion of coherency guards a community against arbitrariness. He argues that the proposed change must make sense for the whole of the tradition of behaviour. In this respect, Oakeshott asserts that in a tradition of political behaviour 'everything figures by comparison, not with what stands next to it, but with the whole'.[51] In other words, political activity is taking a given world of ideas, a tradition of behaviour, and making it more of a world. Political change must make sense for the whole of tradition and make it more coherent.

Political activity thus requires a profound knowledge of the tradition of political behaviour. Oakeshott argues that 'what has to be learned is not an abstract idea, or a set of tricks, not even a ritual, but a concrete, coherent manner of living in all its intricateness'.[52] We find here again the criterion of coherence. Once more, Oakeshott rejects the argument that an abstract idea may serve as a foundation for the

47 *RP*: 56–57.
48 *Ibid.*
49 *RP*: 57.
50 *RP*: 56–57.
51 *RP*: 61.
52 *RP*: 62.

political. Moreover, he also refutes the idea that political knowledge may be gained by means of an abstract idea or other such 'tricks'. What has to be learned is a manner of living which is concrete and coherent and, consequently, satisfactory and complete. This concurs with Oakeshott's discussion of the truth of a mode of experience in *Experience and its Modes*. In so far as politics is a modulation of the mode of practice, its truth is 'relative to the degree of completeness which belongs to its world of ideas, its organization of reality'.[53] [54] In sum, for Oakeshott, a tradition of political behaviour avoids the defect of arbitrariness because it must achieve complete coherence. A modification of the arrangements of a community must therefore make sense for the whole of tradition and amplify its coherence.

For Oakeshott, then, what has to be learned in politics is a tradition of political behaviour. However, he himself acknowledges that a tradition of behaviour is a 'tricky thing to get to know'.[55] How can members of a community know whether a change makes sense for the whole of tradition? How is knowledge of a tradition of behaviour acquired? The acquisition of the knowledge of a society is made all the more difficult since a tradition is perpetually undergoing transformation. It may thus appear to be unintelligible since it is 'neither fixed nor finished'.[56] In other words, in a tradition everything is temporary and no part of it is immune from change. Once again, it should be noted that Oakeshott expressly rejects foundations understood in Edenic terms. Knowledge cannot anchor itself to a changeless centre since every part of the tradition inevitably undergoes transformation.[57] Although he acknowledges these difficulties, Oakeshott nevertheless argues that a tradition of behaviour is not devoid of identity and that it is thus a possible object of knowledge since all of its parts do not change at the same time. In other words, a tradition of political behaviour is 'steady' enough to get to know because 'though it moves, it is never wholly in motion; and though it is tranquil, it is never wholly at rest'.[58] The challenge for Oakeshott is to find a manner to get to know a tradition of political behaviour without falling prey to Rationalism and simply being content with a list of abstract ideals. In the essay 'Political Education', Oakeshott argues once more that the answer to the problem is legends. He argues that every society (and not just the Romans) has recourse to legends as a means of political education. He

---

53   *RP*: 493.
54   *EM*: 77.
55   *RP*: 61.
56   *Ibid.*
57   *Ibid.*
58   *Ibid.*

asserts that a society 'by the underlinings it makes in the book of its history, constructs a legend of its own fortunes which it keeps up to date and in which is hidden its own understanding of its politics'.[59] Legends, as Oakeshott understands them, are essentially a representation of the manner of a society's political thinking.[60] Rather than abridging a political tradition and translating it into a system of foundational abstract principles, a legend represents the tradition and reflects it back to society. By familiarizing oneself with a society's political legend it is possible to acquire the requisite political knowledge. Legends thus constitute stabilizing constructs for society and the political. They ensure a society's self-knowledge and self-understanding. Moreover, their study becomes an integral part of a political education. I will pursue this idea further on in the section devoted to history.

The point of the preceding discussion was to show the link between Oakeshott's idealism, politics, knowledge and legends. Returning to the subject at hand, Oakeshott's idealism and his theory of modes, it will be recalled that in *Experience and its Modes* he distinguishes between the whole of experience, which is a concrete and coherent world of ideas, and the modes of experience, which he defines as abstract worlds of ideas that perceive the whole of experience from a limited standpoint. As explained earlier, in *Experience and its Modes*, Oakeshott identifies three modes of experience: science, history and practice. He does not attribute the status of mode to poetry or aesthetics. Rather, poetry is deemed to be a part of practice. He argues that whereas philosophy, science and history are attempts to escape from the conduct of life; art, music and poetry are 'wholly taken up with practical life'.[61] However, the status of poetry changes in the essay 'The Voice of Poetry in the Conversation of Mankind', which is part of the collection *Rationalism in Politics*. In the preface to that book, Oakeshott explains that 'the essay on poetry is a belated retraction of a foolish sentence in *Experience and its Modes*'.[62] The sentence Oakeshott is referring to is the one quoted above. 'The Voice of Poetry in the Conversation of Mankind' is meant as a rectification of the status of poetry as well as a revision and augmentation of his theory of modes. (The status of poetry in Oakeshott's thought is a question I will return to later in Chapter 4.) As the title of the essay indicates, Oakeshott now conceives of modes as 'voices' or 'idioms' engaged in 'conversation'. Whereas in *Experience and its Modes* Oakeshott argues that the modes are wholly and absolutely independ-

---

59 *RP*: 63.
60 *Ibid.*
61 *EM*: 297.
62 *RP*: preface.

ent of each other and that there is no direct relationship between them, in his revised position he believes that the diverse idioms of utterance which make up human intercourse have 'some meeting-place'.[63] This meeting-place is a conversation. For Oakeshott, a conversation does not compose an argument, an enquiry or a debate. Consequently, it remains impossible to pass in argument from one mode to another since in conversation the voices or idioms are 'not concerned to inform, to persuade, or to refute one another'.[64] In a conversation, Oakeshott maintains, there is 'no "truth" to be discovered, no proposition to be proved, no conclusion sought'.[65] Rather, it is a meeting-place where different universes of discourse 'meet, acknowledge each other and enjoy an oblique relationship'.[66] Each voice engaged in the conversation is a reflection of a human activity. In this essay, Oakeshott distinguishes four participant voices in the conversation: poetry, history, science and practice. Briefly, it is of interest to note that Oakeshott also refers to this idea of conversation when defining culture. In this respect, in the lecture 'A Place of Learning', which he first delivered in 1974, he conceives of culture as 'a variety of distinct languages of understanding'.[67] Put another way, Oakeshott asserts that the components of a culture may be thought of as voices 'each the expression of a distinct and conditional understanding of the world and a distinct idiom of human self-understanding'.[68] As for the relationship of its components, Oakeshott explains that culture should be understood as these voices joined in conversation.[69] Finally, Oakeshott maintains that a culture also comprises myths, stories and poems 'expressing fragments of human self-understanding'.[70] In short, culture for Oakeshott 'is a historic contingency'.[71]

'The Voice of Poetry in the Conversation of Mankind' also offers Oakeshott the opportunity to revise his conception of the real world as well as of the activity of thought. Oakeshott defines the real world as a world of experience where 'self and not-self divulge themselves to reflection'.[72] The self, Oakeshott argues, appears as the activity of imagining which is nothing more than the self 'making and recognizing

---

63   *RP*: 489.
64   *Ibid.*
65   *Ibid.*
66   *RP*: 490.
67   *VL*: 29.
68   *VL*: 30.
69   *Ibid.*
70   *VL*: 17
71   *Ibid.*
72   *RP*: 495.

images, and moving about among them'.[73] It should be noted that
Oakeshott has substituted imagining for thinking and images for ideas.
The not-self is composed of images which are not 'given', but which are
'made'. Nevertheless, despite the fact that the self makes images,
Oakeshott insists that the self and the not-self, imagining and image are
'neither cause and consequent nor consciousness and its contents'.[74]
This is the case because images are nothing if they are not in relation
with a self and a self cannot appear or constitute itself without images.
Moreover, images are always specific in character since they correspond to a specific mode of imagining. Finally, imagining for Oakeshott
is not an activity which precedes and provides the materials for
thought. The activity of imagining is not a condition of thought. Rather,
it is one of the modes of thought.[75]

W.H. Greenleaf provides a convincing argument explaining why
Oakeshott is obliged to change his view of experience and modes, and,
more specifically, his conception of thought, when he changes the
status of poetry. He points out that as opposed to science, history and
practice, poetry is not judgment. However, in order for poetry to constitute a mode it must be a separate, homogeneous world with con-
siderabilities of its own. These must be of the same status, but not of the
same kind as science, history and practice.[76] For Greenleaf, this means
that Oakeshott's account of the modes of experience has to be 'translated [...] into a new terminology of wider application which will be
suitable for the exposition of all four modes of experience in similar
terms'.[77] For this reason, the meaning of experience or thinking must be
expanded in order to include all forms of mental activity. Oakeshott
uses the word 'imagining' to define this expanded meaning of thinking.
Greenleaf believes that this revised and augmented account of experience achieves a 'new level of coherence in the account of experience'.[78]

In order to determine what legends and myths are, the mode to
which they belong must first be established. Although it is safe to
assume that legends and myths do not belong to the mode of science, a
strong case can be made for the other modes.[79] It might be argued that
political legends and myths are to be understood as history, poetry and

---

[73] *RP*: 496.
[74] *Ibid.*
[75] *RP*: 497.
[76] W.H. Greenleaf 1966: 34.
[77] *Ibid.*
[78] *Ibid.*: 35.
[79] This statement would be contested by those who defend the idea that the nature
      of narrative is determined by human evolution. See Gottschall, J. and Sloan
      Wilson, D. (eds.) 2005, *The Literary Animal: Evolution and the Nature of Narrative*.

even philosophy. The relationship of legends and myths to philosophy, history and poetry will be examined in turn. It will become evident throughout the discussion that legends' practical element is undeniable. The question then is: are legends solely practical experience or do they belong to another mode of experience as well? In spite of Oakeshott's claims to the contrary, do legends transcend one single mode of experience and pass in argument from one mode to another, thus constituting a synthesis of two or more modes?

Legends of Political Life and Philosophy

It may be argued that legends or myths are instances of philosophical reflection. In the case of the Romans, Oakeshott argues that the intellectual organization of that society, which was remarkably firm and profound, was a legend of political life. That is, the manner in which they governed and were governed was turned into a legend and thus endowed with universal significance.[80] Furthermore, in 'Political Education', Oakeshott asserts that every society constructs a legend which expresses its own understanding of its politics. This understanding is the history of the manner of a society's political thinking. Hidden in a legend is what people have thought and said about their society's manner of governing.[81] Therefore, there are what are commonly thought of as philosophical elements involved in legends such as intellectual organization, universality and reflection about politics. For Oakeshott, however, to view legends as philosophy is erroneous since it is to misunderstand the role and purpose of philosophy.

In *Experience and its Modes*, Oakeshott defines philosophy as 'experience without presupposition, reservation, arrest or modification'.[82] Philosophical experience is critical and reflective throughout. It loses its character when it becomes distracted or hindered by what is partial and abstract.[83] This means that philosophy must not be distracted or hindered from its purpose by the abstract mode of practice and its modulation, politics. Oakeshott pursues the idea that philosophy is 'unhindered reflective enterprise' in the essay 'Political Philosophy' which has been dated to 1946–1950.[84] In this essay, he explicitly argues against the position that philosophy requires foundations. To this end, he posits that all of the different kinds of reflective enterprises begin with knowledge and with the presupposition that that knowledge is

---

80   *LHPT*: 208.
81   *RP*: 63.
82   *EM*: 2.
83   *EM*: 3.
84   *RPML*: 144.

infected with ignorance. Oakeshott distinguishes between those reflective enterprises which involve a partial subversion of the knowledge they begin with and philosophical reflection which is radically subversive.[85] Subversion is limited by a kind of reflective enterprise which presupposes that 'it is possible to establish a body of opinions so firmly that it can be given the name of "fact" or "thing"'.[86] Firmly establishing a body of opinions allows this kind of reflection to increase its knowledge of something whose identity is fixed. Put another way, this kind of reflective enterprise 'takes on the appearance of building a structure upon an assured foundation'.[87] Oakeshott acknowledges that there are times when a term is put to subversiveness and firm anchorages are laid out for reflection, the intention being that it will not move beyond these fixed limits.[88] Philosophy, however, is reflective enterprise the precise purpose of which is to avoid all fixed points of reference. It is reflection which is designed to remain fluid. As such, it appears only when firm anchorages have been rejected. Thus, for Oakeshott, philosophy is radically subversive reflection.[89]

This understanding of philosophy is most comprehensively developed in the first essay of *On Human Conduct,* 'On the Theoretical Understanding of Human Conduct'. There, he defines theorizing as the 'unconditional engagement of understanding'.[90] Its unconditionality stems from its principle which is to 'never ask the end'.[91] Theory, as does all reflection, begins in an already understood. In other words, theorizing does not begin in pure ignorance. It begins with knowledge which, for the purposes of reflection, is assumed to be ignorance or not true. All reflection springs from the paradox that 'we know and that at the same time we do not know'.[92] In the enterprise of theorizing, understanding begins with a 'fact' which is a 'first and conditionally acceptable understanding of a "going-on"'.[93] From this primary form of knowledge it is possible to further abate the unintelligibility of the world by detaching a going-on from its contingent circumstances and identifying it in terms of an ideal character. Ideal characters are theoretical instruments of identification and as such are reflective com-

---

85 *RPML*: 138–140.
86 *RPML*: 141.
87 *Ibid.*
88 *Ibid.*
89 *RPML*: 141–143.
90 *HC*: 1.
91 *HC*: 2.
92 *RPML*: 138.
93 *HC*: 2.

positions of characteristics.[94] Identification specifies 'a *this* in terms of an ideal character composed of characteristics'.[95] Facts thus understood become identities. Although a going-on is now identified in terms of an ideal character understood in terms of characteristics, and even though such identities may be related to one another, thus allowing for a more satisfactory level of understanding to be achieved, this nevertheless remains conditional understanding. It corresponds to what Oakeshott refers to as platforms of conditional understanding.[96] Since theorizing is a continuous, self-moved and critical enterprise, it remains unsatisfied with conditional understanding.[97] For the theorist, a platform of conditional understanding is akin to 'a prison from which he seeks release'.[98] Theory finds a release from conditionality in the recognition that identities, although conditionally understood, are also not-yet-understoods. They are invitations to understand which allow theory to move beyond platforms of conditional understanding. What is not yet understood is the conditionality of identities. Thus, theory seeks to make identities more intelligible by understanding them in terms of their postulates or conditions. By turning its attention to the conditionality of identities, theory is able to move beyond its current and unsatisfactory understanding.[99] For Oakeshott, theory, in making these postulates the terms of its understandings, comes 'to occupy a new platform of conditional understanding'.[100] Simply put, theory has transferred its attention from the characteristics of identities to its postulates. The postulates which are used for understanding a particular identity themselves demand to be recognized as identities in their own right and so on and so forth.[101] Thus a theorist, by attending to postulates as identities which need to be understood, finds himself 'embarked upon an adventure in understanding which must soon carry him far out of sight of what he purports to be seeking to understand'.[102] This, for Oakeshott, is what philosophical activity consists in. Theory, he argues, is an 'unconditional adventure in which every achievement of understanding is an invitation to investigate itself'.[103] Thus, theory continually generates 'not-yet-understoods' which must be investigated. In this

---

[94] *HC*: 4.
[95] *HC*: 5, original emphasis.
[96] *HC*: 6–8.
[97] *HC*: 2.
[98] *HC*: 8.
[99] *HC*: 8–9.
[100] *HC*: 9.
[101] *HC*: 10.
[102] *Ibid.*
[103] *HC*: 11.

sense, Oakeshott asserts that theorizing is to be 'perpetually *en voyage*'.[104] In sum, what constitutes the unconditionality of the engagement of understanding is 'the continuous recognition of the conditionality of conditions'.[105]

In the case of human conduct, to understand it theoretically is therefore to understand it in terms of its postulates or conditions. At the end of the essay 'On the Theoretical Understanding of Human Conduct', Oakeshott provides a detailed exposition of the enterprise of theorizing human conduct, and, in so doing, he explicitly distinguishes between theory and myth. To theorize human conduct is to understand contingency, that is:

> a relationship between 'goings-on' identified as individual occurrences exhibiting intelligence (human actions and utterances) in which they are understood in the only way in which their formal character as such individual occurrences allows them to be understood, namely, in terms of their dependent connections with other such occurrences.[106]

For Oakeshott, understanding in terms of contingent relations is contextual.[107] A contingent relationship, he argues, is a 'sequential relationship of intelligent individual occurrences where what comes after is recognized to be conditional upon what went before'.[108] Intelligent individual occurrences, or human actions and utterances, are intelligible because they are conditional upon what precedes them. In this sense, Oakeshott argues that occurrences are intelligible because they 'touch'. In 'touching', occurrences not only 'identify themselves as belonging together', they also identify themselves as 'composing an intelligible continuity of conditionally dependent occurrences'.[109] That is, the contingent relationship theory is engaged to understand is the one between each occurrence and the one preceding it. This means that 'every antecedent is itself a subsequent and every sequel is an antecedent'.[110] In this sense, human actions and utterances compose an intelligible continuity of occurrences each conditionally dependent on the one preceding it. Each antecedent occurrence is an action which calls for a response and that response is identified as the acknowledgment of the preceding action. It is the congruity of what came after

[104] *HC*: 11, original emphasis.
[105] *Ibid.*
[106] *HC*: 103.
[107] *HC*: 105.
[108] *HC*: 104.
[109] *Ibid.*
[110] *Ibid.*

with what came before which constitutes the intelligibility of contingent relationships.[111]

To theorize a contingent relationship is to 'put it into a story in which it is recognized to be an occurrence contingently related to other occurrences'.[112] A story clearly establishes how occurrences are contingently related to one another, thereby making contingent human actions and utterances intelligible. Oakeshott is at pains to show that such a story is conditional in character. It begins with the conditional 'Once upon a time' and not with the unconditional, Edenic, 'In the beginning'. Moreover, such a story does not have an unconditional conclusion since its end, that is an action, is the beginning of another story. Finally, this theoretical story has no overall meaning. Oakeshott is adamant that the teller of such a story, that is the theorist, has no other message but the intelligibility with which he has endowed occurrences by putting them in a story.[113] Here, Oakeshott explicitly distinguishes between theory and myth. He concedes that a story may be used 'to point a moral, to serve as an authority for future conduct, to teach its hearers how to perform actions likely to have wished-for outcomes, to assure them of a golden destiny, or to reconcile them to an unhappy fate'.[114] However, the teller of such a story is no longer engaged in theory but, rather, is constructing a myth. He is no longer concerned with the topical and transitory, but with unconditional certainty.[115] In sum, it is Oakeshott's position that a story concerned with relaying a moral, or which serves as an authority for conduct, is not a story at all: 'It is not to tell a story but to construct a myth.'[116]

Oakeshott is unequivocal: myths and legends are not philosophy. Their prescriptive character and the element of permanence they possess exclude them from that world. A myth has an unconditional beginning and conclusion, it has an overall meaning, it has an overall message, it points to a moral and it serves as an authority for future conduct.[117] The prescriptive character of myths and legends is abundantly clear in Oakeshott's interpretation of Roman politics. He claims that the Romans' political experience was turned into a legend which endowed it with universal significance. The events and fortunes which marked the history of the Roman people were transformed into a work of art, a drama or a story, the moral of which was made explicit in

---

[111] *HC*: 104–105.
[112] *HC*: 105.
[113] *Ibid.*
[114] *Ibid.*
[115] *Ibid.*
[116] *Ibid.*
[117] *Ibid.*

events.[118] For Oakeshott, a prescriptive story which opens with the unconditional 'In the beginning' and ends with an unconditional conclusion cannot be philosophy. His writings on philosophy are unambiguous and unequivocal on the matter of the relationship of philosophy to politics. Philosophy, he maintains, serves no practical or political purpose. Oakeshott thus establishes a strict division between philosophy and practice. In *Experience and its Modes*, he contends that philosophy is 'without any direct bearing upon the practical conduct of life, and that it has certainly never offered its true followers anything which could be mistaken for a gospel'.[119] Philosophy must be pursued for its own sake and Oakeshott perceives practical life as posing a threat to its independence. In this sense, he argues that 'it [philosophy] depends for its existence upon maintaining its independence from all extraneous interests, and in particular from the practical interest'.[120]

The strict division also holds true for political philosophy. Although politics is a modulation of practice, it may nevertheless be reflected upon philosophically. Oakeshott asserts in *Experience and its Modes* that philosophy has the responsibility of accounting for the modes of experience and determining their character.[121] He reiterates this argument in *On Human Conduct* when he claims that theorizing may be arrested without denying its character as the engagement to understand. Oakeshott argues that 'the theorist who drops anchor here or there and puts out his equipment of theoretic hooks and nets in order to take the fish of the locality, interrupts but does not betray his calling'.[122] In fact, it is necessary for the unconditional engagement of understanding to be arrested if any identity is to be understood in terms of its postulates.[123] Thus, philosophy has the responsibility to understand politics in terms of its postulates. Oakeshott discusses political philosophy in detail in the essays 'The Concept of a Philosophy of Politics' (which has been tentatively dated to 1946) and 'Political Philosophy'. In 'Political Philosophy', Oakeshott contends that the impulse in political philosophy is 'the impulse to detect *the permanent character of political activity*'.[124] To understand the permanent character of political activity is to view the character of political life from the concrete standpoint of the totality of experience.[125] More pre-

---

[118] *LHPT*: 208.
[119] *EM*: 1.
[120] *EM*: 3.
[121] *EM*: 4.
[122] *HC*: 11.
[123] *Ibid.*
[124] *RPML*: 151, original emphasis.
[125] *RPML*: 126.

cisely, political philosophy is the attempt to define the body of political concepts which comprise the world of political activity by relating them to the totality of experience.[126] There are purposes political philosophy cannot serve, following Oakeshott's conception of it. First and foremost, political philosophy cannot serve as a guide to politics. In this sense in 'The Concept of a Philosophy of Politics', Oakeshott asserts that political philosophy is 'unable to give guidance for action […] It is not itself a political programme; it is not a foundation or basis, a body of general principles upon which a political programme might be constructed'.[127] The argument in support of a strict division between philosophy and politics is also central to the essay 'Political Philosophy' where Oakeshott concludes that 'we must expect from political philosophy no practical political conclusions whatever. Political philosophy can provide no principles to be "followed", no rules of political conduct to be observed, no ideals of policy or arrangement to be pursued'.[128] In sum, political philosophy must be understood as an explanatory and not as a practical activity.[129] Consequently, myth and legend are not philosophy.

Although myths and legends are not philosophical reflection, we may nevertheless legitimately enquire into the kind of reflection of which they would consist. As the example of the Roman legend shows, myths and legends are clearly a kind of reflection upon politics. Oakeshott never specifies what kind of reflection myth and legend consist in, but I posit that if we consider his writings on political reflection that it is possible to make the case that myth and legend are instances of the reflective enterprise the aim of which is the construction of a political doctrine. However, while they may consist in the same kind of thinking, legends are not political doctrines. Rather, they are a legitimate alternative to doctrines, constructed narratives which allow for a political society's identity to be founded.

In the essay 'Political Philosophy', Oakeshott distinguishes three kinds of reflection on politics: reflection in the service of politics, reflective enterprise turned towards the construction of a political doctrine and political philosophy. These are what David Boucher refers to as the three levels at which political thinking takes place.[130] Reflection in the service of politics is concerned with the arrangements of a society. Political reflection of this order considers whether the

---

[126] *RPML*: 127.
[127] *RPML*: 137.
[128] *RPML*: 153–154.
[129] *RP*: 66.
[130] D. Boucher 2007: 72–73.

current arrangements are satisfactory to the desires approved by a society. We find here Oakeshott's conception of political activity. This kind of political reflection results in policy, that is, recommendations about the political ends which should be pursued and the means which should be used to attain them. An impulse of radical subversion is completely absent from this kind of reflection on politics.[131] It may safely be concluded that legends and myths are not reflection in the service of politics. The purpose of the Roman legend is not to analyse the appropriateness of current arrangements and recommend policy. Rather, a legend or myth is a different sort of reflection about a people and its manner of governing. What is at once represented in, and created by, a legend or myth is a people's sense of identity. A society's identity and knowledge of itself is thus confirmed in a legend. Therefore, the reflection involved in myth and legend offers a more profound understanding of a society than reflection in the service of politics is able to. Yet this is not philosophical reflection, according to Oakeshott, since it is not concerned with 'the place of political activity itself on the map of our total experience'.[132]

I posit that myths and legends are forms of the second kind of political reflection Oakeshott identifies: reflective enterprise turned towards the construction of a political doctrine. Both legends and doctrines relate to what Oakeshott terms communal self-consciousness. In the lectures entitled 'The Socio-Political Doctrines of Contemporary Europe', which Luke O'Sullivan specifies he gave in the late 1930s to accompany the book of the same name, Oakeshott distinguishes between two kinds of communal self-consciousness: patriotism, that is, the emotional self-consciousness on which the solidarity of society rests and the kind of intellectual self-consciousness which social and political doctrines produce.[133] [134] While Oakeshott does not elaborate on his understanding of patriotism in these lectures, I argue that the emotional self-consciousness on which the solidarity of a society rests is generated by legends of political life. The distinction Oakeshott draws between emotion and intellectual reflection seems to suggest that patriotism, and consequently political legends, is not the result of intellectual activity, but is purely emotional. I argue that this is not in fact Oakeshott's position. Patriotism and solidarity do involve reflection on the political as it would be difficult for one to be patriotic about a political tradition one does not understand or has no know-

---

131 *RPML*: 146–147.
132 *RP*: 65.
133 L. O'Sullivan 2004: 13.
134 *WH*: 153–154.

ledge of. Only, as we will see, the political reflection involved in patriotism and solidarity takes a different form from that found in political doctrines. Briefly, rather than rationalizing the life of a political society into abstract ideas or general principles, legends of political life are narrative constructs which endow a political society with self-understanding and self-knowledge. This will be explained in greater detail further on. Finally, Oakeshott does not establish a strict dichotomy between emotional and intellectual self-consciousness as he asserts that doctrines can contribute to patriotism by giving it an intellectual content and coherence that it otherwise lacks.[135]

Thus, communal self-consciousness is the root of social and political thought defined as 'thinking about the social and political conditions and institutions of the community in which we live'.[136] Oakeshott identifies three conditions which must be present before a community thinks of itself as an entity. Firstly, it must have long established customs, laws and institutions. Secondly, it must be able to contrast its way of living with another civilization. Finally, the community must have achieved a high degree of intellectual development. It is only once these circumstances prevail that a social and political doctrine can emerge, Oakeshott argues. In this regard, he asserts that a doctrine 'is something which follows upon a high degree of institutional and legal organization in a society'.[137] In other words, a social and political doctrine cannot emerge unless a high degree of social self-consciousness already exists.[138] For Oakeshott, a social and political doctrine is an attempt 'to think about and to rationalize the social and political life of a community'.[139] By rationalizing, Oakeshott means setting down in the language of abstract ideas the relationships and institutions of a society.[140] Put another way, the essential character of a social and political doctrine is to rationalize the life of an existing society into instances of general principles.[141] More specifically, a social and political doctrine is the result of the intelligence of a society turning back upon the structure of the society and making the character of that society known to itself.[142] Thus, one of a doctrine's most important effects is to increase and to deepen social self-consciousness.[143]

---

[135] *WH*: 154.
[136] *WH*: 150.
[137] *WH*: 153.
[138] *WH*: 152.
[139] *WH*: 151.
[140] *Ibid.*
[141] *WH*: 152.
[142] *Ibid.*
[143] *Ibid.*

Hence, social and political doctrines are 'neither to be despised nor overrated', according to Oakeshott.[144] He maintains that we should expect enlightenment of a certain sort from political doctrines, but not practical guidance in political activity.[145] Moreover, although a political doctrine heightens a society's sense of self-consciousness, its tendency is to fix a civilization by making firmer, more rigid as well as more coherent the life of a society.[146] This poses a danger in his view as the possession of a doctrine makes it less easy for a society to change.[147] As we will see, this is not the case for legends of political life which, I posit, are contingent foundations for the political and therefore fix a society's identity while also allowing for change.

In the later essay 'Political Philosophy', Oakeshott examines in greater detail the thinking and analysis that characterizes political doctrines. It should be noted that he also refers to this kind of reflection as explanation of political activity. He asserts that this kind of reflection appears when a society has achieved a settled manner of existence.[148] In these circumstances he claims that 'an almost self-conscious coherence or uniformity of character is generated'.[149] That is, an identity is generated upon which reflection may focus its attention. When reflection is directed to the detection and exploration of this character, thereby 'extrapolating its tendencies, fixing its elements and making firm its outline', the result, Oakeshott argues, is a political doctrine.[150] A political doctrine may spring 'not only from an actual, but also from an imaginary political experience'.[151] For him, it is irrelevant whether the political experience in question is actual or imaginary since 'whatever offers opportunity for analysis and more orderly reconstruction may be expected to feel the touch of this explanatory device'.[152]

A reflective enterprise concerned with the explanation of political activity 'falls far short of being radically subversive' since its purpose is to reconstruct political experience by fixing the elements of its identity and making firm its outline.[153] This kind of reflection corresponds to the partially subversive and foundational reflective enterprise, referred to earlier, which 'takes on the appearance of building a structure upon an

---

144 *RPML*: 149.
145 *Ibid.*
146 *WH*: 154.
147 *Ibid.*
148 *RPML*: 147.
149 *Ibid.*
150 *Ibid.*
151 *Ibid.*
152 *Ibid.*
153 *RPML*: 148.

assured foundation, of getting to know *more* about something whose identity [...] is in some way already fixed'.[154] Political reflection whose purpose is explanatory, then, is concerned with setting-up landmarks and laying-out firm anchorages. In this sense, Oakeshott asserts that for 'every "certainty" it displaces it offers another in return'.[155] Moreover, this reflective enterprise is 'incapable of throwing off entirely its allegiance to the political experience from which it springs'; consequently, it 'never loses its character of being an explanation *of* something whose character is already fixed'.[156] The subversiveness of reflection is limited and, for this reason, Oakeshott claims that a political doctrine is 'never so subversive as to represent itself as anything other than knowledge of an already familiar political world'.[157] Consequently, explanatory political reflection turned towards the construction of a political doctrine possesses a definite foundational element since it deals in certainties and aims to increase knowledge of a fixed political identity. A political doctrine is knowledge of a political world and, for this reason, this kind of political reflection remains tied to the political experience it springs from.

Oakeshott's contention, then, is that explanatory, partially subversive, foundational reflection upon politics results in a political doctrine. Although Oakeshott never makes this argument, I posit that this kind of reflection may also result in a legend or myth. That is, explanatory political reflection may be turned towards the construction of a political doctrine, but it may also be turned towards the construction of a legend. Myths and legends, in terms of the role they play in relation to the political, meet the criteria (if we can call it that) set out by Oakeshott in regards to political doctrines. In *Lectures in the History of Political Thought*, Oakeshott argues that every society which is awakened to political self-consciousness constructs a myth or an imaginative interpretation of how it came to be.[158] In his lecture 'Roman Political Thought (1)', Oakeshott suggests that a myth or legend, that is, an imaginative interpretation of a people's political experience, is an acceptable alternative form of intellectual organization to a political doctrine, a system of abstract ideals or an ideology, which he rejects because of their rationalist nature. In this respect, he contends that the political practice developed by the Romans over a period of a thousand years was never turned into a coherent system of abstract ideas. That is

---

154 *RPML*: 141, original emphasis.
155 *RPML*: 148.
156 *Ibid.*, original emphasis.
157 *Ibid.*
158 *LHPT*: 46.

not to say that Roman political experience lacked intellectual organization, only that instead of a doctrine, it took the form of a legend.[159]

The underlying idea is that political doctrines and legends are both
engaged in the same kind of explanatory, foundational reflection upon
politics. If we examine the criteria Oakeshott uses to define reflection
turned towards the construction of a political doctrine, we see that this
is indeed the case. Reflection in both political doctrines and legends is
centred on the fixed identity constituted by the political experience of a
society, be it actual or imaginary. Oakeshott's definition of legend confirms that it is knowledge of an already familiar political world and it
remains tied to the political experience from which it springs, as is the
case with a political doctrine.[160] Consequently, myth and legend are an
'explanatory device' as is a political doctrine which engages in the
'orderly reconstruction' of a society's political experience.[161] In sum,
although myth and legend are not engaged in philosophical reflection
upon political activity, they are nevertheless a reflective enterprise
centred upon politics, but the kind of reflection involved is explanatory
and foundational in nature. The political identity a legend founds, or
'fixes', is a political society's identity. What it increases is knowledge of
a political society. It is for this reason that political societies awakened
to self-consciousness construct a myth. It is such a constructed
narrative which allows them to found their identity. The relationship
between self-consciousness and myth is bidirectional. A society
awakened to self-consciousness fixes its identity by means of a myth,
but the narrative also endows society with its sense of identity. Finally,
although political legends fix a political society's identity, they do not
translate its political experience into an ideology or a doctrine. As I
argue throughout the book, legends of political life are contingent
foundations in that the story they tell may always be augmented as
opposed to political doctrines and ideologies which are fixed and
finished. Therefore, political legends are a legitimate form of foundational reflection upon the political.

A more defined portrait of myths and legends is beginning to
emerge. First, myths and legends are a kind of reflection on politics, but
they are not philosophical reflection. Instead, they belong to a partially
subversive reflection on politics; one that is explanatory and foundational. Secondly, as to its structure and content, a myth or legend opens
with an unconditional beginning and ends with an unconditional conclusion. They have an overall meaning and, as such, have a clear

---

[159] *LHPT*: 208.
[160] *RPML*: 148.
[161] *RPML*: 147.

message. They point to a moral and serve as an authority for future conduct. Central to myths and legends, then, is a practical element which is not congruent with the strict division Oakeshott establishes between philosophy and practice. They are prescriptive and, as such, as the example of Rome shows, they function as constructed foundations for the political. Myths and legends are constructions which inform society of its political practice and establish the boundaries of that practice. Moreover, they serve as a moral guide and as an authority for future political activity. Thus, myths and legends serve as stabilizing constructs for the political practice of a society.

Legends of Political Life and History

Legends and myths tell the story of past events, of happenings and of the deeds, misdeeds or feats of heroes, men or even political figures. The Roman legend tells the story of the events and of the fortunes which shaped the Roman people. Moreover, it relates the manner in which the Romans governed and were governed. In short, the Roman legend tells the story of that society's political experience. Legends, therefore, tell stories of human actions and of events. Since they relate past events, legends and myths may be deemed by some to be history. In the essay 'Political Education', Oakeshott describes a legend as the 'underlinings' made by a society in the book of its history. Furthermore, the study of a legend, in the same way as the study of history does, reveals 'in its backward glances the tendencies which are afoot' in a society.[162] In this particular essay, Oakeshott establishes a direct relation between legends and history. However, the implication is that legends only retain what is spectacular, dramatic and universal and discard nuance and detail.[163] For this reason, Oakeshott argues that the historical investigation of a legend, the aim of which is to understand its prejudices, for that is what it retains and relates of history, is not a genuine study of history, but, rather, constitutes what he terms 'quasi-history'.[164] What Oakeshott means by this term is unclear. What is 'quasi-history'? In this section, I propose to determine the relationship between legend and history in Oakeshott's thought. For this purpose, I will focus on Oakeshott's writings on history in *Experience and its Modes, Rationalism in Politics, On History, What is History?* and *Lectures in the History of Political Thought*. The discussion will show that because of the practical element which is at the heart of legends' character, they in effect fail as history. Legends evoke a different kind of past, and it is

---

[162] *RP*: 63.
[163] *WH*: 367–368.
[164] *RP*: 63.

doubtful whether it is even a past at all. The exploration of Oakeshott's distinction between legend and history will allow for a better under-standing of a legend's character and to see how it serves as a contingent, constructed foundation for the political.

History, like all of the modes, is nothing but experience. Since it is experience and experience is thought, it follows that history begins with a homogeneous world of ideas. More precisely, history is the historian's world of experience and his world of ideas. The end in history is to take this given world of ideas and make it more coherent.[165] Since history is experience, all historical facts and events are experience and therefore ideas. Events are not independent from experience.[166] Moreover, since history is specifically the historian's experience, history is consequently 'made' by the historian. In this sense, Oakeshott argues that 'to write history is the only way of making it'.[167] Since discovery without judgment is impossible, Oakeshott maintains, all historical facts are the result of the historian's judgment and all events stem from inference. In writing history, the historian makes it by judging facts and inferring events from antecedent ones.[168] The historical past, therefore, is 'always an inference; it is the product of judgment'.[169] Since the past in history is inference and judgment, it can only be what the evidence obliges the historian to believe. In sum, the historical past is 'the whole of reality subsumed under the category of the past'.[170]

However, the category of the past is large. The fact that the histori-cal past is subsumed under a more general and broader category of the past implies that it contains more than one kind of past. That there are different kinds of past is confirmed by Oakeshott in his essay 'Present, Future and Past' which forms part of the collection *On History*. The question that arises, then, is whether legend belongs to history, or if it evokes a different kind of past. Oakeshott addresses the issue in the essay. He argues that there are different modes of past which may be distinguished in terms of the present they are related to.[171] He is con-cerned with two different modes of past: the historical past which is related to the present-past, and the practical past which is related to the present-future of practical engagement. Oakeshott's discussion of his-tory concurs with and builds upon the understanding he provides in *Experience and its Modes*. History, he asserts, is unique in being exclu-

---

[165] *EM*: 93, 99, 101.
[166] *EM*: 99.
[167] *Ibid.*
[168] *EM*: 94, 100, 108.
[169] *EM*: 108.
[170] *EM*: 118.
[171] *OH*: 10.

sively concerned with the past.[172] This exclusive concern with the past implies a distinctive present to which history and the past it evokes are related. For Oakeshott, the present in historical understanding is distinguishable as 'a subject exclusively concerned with past (an "historian" as such) related to objects which speak only of past (that is, things understood exclusively in terms of their relation to past)'.[173] Crucial to the understanding of the historical present is the character and status of the objects history is concerned with. Oakeshott maintains that the historical present is 'exclusively composed of objects recognized, identified and understood as survivals from past'.[174] If an object does not fit this criterion it cannot be the object of historical study. The objects history is concerned with are survivals from the past; they are not objects which have simply survived. The present in historical understanding is, therefore, composed of objects recognized 'solely and expressly as survivals, vestiges, remains, fragments of a conserved past'.[175] Since the objects which compose the historical present are survivals of a conserved past, they are consequently incapable of evoking a future. Therefore, Oakeshott argues that the historical present is in fact a past. It is a present-past, or put another way, it is a past which has itself survived and is present.[176] Historical investigation begins in the present-past from which the historian infers the historical past. The historically understood past can only be inferred since it is not a past which could have survived and consequently was never itself present.[177] The historical past, then, is the 'conclusion of a critical enquiry of a certain sort; it is to be found nowhere but in a history book'.[178] Oakeshott identifies this enquiry as an enquiry in which survivals from the past are dissolved into their component features and are used as circumstantial evidence from which to infer a past which has not survived. This past is composed of passages of related historical events which are assembled as answers to questions formulated by an historian.[179] These historical events have no message since their meanings lie in their unrepeatable conditions. That is, they cannot be detached from their circumstantial conditions without losing their

---

172 *OH*: 30.
173 *Ibid.*
174 *Ibid.*
175 *Ibid.*
176 *OH*: 30–32.
177 *OH*: 34–36.
178 *OH*: 36.
179 *Ibid.*

meanings.[180] The meanings of historical events are neither universal or timeless, but rather contingent and circumstantial.

From what has been ascertained so far about legend, we know that it is prescriptive, authoritative and that it carries a message and a moral. In other words, a legend refers to and has a bearing upon the future. It projects a political society into the future. Consequently, although a legend deals with the past, it does not evoke the historical past, but rather a different kind of past. This is precisely Oakeshott's argument in 'Present, Future and Past'. He contends that what he terms 'legenda' belongs to the practical past.[181] Like history, the practical past is related to a present, in this case to the present-future of present-engagement.[182] I will briefly discuss this present in order to better understand the past it is related to and the issues Oakeshott raises in regards to it.

The present-future of practical engagement is what Oakeshott refers to elsewhere as a practice or a tradition of behaviour. The practical present is composed of 'subjects of a certain (optative) character related to one another in terms of their desires, purposes and action'.[183] What is of particular interest in this essay is his focus on the relation of subjects to objects in a practice. The relation between objects and subjects is central to the mode of practice both in its present and past tenses. Moreover, the role played by objects in the practical present and the practical past is a key element of my argument which aims to make the case that legends serve as constructed foundations for the political.

In the practical present, the objects of attention and concern are recognized by subjects in terms of their qualities and of the expectations they evoke. Subjects' responses to objects are appreciations of their current meaning and worth to themselves. In other words, objects are understood in relation to subjects as agents.[184] Subjects come to inhabit a present of common discourse by learning to recognize the meaning of objects and their worth in relation to their wants and purposes as well as in relation to the actions and utterances in which they seek to satisfy those wants.[185] Furthermore, subjects, in order to function within a practice, must also learn where to find these objects, how to assemble and enjoy them and how to understand them.[186] In

---

180 *OH*: 42.
181 *OH*: 19, 44.
182 *OH*: 21.
183 *Ibid.*
184 *OH*: 12.
185 *OH*: 12-13.
186 *OH*: 11-13.

other words, for Oakeshott, objects themselves compose the practical present since they are:

> the language in which we compose our wants and conduct the transactions designed to satisfy them, the terms of our habits, the steps of our wanderings to and fro. Every such object noticed and attended to is a distinct happening recognized in relation to ourselves as agents, responded to, valued, used, put by, ignored or rejected.[187]

In sum, the self as agent and the object are distinguishable but inseparable counterparts.[188]

The objects which compose the practical present are recognized in terms of time understood as a relation between a present and an imagined future. That is, the practical present evokes a future condition of things which is evoked in every want and which every action seeks to realize. Given that the practical present is intertwined with the future, Oakeshott argues that it is itself a present-future.[189] In other words, a present of common discourse lives in the future. In this context, objects are recognized in terms of their worth and ability to satisfy agents' wants and to realize their practical engagements.[190] Objects in the present-future of practical engagement are recognized 'in terms of the future they foretell'.[191]

Although the present-future of practical engagement evokes the future, it is nevertheless also related to a past. The past it evokes must be related to its particular present and, consequently, this past must be of worth to the current practical engagements of the practical present. In this respect, Oakeshott argues that 'our practical concern with past is our concern with present objects in relation to ourselves, to ascertain their worth to us and use them for the satisfaction of our wants'.[192] Objects which are of worth to the practical present may be objects which have survived from a near or distant past. The past is evoked from the present in a procedure of recollection. That is, objects of worth which have survived from the past become available to agents in a procedure of recall to mind.[193] The procedure of recollection, as it is understood by Oakeshott, is 'joining a puzzling or intractable present with a known and unproblematic past to compose a less puzzling or more manageable present'.[194] This is a significant assertion. Oakeshott claims

---

187   *OH*: 13.
188   *Ibid.*
189   *OH*: 14–15.
190   *OH*: 15.
191   *Ibid.*
192   *OH*: 15.
193   *OH*: 18–19.
194   *OH*: 18.

that the practical past's usefulness and worth is derived from the fact
that it contributes to composing a less puzzling and more manageable
present. That is, the practical past offers stability and sense to the
present-future of practical engagement. Objects which are recalled to
mind for practical purposes are fragments of a past which have survived. Oakeshott contends that the practical present contains an 'ever-
increasing deposit' of these fragments which are available to be listened
to and consulted.[195] These fragments are relevant to present circumstances and, as such, may be related to current conduct.[196] These
recalled fragments consist in artefacts (which, Oakeshott suggests, may
serve as models to be copied), recorded anecdotes and episodes of
bygone human fortune used to elaborate stories of past human circumstance, examplars of human character and images of human conduct.[197]
The virtue of these fragments lies in their familiarity and usefulness to
the practical present. They are useful in that they communicate useful
information or advice, and in that they may be listened to, consulted
and used. In this sense, authority may be attributed to these fragments
which have survived from the past.[198] In sum, Oakeshott posits that
these fragments or objects compose 'legenda' which he defines as 'what
is "read" and what may be read with advantage to ourselves in our
current engagements'.[199] Put another way, the fragments which have
survived from the past constitute a present in the sense that they are
objects:

> [...] accepted, understood in terms of their qualities and attended to in
> terms of their meaning and worth [...] to ourselves in pursuing our
> current purposes, distinguished only in purporting to be voices from the
> past.[200]

Survivals, in order to be recognized by subjects engaged in the practical
present, must be of worth and useful to the realization of current
engagements and purposes. They are only distinguished from other
objects in that they purport to originate in the past.[201]

Oakeshott asserts that every society has an inheritance of such survivals from the past. He refers to this past as a 'living' past which may
be either actual or imaginary. The fact is irrelevant since what is
important is what the past can teach a society and tell its members

---

195   *Ibid.*
196   *Ibid.*
197   *Ibid.*
198   *OH*: 18–19.
199   *OH*: 19.
200   *Ibid.*
201   *Ibid.*

about themselves.[202] In this sense, Oakeshott argues that the provenance of survivals in the past is of no importance since what they mean to members of a society is whatever they may be made to mean and, consequently, it follows for him that 'whether or not these survivals are scenes from a mythology, products of poetic imagination or alleged bygone exploits is often a matter of indifference'.[203] Part of the 'living' past is an actual or imaginary ancestral past in which members of a society locate the society to which they belong. Therefore, the identity of a society and the knowledge its members have of it are directly related to the practical past.[204] It is a living past which teaches by example and, more importantly, Oakeshott argues that it is this past which affords us a 'current vocabulary of self-understanding and self-expression'.[205] Both an individual's and a society's self-understanding and self-expression stem from the practical past. As regards the self-understanding of a society, Oakeshott argues that when considerable passages of the practical past are assembled by putting together fragmented survivals they 'yield important conclusions about ourselves and our current circumstances'.[206] These conclusions may reveal that it is a past which 'displays a "progressive" movement to which our own times belong; that it exhibits a darkness to which our own enlightenment is a gratifying contrast; that it tells a story of decline and retrogression of which we are the unfortunate heirs'.[207] The fragments which have survived from the past, when they are assembled and are made to tell a story, are the source of a society's self-understanding. Furthermore, it is the form its self-expression takes. These stories carry prescriptive messages. For instance, when the story is one of decline and retrogression the implication is that the society in question must turn its fortunes around, perhaps by recalling or remembering its past glories, accomplishments or genius. In other words, survivals from the past may under certain guises tell the stories of civilizations and societies. Thus, it is the authoritative character of fragmented survivals which motivates their recall to mind.[208]

Survivals, Oakeshott observes, occupy a large place in the practical present. This is due to the fact that they reveal themselves to be of worth and useful for the current practical engagements of a society and

---

[202] *OH*: 18.
[203] *OH*: 18–19.
[204] *OH*: 19.
[205] *OH*: 21.
[206] *Ibid.*
[207] *Ibid.*
[208] *OH*: 19.

its members.[209] These survivals are always at the ready to be recalled and 'to be noticed, enjoyed or employed for what they may be made to mean or for whatever they may be worth in respect of current practical engagements'.[210] However, Oakeshott is dubious about the provenance of these objects which have survived from the past. When defining the practical past, he specifies that it is 'composed of artefacts and utterances *alleged* to have survived from past'.[211] Moreover, when discussing the procedure of recollection, he states on at least two occasions that survivals are recalled from 'where they lie scattered in our present'.[212] Oakeshott proceeds to consider the doubts he entertains about survivals and concludes the essay by arguing that fragments which are alleged to have survived from the past are not in fact recalled from the past, but are recalled from where they lie in the present.[213] He asserts that a survival is a 'transparent item recalled, not from the past, but from where it lies in a perpetually accumulating collection of unmistakable present artefacts and utterances'.[214] The practical past, then, is not past at all. Rather, what Oakeshott alternatively terms the didactic or living past is 'the present contents of a vast storehouse into which time continuously empties the lives, the utterances, the achievements and the sufferings of mankind'.[215] Thus, the practical past is that part of a present-future of practical engagement which is composed of objects recognized 'not as survivals but merely to have survived'.[216] Following Oakeshott, objects of the practical past are not survivals of the past, but are objects which have merely survived and are stored in the practical present. They are readily at hand to be recalled to mind for use in current practical engagements.[217]

The distinction Oakeshott draws between historical survivals and survived objects is central to his understanding of the practical past and 'legenda'. He posits that the meaning of historical survivals lies 'in their unrepeatable conditions and in the wants and designs of agents who were alive and are now dead beyond recall'.[218] In other words, the meaning of authentic survivals cannot be divorced from their conditions. The survivals which compose the historical present-past could

---

[209] *Ibid.*
[210] *OH*: 39.
[211] *OH*: 38, emphasis mine.
[212] *OH*: 19, 39.
[213] *OH*: 41.
[214] *OH*: 40.
[215] *OH*: 43.
[216] *OH*: 41
[217] *Ibid.*
[218] *OH*: 41–42.

not 'endure detachment from their circumstantial conditions, and they can have no message for us'.[219] Historical survivals, then, cannot be detached from their circumstantial conditions in order for their meaning to be made into a useful message for the practical present. The very opposite is true of survived objects. Objects which are valued for their usefulness in current practical engagements are divorced from their circumstantial conditions. Oakeshott asserts that they are 'abstracted from record in a reading which divests them of their contingent circumstances and their authentic utterance'.[220] From authentic and circumstantial historical meanings, survivals are transformed into emblematic characters and episodes, symbolic and stereotypic *personae*, actions, exploits and situations.[221] Oakeshott argues that as objects pour into the vast storehouse which composes part of the present-future of practical engagement they undergo a:

> process of detachment, shrinkage and desiccation [...] in which [they] are transformed from being resonant, ambiguous circumstantial survivals from bygone human life into emblematic actions and utterances either entirely divorced from their circumstances or trailing similarly formalized circumstances: occurrences, artefacts and utterances, transformed into fables, relics rather than survivals, icons not informative pictures.[222]

Survived objects, which are detached from their contingent circumstances and thus take on a universal character, may take the form of fables, relics and icons. In short, they compose 'legenda'. What characterizes 'legenda' is its usefulness for the practical present. For Oakeshott, some of its items are so often and widely used in the practical world that they in effect constitute a vocabulary of practical discourse.[223] This vocabulary is composed of symbolic characters and contains 'emblems of all the virtues, vices and predicaments known to mankind, continuously added to and continuously recalled for use'.[224] As regards the political, Oakeshott argues that it is in this storehouse, or symbolic vocabulary of practical discourse, that 'we may hope to find the "original contract" legitimizing a current government'.[225] Clearly then, political authority and legitimacy may stem from a symbolic discourse.

---

219 *OH*: 42.
220 *Ibid.*
221 *Ibid.*
222 *OH*: 43.
223 *OH*: 44.
224 *Ibid.*
225 *OH*: 45.

The practical past, therefore, is a collection of symbols. More precisely, it is the part of the present-future of practical engagement composed of objects recognized to have survived. Oakeshott portrays it as
'an accumulation of symbolic persons, actions, utterances, situations
and artefacts'.[226] These symbols are the products of the practical
imagination.[227] Although the practical past is not history, Oakeshott
does not for that reason look negatively upon it. On the contrary, he is
adamant that the practical past is an 'indispensable ingredient of an
articulate civilized life'.[228] In sum, the practical past recalls symbols
which are the product of the practical imagination in order to compose
a less puzzling and more manageable present. In the case of politics,
this means founding the legitimacy of government on symbols
generated by the practical imagination.

It should be clear that for Oakeshott the practical past, or the prac-
tical attitude towards the past, is not an illegitimate form of the past.
He argues the point vigorously in the essay 'The Activity of Being an
Historian'. There he asserts that:

> the use of a practical idiom in speaking about the past, certainly cannot
> be dismissed as merely illegitimate. Who are we to forbid it? On what
> grounds should the primordial activity of making ourselves at home in
> the world by assimilating *our* past to *our* present be proscribed?[229]

Not only is the practical past indispensable to civilized life, but making
ourselves at home in the world by constructing a living past is primordial. For Oakeshott, the practical past is 'not the enemy of mankind, but only the enemy of "the historian"'.[230] The practical attitude
towards the past is the chief undefeated enemy of history. It has proven
to be a very difficult enemy to defeat, according to Oakeshott, given the
difficult process of emancipation of history from the authority of practice, or, as he puts it, from the 'primordial and once almost exclusive
practical attitude of mankind'.[231] The idiom of practice, he maintains,
has imposed itself upon all enquiry into the past and for so long that its
hold 'cannot readily be loosened'.[232] Of the different modulations of the
practical idiom, Oakeshott argues that it was once religion that
impeded the emergence of the historical past, but that in modernity it is

---

[226] *OH*: 48.
[227] *Ibid.*
[228] *Ibid.*
[229] *RP*: 180, original emphasis.
[230] *Ibid.*
[231] *RP*: 171.
[232] *RP*: 181.

politics which is now the principal impediment.[233] Whatever the modulation, it is always a practical disposition which is determined to 'recall [events] from the dead so that they may deliver their messages. For it wishes only to learn from the past and it constructs a "living past" which repeats with spurious authority the utterances put into its mouth'.[234] The constructed living past recalled by the political may take the form of a legend or saga, a kind of past which Oakeshott qualifies as poetic and defines as a 'drama from which all that is casual, secondary and unresolved has been excluded: it has a clear outline, a unity of feeling and in it everything is exact except place and time'.[235] This concurs with the argument I put forward in Chapter 4 that legend and myth are poetic constructs. However, no matter the kind of construct, Oakeshott's point is that humans, because of their primordial, practical attitude, assimilate the past to the present in order to build a world of sense for themselves and for generations to come.

For a fuller understanding of the practical past it is helpful to examine Oakeshott's essay 'The Emergence of the History of Thought' written in 1967 and which forms part of the collection *What is History? and other essays*. There, he distinguishes between the past concerned with action (the practical past or the legendary past), the legendary intellectual past, which is concerned with ideas, and the history of thought which, Oakeshott posits, emerged out of the legendary intellectual past. For the purposes of the present argument, I will focus on the two forms of legendary past.

The past concerned with action or performative utterances is what Oakeshott refers to as the practical past in the essay 'Present, Future and Past'. He asserts that the attention of most people in the present is 'focused upon where in the world they are located, upon what they are doing and upon the imagined outcome of their choices and actions'.[236] In order to enhance their self-awareness and to confirm their sense of their own identity, they turn to a past which tells a story of how they came to be where they are and to be doing what they are doing.[237] Oakeshott's position is that human self-recognition has to be learned and that it is by means of recourse to the past that an agent may identify himself or confirm his identity.[238] In other words, an evoked past, Oakeshott contends, is 'the condition of all human self-

---

233   *RP*: 182.
234   *RP*: 181.
235   *RP*: 182.
236   *WH*: 349.
237   *Ibid*.
238   *WH*: 345.

consciousness'.[239] For Oakeshott, identity and self-consciousness stem from being aware of 'belonging to a present of understandings, engagements, achievements and relationships which stretches back into a past'.[240] The implication, which is crucial to Oakeshott's argument, is that consciousness is not the resultant of subjects sharing a common human nature. Rather, Oakeshott argues that *Humanitas* is awareness of this past and its cultivation. It is this which constitutes the education which endows subjects with an identity.[241]

A past of this kind, Oakeshott asserts, is not a gift, but a construction. More precisely, it is an 'evoked past, a work of art, a legend of past which has to be created, learned, cared for and cultivated. And to call it a "legendary" past is to distinguish, not to denigrate it'.[242] A past concerned with action, then, is a constructed legendary past. Moreover, Oakeshott reasserts that it is not an inferior kind of past since it is indispensable to civilized life as he argues in 'Present, Future and Past'. The legendary past is constituted in recollection. As such, it is an imagined past composed of recalled symbolic events. Its components are symbolic occurrences such as the deeds, sufferings, engagements, achievements, shortcomings and failures of forebears. Persons in a legendary past are most often presented as emblems or as authors, originators and progenitors. We will see in Chapter 5 that this idea is fundamental to the Roman legend of politics which places at its centre the original act of the foundation of Rome by Romulus. In short, the legendary past is composed of heroic and symbolic events.[243]

The legendary past, then, endows persons and associations of persons with their sense of identity. It achieves this by means of the messages it delivers, the lessons it teaches and the authority and confidence it gives to the current engagements of the practical present, thereby endowing persons and associations of persons with 'an unequivocal lineage and character'.[244] The legendary past's principle virtue is to make them at home 'in an otherwise mysterious and menacing universe'.[245]

The past which is concerned with action and performative utterances takes the form of a legend or saga. The past symbolic event expressed in a legend may be contracted into a 'single overwhelming

---

[239] *WH*: 346.
[240] *Ibid*.
[241] *WH*: 346–347.
[242] *WH*: 347.
[243] *Ibid*.
[244] *Ibid*.
[245] *Ibid*.

event'.[246] Oakeshott gives as an example of such an event the foundation of an institution. Here it may be assumed that the term 'institution' includes political institutions such as the state or, more simply, the act of instituting the political or society. The foundation of the Roman republic is a case in point of such an institution. Or, the narrative form of the past may be an epic, that is, a story of many related happenings.[247] In either case, the stories these narratives relate are stories of past deeds and sufferings and epics of doings and happenings. Those who unfolded these stories by the same token endowed their communities and societies with an understanding of themselves. Oakeshott includes Herodotus, Livy, the historiographers of the ancient Hebrews, the early legend-makers of the inhabitants of England, Geoffrey of Monmouth, who forged an identity for Britain by relating how it emerged from Albion, and Machiavelli among those figures engaged in legend-making.[248] It may be concluded from these examples that legend-making is of significant importance for the political. Oakeshott confirms this when he states that rulers seeking the authority to rule and subjects vindicating their liberties to act are among those for whom the 'need for the self-understanding which a past-relationship promotes is most immediately and most urgently felt'.[249] The legendary past, then, endows and confirms the identity, self-understanding and self-consciousness of persons and of political associations. It relates the story of their foundations or of the epic story of their pasts with which they identify.

In addition to the legendary past, Oakeshott identifies the legendary intellectual past which is composed of thoughts, beliefs, ideas and arguments. In short, this past is concerned with what persons have thought or with the manner of thinking of a political association.[250] The purpose of this past is to construct an intellectual legend as a 'celebration or a confirmation of a man's or an association's sense of identity'.[251] Oakeshott cites Diogenes' *The Lives of the Philosophers*, which he describes as a constructed legend of Greek philosophical reflection, and Livy's *History*, an expression of pride in the civil and martial exploits of the Roman people, as notable examples of such celebrations and confirmations.[252] As regards modern intellectual heritage, he argues that at least three major intellectual legends of modern Europe have emerged:

---

[246] *Ibid.*
[247] *WH*: 347–348.
[248] *WH*: 348–349.
[249] *WH*: 350.
[250] *Ibid.*
[251] *Ibid.*
[252] *WH*: 351.

the humanists and humanism, the Baconian version of the legend and
finally the French Enlightenment and the *philosophes*. He also notes the
legend-making efforts of De Maistre in constructing a critique of the
Enlightenment legend.[253] As is the case with the practical past, which
Oakeshott maintains is an indispensable ingredient of civilized life, he
contends that modern individuals need an intellectual legend and the
one in terms of which they are still apt to identify themselves intellectu-
ally is with the Enlightenment legend. Legends of intellectual past,
then, confirm and celebrate a person's or an association of persons'
sense of identity, and, in order to perform this function, ideas must
necessarily be understood as solid and timeless products of a changeless and universal human mind.[254]

Therefore, although legends tell the story of past events, they do not
on that account constitute history. This is incontestably a kind of past,
only it is the practical, legendary or living past, as Oakeshott alternatively refers to it, and not the historical past. The legendary past has
two facets. It tells the story both of symbolic events, actions and performative utterances as well as of timeless and solid ideas, thoughts
and beliefs. The practical past is evoked by a procedure of recollection
to mind. The historical past for its part is the conclusion of a critical
enquiry designed and devised by an historian. As such, it is to be found
only in books. The distinction made by Oakeshott between the practical
and historical pasts is consistent with his theory of modes which stipulates that it is impossible to pass in argument from one mode to
another. In this sense, Luke O'Sullivan observes that 'the purpose of the
distinction of the historical from the practical past remained
unchanged; it was to protect the autonomy of historical knowledge
from reduction to a pragmatic view of the past'.[255] As a consequence,
O'Sullivan notes that for Oakeshott 'the historical past is not to be identified with either the remembered or recollected past, both of which
belong to the "practical" self'.[256] David Boucher concurs with this
analysis and points to the fact that history's character is 'incapable of
being compromised by the intrusion of conclusions appropriate to any
other mode of understanding'.[257] For this reason, Boucher explains that
for Oakeshott a 'living past, relevant to the present or evocative of a
future state of affairs, is modally irrelevant to history and belongs in
the substantive world of practical affairs'.[258] However, Thomas Smith

---

253 *WH*: 354–364.
254 *WH*: 368.
255 L. O'Sullivan 2003: 228.
256 *Ibid.*: 231.
257 D. Boucher 1984: 213.
258 *Ibid.*

wonders whether Oakeshott's narrow conception of history allows for the breadth of knowledge and understanding that he himself longs for. Oakeshott greatly admires Hobbes and considers *Leviathan* to be one of the greatest accomplishments in the history of political thought. However, Oakeshott reads *Leviathan* as a myth and Smith contends that 'nothing of this scope resides within the confines of history. Constricted by method and single-mindedness, Oakeshottian history ("always on the verge of passing beyond itself") is enticed by this mythic "extravagance of the imagination"'.[259] Smith observes that Oakeshott makes an important concession to myth and legend as regards historical understanding. In this respect, Smith asserts that 'in the end, Oakeshott appears to yield—as, I suppose, a fallen historian—to the resolution and unity of a practical, even mythical view of the past'.[260]

The practical past, then, is most often discussed by commentators in the context of studies of Oakeshott's conception of history. The practical or legendary past itself is of secondary importance. It is referred to in order to clearly distinguish, or point to weaknesses in, Oakeshott's understanding of the historical past. In short, little attention is paid to the practical or legendary past for its own sake. My focus is on the legendary past since its examination reveals that it is rich in possibilities for politics, in particular for a political society's identity. It supports the argument that legends serve as constructed contingent foundations for the political. The practical past is in fact a constitutive element of Oakeshott's weak foundationalism.

Although commentators largely ignore the practical past, it is, nevertheless, central to Oakeshott's thought. His critique of Rationalism essentially amounts to a plea for the restoration of the practical past in modern politics. In the essay 'Rationalism in Politics', Oakeshott reserves perhaps his harshest judgment for the United States of America, an example of a new society which is guilty of Rationalism for having purposefully and intentionally rejected the English tradition of politics, that is, the practical past, in order to begin anew and found the political upon abstract principles.[261] More than this, however, Oakeshott is not only critical of the rejection of the practical past, but he also engages with the practical past in terms of the kind of reflection he pursues upon the intellectual past. The dichotomy between the traditional manner of political behaviour and Rationalism which is at the core of 'Rationalism in Politics' also structures Oakeshott's entire political thought. What we find in all of his writings, albeit expressed in

---

[259] T.W. Smith 1996: 613.
[260] *Ibid.*: 614.
[261] *RP*: 31–33.

different manners, is a dichotomy between two polar opposite conceptions of the political, the one overly reflective (Rationalism) and the
other traditional (or a practice in later works) and largely unreflective.
Oakeshott constructs two legends, the legend of the traditional manner
of political behaviour and the counter-legend of Rationalism with these
two conceptions of the political. I explore this idea in Chapter 5 where I
make the claim that 'Rationalism in Politics' is best understood as a
warning in regards to what he believes is the corruption of the modern
European consciousness by Rationalism. That is, the legend of the
traditional manner of political behaviour which endows Europe with
its identity is in the process of being corrupted by the rationalist
counter-legend. What I want to point out at this stage is that when
Oakeshott is engaged in reflection upon the intellectual past and the
evolution of ideas, be it in relation to manners of behaviour, the
character of the modern European state or political practices, he is not
engaged in intellectual history proper since his concern is not
specifically historical, but rather practical and political. Oakeshott's aim
is to lay the groundwork for the legends' respective identities, and to
this end, the practical past is indispensable. He constructs legends of
intellectual past, but also recounts various versions of the legend of
political modernity which have fixed themselves securely in European
thought and, as such, have never been dislodged. The distinction
between the history of thought and the legendary intellectual past is
one he makes in 'The Emergence of the History of Thought' and he
acknowledges himself in *Lectures in the History of Political Thought* that
he is not lecturing on '"*the* history of political thought"'.[262] Put another
way, he affirms that he cannot 'detect a history of political thought
which reveals a gradual accumulation of political wisdom and understanding'.[263] That Oakeshott's concern is with the legendary intellectual
past is confirmed in 'The Emergence of the History of Thought' where
he asserts that modern Europe's three major intellectual legends, of
which the Baconian and Enlightenment versions are constitutive
elements of Rationalism, are intellectual legends because they express
ideas and not thoughts in the mind of a thinker. Moreover, these ideas
are solid, fixed, independent 'thought-units' which are known for their
truth or falsity.[264] The same may be said of the legend of the traditional
manner of behaviour which largely rests on the English political experience which, Oakeshott claims, constitutes a legend of political life. I
explore the English political legend in Chapter 5. Oakeshott's purpose,

---

[262] *LHPT*: 32, original emphasis.
[263] *Ibid.*
[264] *WH*: 367.

therefore, is to construct a legend and counter-legend in order to reject Rationalism and plead for the restoration of tradition and practice in modern politics. Consequently, he is not writing the history of thought; rather, he is engaged in the legendary intellectual past. This explains the impressionistic nature of his writing which treats the past. He moves from one dramatic peak of the story to the next, instead of exploring the valleys and filling in the gaps of the legend.

Conclusion

The study of the practical past in Oakeshott's thought allows for an enriched understanding of legends. Legends are an indispensable ingredient of an articulate civilized life. They are constructs of the practical imagination composed of symbolic persons, actions, utterances, situations and artefacts and constitute a symbolic vocabulary of practical discourse.[265] They tell the story of past events, actions and performative utterances as well as of ideas, thoughts and beliefs. In so doing they endow persons and associations of persons with a sense of identity, of self-understanding and of self-consciousness. In other words, they found a political society's identity. This is the principal and, by far, the most important purpose they serve. The practical present or 'natural' present is a puzzling, mysterious and menacing world. The sense of identity legends confirm and affirm allows persons and associations of persons to know where they are in the world, how they came to be there and how they came to be doing what they are doing. Put another way, legends stabilize an otherwise problematic present. Awareness and cultivation of this past gives persons the sense of belonging to a common *Humanitas*. Moreover, legends are prescriptive in that they deliver messages and transmit solid, timeless and universal (in so far as they are removed from their contingent circumstances) truths which serve as a guide to both personal and political action.

The discussion of philosophy and of the mode of history allows us to begin to identify the criteria which define Oakeshott's concept of legend. First, legend is reflection upon the political at the second, or foundational, level of reflection. That is, legend is not philosophy since it is not radically subversive. A legend of political life does not seek to understand the place of political activity on the map of human activity. Rather, legend seeks to gain knowledge of a fixed identity. Oakeshott argues that any given society over a long period of time eventually achieves a settled manner of existence at which point an almost self-

---

[265] *OH*: 48.

conscious, coherent and uniform character is generated.[266] I contend
that it is not only a political doctrine which directs its reflective impulse
to detecting and exploring this type of character and which seeks to
extrapolate its tendencies, to fix its elements, and to make firm its
identity, but also legend. In so doing, legend engages in a reflective
enterprise concerned with building a stabilizing construct. Its aim is to
know more about something, in this case a society, whose identity and
whose character is in some way already fixed. In other words, legend is
reflective enterprise concerned with fixing or founding a society's identity and increasing the knowledge of it. To this end, legend is always
knowledge of an already familiar political world and this kind of
reflection upon the political remains tied to the political experience it
springs from. Legend, then, is foundational reflection upon the
political. Secondly, legend belongs to the practical past. The practical
past constructs a 'living past' by recalling an artefact, a symbolic person, a past event, an action or an utterance. In so doing, it assimilates
the past to the present, thereby stabilizing an otherwise problematic
present. An important consequence of this is that legend endows a
society with its identity and sense of self-consciousness as well as
knowledge of itself. That is, legend allows humans to feel at home in an
otherwise mysterious and menacing world. As such, this narrative construct serves as a contingent foundation for the political. The construction of legends, then, is a primordial and indispensable ingredient
of civilized life. In sum, far from being devoid of foundations,
Oakeshott's political thought, with its emphasis on the past, belongs to
the Arendtian constructivist tradition.

---

[266] *RPML*: 147.

Chapter Three

Legends of Political Life: Permanence and Change United

Introduction

The character of modern politics, Oakeshott declares, is 'unavoidably complex'.[1] It is characterized by two extremes: contingency and permanence. The principle virtue of the complexity of modern politics is that it offers a 'habitable middle region', a manner of escaping the 'self-destructive extremes'.[2] Oakeshott's concern is with ensuring a world fit for human life. A liveable world is one that avoids the extremes and exploits the middle region of politics. In other words, Oakeshott defends a mixed form of politics. I contend that this mixture of contingency and permanence implies foundations for the political. Oakeshott commentators argue that he is antifoundationalist or that his political thought is devoid of foundations. I concur in so far as the sort of foundations they refer to are what John Seery terms Edenic foundations. My position, however, is that Oakeshott's concept of the principle of the mean in action implies contingent foundations in the Arendtian constructivist tradition. The principle criterion these foundations must respect is that the contingent element must dominate the mixture. I argue that legends of political life respect this understanding of foundations. In Chapter 2, I showed that legends are a type of foundational reflection upon the political and that they invoke the practical past. What is more, they are deeply poetic. Legends, so I argue, are poetic constructs and it is my contention that it is their poetic character which unites contingency and permanence. Put another way, poetry allows for the resolution of the dichotomy between contingency and permanence. At the end of the present chapter, I show that it is legends'

---

1 *PFPS*: 121.
2 *Ibid.*

poetic character which ensures the contingency of the foundation. In Chapter 4, I make the case that it is poetry which ensures the permanence of a society's identity.

Oakeshott and Edenic Foundations

The question I wish to explore is whether Oakeshott's conception of the political rests on an Edenic conception of foundations. If we recall the discussion of foundations from Chapter 1, it is fair to say that he is clearly not Edenic in this sense, although, as Seery points out in regards to Rorty and Butler, he may nevertheless conceive of foundations exclusively in these terms and operate within an Edenic framework.[3] From a general point of view, commentators point out that Oakeshott defends a strictly contingent conception of the political and morality. David Mapel argues that the idea of contingency is the key to understanding his 'decidedly idiosyncratic yet valuable contribution to the theme of antifoundationalism in politics'.[4] He asserts that Oakeshott defines contingency as 'the absence of any necessary foundations for human practices themselves'.[5] Chief among these practices are politics, law and morality, the authority of which, since they are human inventions, is ultimately grounded in the 'continuing acknowledgement of those who participate in them'.[6] Mapel maintains that, for Oakeshott, 'they have no further foundational purpose that can be located in a human nature, a religious duty, or a set of timeless philosophical truths'.[7] Bruce Haddock concurs with this analysis and argues that Oakeshott 'cannot allow reference to "first principles" that are exempt from the transience that conditions all our practical experience'.[8] For him, 'a principle cannot be treated as "a criterion which is reliable because it is devoid of contingency"'.[9] For Rorty, Oakeshott's conception of the political as contingent 'helped undermine the idea of a transhistorical "absolutely valid" set of concepts which would serve as "philosophical foundations" of liberalism'.[10] In this sense, Andrew Vincent points out that, for Oakeshott, 'morality and politics are not and never can be universals. There are *no* external metaphysical or moral foundations'.[11] Moreover, to emphasize the point, he adds that Oakeshott contends that 'neither

---

[3]   J. Seery 1999: 471.
[4]   D. Mapel 1990: 392.
[5]   *Ibid.*: 393.
[6]   *Ibid.*
[7]   *Ibid.*
[8]   B. Haddock 2005: 10.
[9]   *Ibid.*
[10] R. Rorty 1989: 57.
[11] A. Vincent 2004: 153, original emphasis.

reason nor justice stand *outside* human conduct. Nothing provides agents with any universal standards, or a "view from nowhere"'.[12]

As Mapel, Haddock, Rorty and Vincent observe, the contingent nature of Oakeshott's conception of the political necessarily excludes Edenic foundations. This is in part due to the fact that the Edenic tradition of foundations corresponds to Rationalism. Prior grounding claims about unquestionable, sacred or natural premises, such as human nature or natural rights, correspond to what Oakeshott terms rationalist 'abstract ideals'. Authentic politics for Oakeshott is 'the activity of attending to the general arrangements of a collection of people, who in respect of their common recognition of a manner of attending to its arrangements, compose a single community'.[13] The arrangements which constitute a community are at once coherent and incoherent, according to Oakeshott. They 'compose a pattern and at the same time they intimate a sympathy for what does not fully appear'.[14] Politics is the exploration of that sympathy for what has not yet fully emerged. Put another way, political activity amends the existing arrangements of a community by exploring and pursuing what is intimated in them. Politics thus constitutes a tradition of behaviour and is devoid of foundations, Oakeshott argues, since it is not the pursuit of general principles, but of the intimations of a flow of sympathy. He maintains that a tradition of political behaviour 'has no changeless centre to which understanding can anchor itself; there is no sovereign purpose to be perceived or invariable direction to be detected; there is no model to be copied, idea to be realized, or rule to be followed'.[15] In short, the political understood as a tradition of behaviour 'deprives us of a model laid up in heaven'.[16]

Natural rights and other such abstract ideals and principles, which correspond to the Edenic understanding of foundations, are abridgments of a tradition of political behaviour. Ideas that we may have about rights, for example, emerge from the practice of politics. Recall the case of freedom and natural rights. Oakeshott argues that both the American Declaration of Independence and Locke's *Second Treatise of Government* are abridgments of the common law rights of Englishmen and, as such, are the products of 'centuries of the day-to-day attending to the arrangements of an historic society'.[17] Natural rights are the reflective abstraction of rights which emerged historically and con-

---

12   *Ibid.*, original emphasis.
13   *RP*: 56.
14   *RP*: 57.
15   *RP*: 61.
16   *RP*: 60.
17   *RP*: 53.

tingently in the course of political activity. Likewise, freedom, Oakeshott contends, 'is not an independently premeditated "ideal" or a dream'.[18] Rather, it is something which is intimated in a concrete tradition of behaviour. 'Freedom', he insists, '[...] is not a bright idea; it is not a "human right" to be deduced from some speculative concept of human nature'.[19] The idea of freedom emerges from the concrete and contingent practice of politics. In this sense, as Rorty asserts, '"moral principles" [...] only have a point insofar as they incorporate tacit reference to a whole range of institutions, practices, and vocabularies of moral and political deliberation. They are reminders of, abbreviations for, such practices, not justifications for such practices'.[20] Consequently, the conception of politics Oakeshott defends in *Rationalism in Politics* is devoid of Edenic foundations. He is adamant that 'principles', which are often conceived of as foundations, are merely the abridgment of traditional manners of behaviour.[21] As Oakeshott succinctly puts it, 'the notion of founding a society, whether of individuals or of States, upon a Declaration of the Rights of Man is a creature of the rationalist brain'.[22]

Contingency also characterizes Oakeshott's later conception of the political in *On Human Conduct*. Overall, his theorization of the political is largely the same as it is in *Rationalism in Politics*; however, it is discussed and presented here in a more detailed and systematic fashion. Again, Oakeshott maintains that politics is devoid of foundations; they are simply impossible and nonsensical. In order to understand what he means by this, I will briefly recall Oakeshott's theorization of the ideal character 'civil association' and the consequences it entails for politics and authority.

The civil condition is a relationship of human beings. It therefore postulates human conduct and it must first be understood in terms of that ideal character. Oakeshott defines human conduct as:

> 'free' (that is, intelligent) agents disclosing and enacting themselves by responding to their understood contingent situations in chosen actions and utterances related to imagined and wished-for satisfactions sought in the responses of other such agents, while subscribing to the conditions and compunctions of a multitude of practices and in particular to those of a language of moral understanding and intercourse.[23]

---

18   *RP*: 54.
19   *Ibid.*
20   R. Rorty 1989: 58–59.
21   *RP*: 68.
22   *RP*: 11.
23   *HC*: 112.

Human conduct is an intelligent, human relationship of free agents which must be learned in order to be enjoyed.[24] It must be noted that Oakeshott identifies human conduct, a contingent human relationship and engagement, and not human nature understood as a prior, unquestionable, natural premise. Civil association, then, postulates a contingent understanding of human character. Civil association or *civitas* is an engagement of human conduct and *cives* are 'free' agents whose response to one another's actions and utterances is one of understanding.[25] Consequently, the civil condition is an understood relationship of intelligent agents.[26] More specifically, the understood relationship of civil association consists in association in terms of a practice defined as a set of conditions which qualify, but do not determine, performances.[27] That is, a practice establishes a number of conditions which are understood and are subscribed to by agents in choosing and acting.[28] A practice is a formal (that is, not a substantial) relationship of equals who have learned and understood how to use and engage in it. In the case of civil association, agents acknowledge themselves to be *cives* in virtue of being related to one another in the recognition of a practice composed of rules.[29] More precisely, *cives* are related in terms of their common recognition of the rules which constitute a practice of civility.[30] Oakeshott contends that the most important postulates of *civitas* stem from this consideration.[31] These postulates are: *lex* (a system of law), adjudication (a procedure in which the meaning of *lex* is significantly, appropriately and durably amplified), legislation (a procedure in which new *lex* is deliberately enacted or current *lex* is expressly amended or repealed), ruling (the exercise of authority to make utterances which require substantive responses from assignable persons in particular contingent situations), authority (relationship in terms of the recognition of rules as rules), obligation (to be related in terms of the acknowledgment of the authority of *respublica* is a relation of obligation) and politics (deliberation upon the desirability of the conditions of civil association).[32] Taken all together, these postulates compose a system of conditions that Oakeshott terms *respublica* and which refers to

---

[24] *Ibid.*
[25] *Ibid.*
[26] *Ibid.*
[27] *HC*: 119–120, 122.
[28] *HC*: 120.
[29] *HC*: 127.
[30] *HC*: 128.
[31] *Ibid.*
[32] *HC*: 128–173.

the public concern or consideration of *cives*.[33] Although Oakeshott claims that each postulate is contingent and devoid of foundations (for instance, in legislating, *lex* cannot be deduced from dictates of Reason), I will focus on the two most important postulates for my argument: authority and politics.[34]

For Oakeshott, the civil condition is relationship in respect of a system of rules, but it is also relationship in terms of the recognition of the rules as rules.[35] Oakeshott's concern is to understand what it means for agents to be related in this manner. He contends that *cives* recognize *respublica* as the system of law which constitutes civil association. In other words, they recognize the authority of *respublica*, and, in so doing, constitute a relationship in terms of a practice.[36] In this sense, Oakeshott claims that 'what relates *cives* to one another and constitutes civil association is the acknowledgement of the authority of *respublica* and the recognition of subscription to its conditions as an obligation'.[37] The tie of civil association is 'continuous assent to this authority'.[38] However, the question arises: What is it that has authority? Or again, why is civil association authoritative? The short answer is that civil association is authoritative because it is acknowledged to be so by *cives*. As Bhikhu Parekh explains:

> It may be asked how *respublica* derives its own authority. In Oakeshott's view its authority is derived from the 'continuous acknowledgement of *cives*', an acknowledgement expressed not in their acts of obedience but in their recognition of the obligation to subscribe to its prescriptions. If they were to cease recognizing its rules as binding upon them, its authority would 'lapse'.[39]

Consequently, civil authority does not derive from the approval by *cives* of the conditions it prescribes, nor is it authoritative because of the consequences related to the enforcement of the rules of civil association. Rather, Oakeshott asserts, civil association is authoritative by virtue of:

> the acknowledgement of *respublica* as a system of moral (not instrumental) rules, specifying its own jurisdiction, and recognized solely as rules; that is, as conditions to be subscribed to in conduct and binding to

---

33   *HC*: 147.
34   *HC*: 139.
35   *HC*: 148.
36   *HC*: 150.
37   *HC*: 149.
38   *HC*: 150.
39   B. Parekh 1979: 496.

consideration independently of their origin or likely or actual outcome in use and of approval of what they prescribe.[40]

In other words, in answer to the question 'why is civil association acknowledged to be authoritative?', Oakeshott contends that it is because 'authority is the only conceivable attribute it could be indisputably acknowledged to have'.[41] That is, the authority of civil association is indisputable because *respublica* understood in terms of its authority is the only understanding of *respublica* which is 'capable of evoking the acceptance of all *cives* without exception, and thus eligible to be recognized as the terms of civil association'.[42] In sum, civil association is authoritative because in order to understand *respublica* and why its members follow the rules, it is necessary to postulate authority. Therefore, *respublica* must necessarily be qualified as being authoritative because, when we examine it, we observe that its members follow the rules.

Civil authority is contingent since it is never acquired in a 'once-and-for-all endowment but only in the continuous acknowledgement of *cives*' of the conditions of *respublica*.[43] Parekh understands this conception of civil authority to be a critique of the contractualist position; he asserts that, for Oakeshott, 'the authority of *respublica* is not a once-and for-all endowment made by *cives* at some specific point in time as some contractualists naively imagine, but the result of a slow and painful historical process'.[44] Authority thus understood necessarily excludes foundations in the Edenic sense. Oakeshott is adamant that the authority of *respublica* cannot:

> lie in the identification of its prescriptions with a current 'social purpose', with approved moral ideals, with a common good or general interest, or a 'justice' other than that which is inherent in *respublica* [...] further, civil authority [...] cannot be derived from their purported access to 'scientific' information about the tendencies of human actions to promote the general happiness or about so-called 'laws of historical development' [...] And if a 'higher law' is postulated such that the authority of *respublica* is conditional upon correspondence with it, this 'law' [...] must itself be shown to have *authority*: mere rationality or wisdom will not do.[45]

Oakeshott's conception of civil authority is, thus, purely contingent and consequently devoid of foundations. As Mapel points out, 'authority is

---

40 HC: 153–154.
41 HC: 154.
42 *Ibid.*
43 *Ibid.*
44 B. Parekh 1979: 496–497.
45 HC: 152–153.

justified in terms of a self-conscious affirmation of the contingency of
rights now described as self-evident'.[46] Jeremy Rayner adds that
Oakeshott's 'Hobbesian approach to authority as an endowment of
those thereby obligated lines him up against those who want to
"ground" authority on God or Nature'.[47]

Like civil authority, the political in civil association is also devoid of
foundations. Oakeshott defines civil association as relationship in terms
of the acknowledgment of the authority of the conditions which constitute *respublica*. However, he also argues that these conditions may be
recognized in terms of their desirability, that is, in terms of approval or
disapproval. Recognizing the authority of *respublica* does not preclude
cives from questioning the desirability of the conditions the system of
law prescribes. Politics, then, is the 'exploration of *respublica* in terms of
the desirability of the conditions it prescribes'.[48] *Cives'* relationship to
respublica is consequently both acquiescent and critical.[49] The concern of
politics is to ensure that *respublica* 'adequately reflect what is currently
held to be civilly desirable'.[50] A rule or condition of *respublica* is deemed
to be desirable in so far as it corresponds to what is currently held to be
civilly desirable. However, politics is not merely the consideration of
the desirability of the conditions prescribed in *respublica*; it is also the
engagement of *cives* to deliberate about the rules of *respublica* in terms
of approval and disapproval.[51] Political action consists in the inspection
in terms of its desirability of a condition prescribed by *respublica* and
imagining it differently from what it is and to undertake (or resist) its
alteration to the allegedly more desirable condition.[52] In other words,
what is expressed in a political utterance is the want that 'all *cives*
should have a civil obligation which they do not already have or
should be relieved (or partly relieved) of a current civil obligation'.[53]
Political utterance and deliberation is persuasive in character. The proponents of change as well as the defenders of the status quo must each
use persuasive and argumentative language in order to persuade *cives*
and the occupants of the legislative office of the justness of their proposal. Oakeshott argues that politics is a 'deliberative and argumentative
engagement directed to reaching conclusions sustained by reasons

---

[46]   D. Mapel 1990: 405.
[47]   J. Rayner 1985: 338.
[48]   *HC*: 164.
[49]   *Ibid.*
[50]   *HC*: 172.
[51]   *HC*: 164.
[52]   *HC*: 163.
[53]   *Ibid.*

designed to persuade others of their cogency'.[54] Politics is deliberative, persuasive, argumentative and not demonstrative.[55]

The persuasive and argumentative character of politics necessarily excludes any type of foundation, Oakeshott contends. He is adamant that conclusions about the desirability of the conditions prescribed by *respublica* cannot be deduced from:

> theorems about the natural conditions of human life, from theorems such as that a man is an organism with an urge to live rather than to perish and that he is ill-equipped to do so, or that there is a natural scarcity of the means of organic subsistence.[56]

Nor can the desirability of a civil prescription be established by 'purporting to connect it inferentially with a superior norm of unquestionable or acknowledged desirability, a moral rule, a prescriptive Law of Reason or of Nature, a principle of utility, a categorical imperative, or the like'.[57] Inference of this kind is impossible, Oakeshott maintains. He holds that 'no civil rule can be *deduced* from the Golden Rule or from the Kantian categorical imperative'.[58] The desirability of a civil prescription cannot be inferred from or modelled upon a superior norm of unquestionable or acknowledged desirability because the conditions prescribed by *respublica* are contingent choices. These choices or political proposals are deliberative conclusions and, as such, belong to the discourse of persuasion and not of proof.[59] Political deliberation is not concerned with demonstrating and proving either that or how a condition connects inferentially with a superior norm and so forth. Demonstrative conclusions are impossible, Oakeshott insists. As Josiah Lee Auspitz observes:

> political deliberation [...] will always be restrained. It will invoke no general principles, for these can never settle a specific political question. Even if all citizens could agree on a common purpose, a higher law, an organic need for society, a social ideal, or a categorical imperative, they would not have therein adequate criteria for the drafting of any given piece of legislation.[60]

Rather, political deliberation is providing reasons which are able to persuade *cives* and the occupants of the legislative office of the cogency of the proposal. In this sense, Oakeshott argues that:

---

54 *HC*: 165.
55 *HC*: 173.
56 *Ibid.*
57 *HC*: 174.
58 *Ibid.*, original emphasis.
59 *HC*: 176–177.
60 J.L. Auspitz 1976: 281.

norms of civil conduct, like other norms of conduct, are contingent
choices which may have reasons but not causes and which are to be
understood in terms of reasons capable of elucidating the alleged
desirability (not the authority) of component prescriptions, current or
projected, of a *respublica*.[61]

The civil condition, therefore, postulates an understanding of politics
which is persuasive and which, consequently, excludes foundations
conceived of in the Edenic sense.

In sum, since the civil condition is a relationship of human beings, it
is a relationship understood in terms of the ideal character human conduct. This entails a conception of the political understood as a practice,
which, in the case of civil association, is conceived of as agents related
in terms of their common recognition of the rules which constitute a
practice of civility. It is alternatively conceived of in terms of a tradition
of behaviour concerned with attending to the arrangements of a
community in *Rationalism in Politics*. Such a conception of the political
is devoid of foundations. The absence of foundations, according to
commentators, means that Oakeshott's conception of the political is
contingent and historical. Vincent argues that for Oakeshott 'all human
conduct is rooted in the diverse conventions (and the ideal characters)
of civilized communities'.[62] He explains that for Oakeshott what con-
strains political conduct is 'the postulates that intelligent reflective
agents utilize for exploring both their own selves and their relation
with others'.[63] Vincent points out that these postulates are, and can only
be, contingent. Furthermore, he adds that for Oakeshott 'no universal
[...] will overcome this contingency'.[64] Rorty concurs with Vincent's
analysis and points out that consequently the only justification for our
practices that is possible with Oakeshott is a circular justification
'which makes one feature of our culture look good by citing still
another, or comparing our culture invidiously with others by reference
to our own standards'.[65] All of these considerations lead Mapel to conclude that 'Oakeshott is certainly radical in his rejection of
foundations'.[66]

---

[61] *HC*: 176.
[62] A. Vincent 2004: 153.
[63] *Ibid.*
[64] *Ibid.*: 154.
[65] R. Rorty 1989: 57.
[66] D. Mapel 1990: 406.

The Principle of the Mean in Action:
A Mixed Form of Politics

But is this really the case? Is Oakeshott radical in his rejection of foundations? Following the exposition of his ideas regarding foundations, it would seem evident that he belongs squarely in the anti-foundationalist camp. However, this is only the case if attention is solely paid to his explicit argument. What the discussion of foundations shows, and what commentators confirm, is that Oakeshott's conception of the political is devoid of a certain sort of foundations: it is devoid of foundations understood in Edenic terms. There are no prior grounding claims about unquestionable, sacred or natural premises understood as human nature, natural rights, abstract ideals, principles of justice or freedom. There are only practices and traditions. This leads to the idea that political institutions are the result of contingent choices and decisions, and, consequently, are historical achievements. Oakeshott is clearly not a philosopher of Edenic foundations. This does not mean, however, that his thought is altogether devoid of foundations. It simply means that he does not belong to the Edenic tradition of foundations. Commentators only address the 'Edenic' side of the equation. None discuss the question of foundations in Oakeshott's political thought in relation to the Arendtian constructivist or building tradition as defined by Seery.

I posit that parallel to his explicit antifoundationalist position Oakeshott also develops an implicit argument in support of foundations, albeit of a different sort. As was discussed in Chapter 1, Oakeshott states that the question of the ties that bind members of a state to one another following the dissolution of communal ties is one of the least tangible of the themes of modern European political thought. Oakeshott, when considering how the state has been conceptualized in modern political thought, asserts that the bond which unites members of an artificial association is fragile and not sufficiently substantial to sustain solidarity amongst strangers. I argued that this echoes my argument that the continued recognition of the rules of association as rules is insufficient to ensure the cohesion of a political association. However, it will be pointed out that Oakeshott does not defend an artificial conception of the state, nor does he conceive of the civil association in artificial terms. Rather, he defends an historical and contingent understanding of the modern state. It may be thought that such an understanding of the state would be devoid of foundations. In this regard, Oakeshott maintains that the bonds which unite members of the state understood as an historical association are circumstantial and contingent. However, the crucial point is that in spite of their contingent nature, they are nevertheless ties or, alternatively, bonds and, as Oakeshott acknowledges, these ties and bonds do manage to become strong.[67] Hence, while they are contingent, the ties that bind the members of a political association to one another are also characterized by an element of permanence. This is precisely what I understand by contingent foundations. Moreover, the ties that bind the members of a political association to one another are constructed or created in that they comprise the 'memory of shared experiences' or 'of the long enjoyment of a common experience of living together'.[68] [69] Oakeshott identifies a common language, a literature, common laws, folktales, legends and songs as being constitutive of 'the total of contingent circumstances' that ensure solidarity amongst strangers.[70] In addition to solidarity, a political society requires a sense of identity. It is for these reasons that I suggest that a careful examination of his thought in regards to the question of the mixed form of politics reveals that there are, at a minimum, foundational elements present in Oakeshott's conception of the political. In other words, it is my position that Oakeshott is foundationalist, but that he belongs to the constructivist, poetic tradition and not to the Edenic tradition. It is a legend of political life, a poetic construct, which founds a political society's identity.

I will begin by examining the question of the mixed form of the political. First, although the contingent conception of the political is dominant in his thought and is most explicitly defended by Oakeshott, I posit that he concurrently and implicitly develops and defends a conception of the political understood as a mixture of the two polar opposite understandings of the political inherent to modernity: that is, the political conceived of as contingent and the political understood as foundational and permanent. Oakeshott's principal claim in *The Politics of Faith and the Politics of Scepticism* is that the political in modernity is 'unavoidably complex'.[71] The complex character of modern politics stems from the fact that political activity fluctuates between two poles or ideal understandings of the political. Oakeshott explains that 'the two dispositions, into which the impulses of the modern European political character have come to group themselves, I have called respectively the politics of faith and the politics of scepticism'.[72] While these two ideal understandings of politics are opposed to one another, Oakeshott argues that they cannot stand alone as independent and

---

[67]   *LHPT*: 422.
[68]   *Ibid.*
[69]   *LHPT*: 425.
[70]   *LHPT*: 422.
[71]   *PFPS*: 121.
[72]   *PFPS*: 117.

fully autonomous forms of the political. They represent extreme understandings of politics and one would self-destruct without the
stabilizing pull exerted by the other. In this respect, Oakeshott asserts
that these polar opposite understandings of the political are the
'"charges" of the poles of our political activity, each exerting a pull
which makes itself felt over the whole range of movement'.[73] Modern
politics, Oakeshott pursues is 'the resultant of both these pulls and not
merely the consequence of one'.[74] To understand the character of
modern politics is to understand its range of motion or movement
within the field of historic possibilities as delimited by faith and
scepticism. Given the complex character of modern politics, the
challenge is to find a way to inhabit and to be at home in such a complex world. This is achieved, Oakeshott maintains, by exploiting the
middle region of the potential range of movement. This habitable
middle region offers an escape from the self-destructive extremes.[75] For
Oakeshott, to be at home in the complex modern world is 'to observe
what may be called the [principle of the] mean in action'.[76] The principle of the mean in action is inherent to a complex style of politics. For
Oakeshott, it is not a fixed point, but rather the middle range of movement between two polar opposite understandings of the political.[77] In
short, 'the principle of the mean in action is, then, the virtue of exploiting the middle range of our political opportunities'.[78]

The principle of the mean in action implies a mixed form of politics.
This view is shared by Ian Tregenza who writes that 'the trimmer
understands that if the boat is to remain afloat the right mixture of faith
and scepticism must be maintained. In other words, faith and scepticism need each other'.[79] As regards the composition of the mixture, I
posit that the principle of the mean in action consists of the politics of
scepticism, but with important modifications which are the result of the
pull exerted by faith. Recall that the ideal understandings of the
political cannot stand alone because they would self-destruct. That
being said, Oakeshott argues that scepticism and faith are not equal in
regards to their ability to stand alone. Oakeshott maintains that without
the pull of scepticism faith faces certain self-defeat, while the politics of
scepticism only faces probable self-defeat in the absence of faith. The
reason for this is that faith 'is incapable of the kind of self-criticism

---

[73] *PFPS*: 118.
[74] *Ibid.*
[75] *PFPS*: 121.
[76] *Ibid.*
[77] *Ibid.*
[78] *PFPS*: 123.
[79] I. Tregenza 2002: 365.

which would enable it to defend itself against its own excesses'.[80] Contrary to faith, scepticism is capable of some self-criticism when it stands alone, Oakeshott contends. He argues that scepticism 'enjoys some reserve and scope for internal movement and self-correction [...] Everything in this style of government is provisional and is constructed so that it may be enlarged or diminished as unfolding circumstances demand'.[81] Consequently, Oakeshott contends that faith and scepticism are not equidistant from the mean. Faith, in its excess, lies further from the mean than does scepticism and its defects. Oakeshott summarizes this idea by quoting Isocrates's observation that 'moderation lies in deficiency rather than in excess'.[82]

Since scepticism lies closest to the middle region of the range of motion of modern politics, this means that the principle of the mean in action comprises the politics of scepticism, but with modifications which resolve its defects. Oakeshott argues that the defects of the sceptical style of politics are the direct result of its principle virtue: its self-limitation.[83] In the politics of scepticism, the role of government is understood to be the maintenance of the system of rights and duties in order to ensure that it corresponds to current social norms and accepted practices. Oakeshott argues that scepticism performs its role sluggishly without the pull of faith. That is, this style of politics is susceptible to political quietism. It underestimates the need for change or modification of the system of rights.[84] In this sense, Oakeshott claims that it 'is apt to be insensitive even to those effects of change which come within its province, namely the appearance of conditions which require an adjustment in the system of rights and duties if a relevant order is to be maintained'.[85] More problematic is scepticism's inability to recognize and act in a genuine emergency. Oakeshott asserts that 'rejecting the call for emergency in its own province, and being reluctant to go beyond its own province, it is liable to confuse a genuine emergency with the counterfeit emergencies of faith, and to discount it'.[86] He maintains that scepticism finds itself handicapped by its own virtue. He argues that 'the energy and enterprise characteristic of modern European communities call for formality in government which the sceptical style can supply; but they call also for readiness in genuine

---

80   *PFPS*: 114.
81   *PFPS*: 114–115.
82   *PFPS*: Isocrates cited by Oakeshott, 115.
83   *PFPS*: 106.
84   *PFPS*: 106–108.
85   *PFPS*: 107.
86   *PFPS*: 108–109.

emergency, and here this style is handicapped by its own virtues'.[87] It is my contention that, for Oakeshott, the remedy for the defects of scepticism is to inject it with certain elements of faith, namely, with the ability to recognize the need for change and readiness for action in genuine emergencies. Faith, in its quest to realize human perfection by means of the political, provides a larger enterprise which ensures that scepticism satisfactorily performs its role of maintaining the 'system of rights and duties relevant to the current activities which compose the community'.[88] In this regard, Oakeshott claims that 'without the pull exerted by faith, without the "perfectionism" which we have seen to be both illusion and a dangerous illusion [...] government in the sceptical style is liable to be overtaken by a nemesis of political quietism'.[89]

Furthermore, I also posit that this mixture of the politics of faith and the politics of scepticism is how Oakeshott conceives of the principle of the mean in action. His discussion of the principle essentially describes this particular mixture of scepticism and faith. Oakeshott addresses the question of the principle of the mean in action by employing the character of the 'trimmer'. His inspiration for this is George Savile, 1st Marquess of Halifax, whom, he asserts, was one of many writers to attempt to elicit 'the principle of "moderation" from the conditions of modern politics'.[90] Recall that Oakeshott contends that the politics of scepticism is the most moderate style of politics. It is largely for this reason that sceptics, according to Oakeshott, were the ones to first discover the principle of the mean in action. Although scepticism is an extreme, Oakeshott contends that its 'extremity is not to impose a single pattern of activity upon a community, and consequently it enjoys [...] a characteristic forbearance of its own which can be seen to intimate a wider doctrine of moderation'.[91] An examination of the trimmer and of his general ideas reveals a close affinity with scepticism. For Oakeshott, the trimmer's guiding notion is the idea that '"it would do as well, if the Boat went even"'.[92] With this in mind, Oakeshott pursues the sailing metaphor and asserts that the trimmer's concern is to ensure that politics does not run to extremes. This means that he believes 'that there is a time for everything and that everything has its time'.[93] For this reason, he faces the direction the occasion requires in order to keep the boat on an even keel. However, changes in direction are neither fre-

---

[87]   *PFPS*: 109.
[88]   *PFPS*: 107.
[89]   *PFPS*: 108.
[90]   *PFPS*: 122.
[91]   *PFPS*: 123.
[92]   *PFPS*: Halifax cited by Oakeshott, 123.
[93]   *PFPS*: 123.

quent, sudden nor great. This is because the changes the movement is designed to counterbalance are not frequent, nor are they sudden.[94] Oakeshott asserts that 'the mean in action is never to be achieved by a general surge this way or that; indeed, such surges are precisely what it is designed to exclude'.[95] To this end, the trimmer believes that a timely, small movement will be less disturbing than a large one at a later stage.[96] We can see why Oakeshott concludes that the 'trimmer' (or the principle of the mean in action) with his moderate character 'has a closer affinity to scepticism than to faith, and he has the advantage of the sceptic in his ability to recognize change and emergency'.[97]

Thus, for Oakeshott, the principle of the mean in action, or the 'middling region', has a closer affinity to scepticism than to faith. However, Oakeshott also argues that scepticism, when it stands alone, reveals a 'certain inappropriateness to the conditions of modern European communities'.[98] An appropriate manner of politics is one that is alive to change and which recognizes the need to act in an emergency.[99] But in the absence of a larger enterprise, Oakeshott contends that the 'sceptical office of keeping the system of rights and duties relevant to the current activities which compose the community may be expected to be sluggishly performed'.[100] In other words, without the pull exerted by faith, the politics of scepticism is susceptible to be overtaken by political quietism. Scepticism is saved from self-destruction by what faith is able to supply, namely, its perfectionism. Thus, while the principle of the mean in action is closer in affinity to scepticism, scepticism itself incorporates a number of elements of faith. Without the pull exerted by faith, scepticism would in all probability self-destruct. Therefore, we find here a mixed form of politics. But above and beyond this, the 'middling region' implies elements of both styles of politics in its quest to avoid extremes. It is a mixture where scepticism (contingency) dominates since its moderate character is in closer proximity to the middle. However, the pull of faith is indispensable, which implies that in the middling region perfectionism interacts with the politics of scepticism. The implication is that in this region consideration is given to perfectionist ideals such as human nature and natural rights, for instance. Consequently, Oakeshott conceives of the principle of the mean in action as a mixture of the contingent and of permanence, per-

---

94   *Ibid.*
95   *Ibid.*
96   *PFPS*: 123–124.
97   *PFPS*: 124.
98   *PFPS*: 106.
99   *PFPS*: 107.
100 *PFPS*: 107–108.

fectionism and foundations where the contingent dominates the mixture. This is not a purely contingent understanding of the political. Rather, it incorporates a dimension of faith and permanence.

The mixture of the contingent and permanence is therefore deemed to be an acceptable and legitimate form of the political by Oakeshott. In fact, the avoidance of extremes, the contingent included, is the only way the complex modern world can be made habitable. However, the principle of the mean in action is not the only mixed form of politics Oakeshott identifies in *The Politics of Faith and the Politics of Scepticism*. He also discusses the mixture of the politics of scepticism and natural rights, which, contrary to the principle of the mean in action, he rejects outright as an illegitimate form of politics. Oakeshott concedes that it is understandable that the sceptical style of politics, the role of which it is to ensure the preservation of rights and duties, 'should be ambitious to establish itself on a firm foundation'.[101] Nevertheless, he contends that this 'impulse' must be 'regarded as an infection caught from faith'.[102] Political foundations, such as the notion that rights and duties are natural and are to be defended on account of their naturalness, belong to faith.[103] The mixture of the politics of scepticism and natural rights is an 'unnatural' alliance and a 'mésalliance' because rights cannot be turned into natural rights without denying them 'that contingency of character which was the heart of the sceptical interpretation'.[104]

The 'Mésalliance' of Natural Rights and Scepticism: The Case of the Foundation of the American Republic

Although Oakeshott is never specific as to which society he is referring to, he most certainly has a case like that of the foundation of the American republic and its Bill of Rights in mind. The question of the Bill of Rights was a highly contentious issue at the time of the ratification of the proposed federal constitution put forward by the delegates of the Philadelphia Convention in 1787. The original constitution which had been submitted for ratification by the state legislatures did not contain a bill of rights. The lack of such a bill was severely criticized by the anti-federalist opponents of the proposed constitution, most notably by the opponent writing under the name of Brutus. In his Letter II dated November 1, 1787, he argues that the lack of a bill of rights was problematic since the constitution as it stood did not adequately protect what he terms public rights against the power and authority of the

---

101 *PFPS*: 82.
102 *Ibid.*
103 *PFPS*: 83.
104 *Ibid.*

federal government. In order to limit and define its powers and guard against the abuse of authority, Brutus maintains that the foundational principles of the social compact 'ought to have been clearly and precisely stated' and, most important of all, that 'the most express and full declaration of rights to have been made'.[105] Brutus argues that in order for civil government to be established, it is necessary for individuals to surrender a certain portion of their natural rights. However, this is done with the knowledge and intention that the natural rights which were not surrendered 'should be preserved'.[106] Following Brutus, this makes clear that at the time of the American Revolution, 'when the pulse of liberty beat high', it was deemed essential and fundamental by Americans 'that such declarations should make a part of their frames of government'.[107]

In response to the letter published by Brutus, the proponents of the proposed federal constitution countered with the Federalist paper 84 written by Alexander Hamilton and published May 8, 1788. The authors of the *Federalist Papers* and Framers of the American constitution, Hamilton, James Madison and John Jay, were opposed to the idea of including a bill of rights in the constitution. They argued that the type of government and society which were to be founded did not require a bill of rights to ensure the freedom of individuals. There are several key elements to the Federalists' response and it is interesting to compare their argument to Oakeshott's position as they reverse his argument and assert that it is a contingent understanding of the political and government that requires a bill of rights to secure rights and freedom. Furthermore, in arguing against the need for a bill, the Federalists have recourse to ideas that are reminiscent of Oakeshott's conception of the political as contingent, tradition and historical. The Federalists integrate elements of both modern conceptions of the political in their understanding of freedom.

Firstly, as was the case with Brutus, the Federalists' argument centres on the need to limit governmental power. In Federalist paper 53, Madison identifies and distinguishes between two types of government. The first type of government he identifies is government for the people. In this type of government, a constitution is established by the people and is therefore unalterable by the government, hence, its foundational nature. Madison argues that the American government is of this sort.[108]

---

[105] Brutus 2003: 447–448.

[106] *Ibid.*: 448.

[107] *Ibid.*: 449.

[108] J. Madison 2003: 260.

The second type of government he identifies is one where the law is established by the government, and, consequently, is alterable by government. In this case, government is of a contingent and historical nature. Madison associates the British political tradition with this type of government. He argues that the supreme power of legislation implies full power to change the government as well as the constitution. In this sense, and in particular in the case of Great Britain, Madison argues that 'it is maintained that the authority of parliament is transcendent and uncontroulable'.[109] Therefore, we can gather that for Madison, Hamilton and Jay, British law and custom do not form a constitution in so far as they do not limit the power and authority of government.[110]

Given the nature of the British political tradition, Hamilton argues that rights and freedom in this type of government are guaranteed by means of bills of rights. Hamilton provides an historical overview of the bills of rights adopted in Great Britain in order to support his argument that they are 'in their origin [...] reservations of rights not surrendered to the prince'.[111] In this sense, contrary to Oakeshott, Hamilton claims that Magna Carta and the Bill of Rights of 1688 (a bill never mentioned by Oakeshott) are both examples of bills of rights since they limit the power of the government. Furthermore, Magna Carta and the other bills of rights form the British constitution.[112] This is the case because the common law and customs are alterable by parliament, which, according to Madison, holds the supreme power of legislation. Since a constitution must ensure the rights and freedom of citizens and limit the power and authority of government, it must necessarily be unalterable by government and, consequently, it is for this reason that in the case of Great Britain their 'several bills of rights [...] form its constitution'.[113] Therefore, we find that in the analysis of the Federalist writers it is the contingent or historical conception of the political and of government, based on custom and common law, which requires bills of rights since it is the only way to secure the rights and freedom of citizens. This position differs substantially from Oakeshott who, as will be discussed in Chapter 5, regards Magna Carta as a charter of recognized and already enjoyed liberties which came about historically, hence the necessity for a contingent type of government.[114]

---

109 *Ibid.*
110 A. Hamilton 2003: 419.
111 *Ibid.*
112 *Ibid.*: 421.
113 *Ibid.*
114 *WH*: 239–242.

In arguing against the need for a bill of rights in the American constitution, Hamilton claims that the first type of government that
Madison identifies, one founded on the power of the people and of
which the proposed constitution is an example, does not require a bill
of rights. Hamilton writes that according to the definition of bills of
rights, 'they have no application to constitutions professedly founded
upon the power of the people, and executed by their immediate
representatives and servants'.[115] Bills of rights do not apply in the case
of a constitution founded on the power of the people because the
people do not surrender any rights and, because of this, there is no
need to establish a list of rights and freedom which have not been
surrendered to the authority of the government. Hamilton concludes
that in the case of the American type of government, which is founded
on the power of the people, the proposed constitution is 'itself in every
rational sense, and to every useful purpose, a BILL OF RIGHTS'.[116] The
constitution is itself a bill of rights in so far as it is foundational and that
it specifies the political privileges of the citizens in the structure and
administration of the government and defines 'certain immunities and
modes of proceeding, which are relative to personal and private concerns'.[117] Therefore, since the constitution is itself a bill of rights, there is
no need to add another one to it.

For Hamilton, a constitution founded upon the power of the people
is a better recognition of rights and freedom than 'volumes of those
aphorisms [...] which would sound better in a treatise of ethics than in
a constitution of government'.[118] Hamilton's argument regarding
founding the political and freedom on declarations and aphorisms
bears a striking resemble to Oakeshott's argument regarding founding
the political on abstract ideals and principles. Hamilton claims that the
constitution and government should rest on something more concrete
and practical than aphorisms. In other words, the constitution defines a
certain number of practices and manners of behaving. Furthermore,
Hamilton specifies that the constitution is 'intended to regulate the
general political interests of the nation'.[119] It should be noted that his
understanding of the role of the constitution and of the function of
government is reminiscent of Oakeshott's conception of the state as
civil association in *On Human Conduct*.[120] In this respect, for Hamilton,
in order to regulate the general political interests of the nation, the con-

---

[115] A. Hamilton 2003: 419.
[116] *Ibid.*: 421, original capitalization.
[117] *Ibid.*
[118] *Ibid.*: 419.
[119] *Ibid.*
[120] *HC*: 313–315.

stitution integrates and specifies a certain number of immunities and proceedings, such as the writ of Habeas Corpus, which ensure the rights and freedom of citizens. The practice of Habeas Corpus is integrated as such into the constitution and its meaning and sense is not simply abstracted into a bill of rights. Therefore, the Framers of the American constitution combine a practice such as Habeas Corpus with a foundational constitutional document in an attempt to secure foundations for a practice which came about contingently and historically.

Finally, Hamilton argues that practice and experience better protect rights and freedom than declarations, aphorisms and bills of rights which often do not mean anything in and of themselves. That is, certain rights only have sense, meaning and content in relation to actual experience. Hamilton gives the example of the liberty of the press. He argues that it is impossible to give a definition of the liberty of the press which does not have some latitude for evasion. Consequently, Hamilton holds that the security of the liberty of the press depends on 'public opinion, and on the general spirit of the people and of the government' and not on 'whatever fine declarations may be inserted in any constitution respecting it'.[121] Implicit in Hamilton's argument is the idea that the security of the liberty of the press depends to a large extent on a practice, or in this particular case on a custom and a tradition. Otherwise, if the liberty of the press simply takes the form of a declaration or of an aphorism in a constitutional document, it is nothing more than an empty shell. Hamilton's argument is remarkably similar to Oakeshott's ideas of a tradition of behaviour and a practice.

Therefore, the Framers of the American constitution do not defend a purely rationalist conception of freedom or one based solely on natural rights. They give importance to the contingent, historical and traditional understanding of freedom and forge their own, original conception of freedom. Practices, procedures and processes are integrated and formalized in foundational documents and institutions. Finally, since it is the people who establish government, this institution can only be instituted through the practice of public deliberation on natural rights. The conception of freedom put forward by the Framers of the American constitution is in fact a synthesis of freedom understood as contingent, traditional and historical, on the one hand and conceived of as foundational, natural and based on reason, on the other.

The founding of the American republic, then, is an alliance between the politics of scepticism and the politics of faith. Although it is a mixed form of politics like the principle of the mean in action; nevertheless,

---

[121] A. Hamilton 2003: 420.

Oakeshott rejects such an alliance since its impulse to found rights which emerged contingently is an infection caught from faith, he argues. Oakeshott's interpretation of the American Revolution is all the more curious since he appears to be uncommonly rigid. That is, he maintains a strict dichotomy between scepticism and faith; more specifically, between their respective conceptions of freedom. In the essay 'Freedom and Power', he distinguishes between two different understandings of freedom, one which he identifies with the American Revolution and the other with the English tradition of politics. Oakeshott claims that the American Declaration of Independence best exemplifies the conception of freedom which is understood to begin with an abstract ideal. Fundamental to this manner of thinking about freedom and power, Oakeshott argues, 'is *the overwhelming experience of submission to power*'.[122] The overwhelming experience of submission to power means that freedom is not a concrete manner of behaviour and, consequently, has never been concretely experienced by society. Since freedom is inexistent as a political tradition of behaviour it has to be 'instituted, introduced from the outside and superimposed'.[123] This manner of thinking about freedom, then, begins with an idea of freedom. Oakeshott claims that in such circumstances, 'nothing is known of freedom, in the first place, except the "idea"'.[124] Freedom in this manner of thinking begins as a dream or ideal which must be made a concrete reality. In other words, the enjoyment of freedom is secured by the 'translation of the idea into practice'.[125] For Oakeshott, it is the analysis of the idea of freedom that leads to its conception as natural rights. He argues that the analysis 'leads to the recognition of certain forms of behaviour as the embodiments of the idea of freedom'.[126] Oakeshott argues that these expressions of freedom come to form the content of a bill of rights, 'a statement of claims to freedom demanding authorization by the established powers'.[127] The established political powers concede to a limitation of their power by recognizing and securing the rights which are understood to embody the idea of freedom. The fundamental point for Oakeshott is the idea that freedom is a concession made by the political power within the context of a society which only has concrete experience of complete submission to power. Freedom understood in this manner 'begins with an abstract idea and ends with

---

[122] *WH*: 237, original emphasis.
[123] *Ibid.*
[124] *Ibid.*
[125] *Ibid.*
[126] *WH*: 237–238.
[127] *WH*: 238.

a Bill'.[128] In other words, the exercise of freedom proceeds from 'principles laid down in constitutional documents'.[129]

For its part, the English tradition of politics is the most accomplished example of freedom understood as contingent, traditional and historical. This manner of thinking is the consequence of a tradition of behaviour. More precisely, it is 'the *experience of a pattern of social life in which the exercise of freedom is a recognizable and independent element*'.[130] In other words, the exercise of freedom is an original and constitutive element of social life. There is no need to theorize or conceptualize freedom because it is already enjoyed by the members of society. Oakeshott argues that there already exist within this pattern of social life a 'number of current forms of behaviour' which he terms liberties.[131] These liberties form a 'concrete model for the exercise of freedom'.[132] Liberties can be recorded and written down in what Oakeshott terms a 'charter of liberties' of which Magna Carta is a prime example. Contrary to a bill of rights, Oakeshott argues, a charter of liberties is not a list of abstract rights and freedoms which need to be instituted. Rather, a charter such as Magna Carta is a '*record of specific liberties* already enjoyed'.[133]

For Oakeshott, then, the aim of the American Declaration of Independence is the realization of the general idea of freedom. In 'Rationalism in Politics', he claims that the Framers of the American constitution have no other alternative since the Revolution represents the rejection of the English tradition of freedom and, having no pattern of social life of their own from which freedom can emerge, the Americans find themselves obliged to invent and dream-up freedom.[134] Oakeshott's apparent outright rejection of natural rights and permanence gives credence to those commentators who contend that Oakeshott's conception of the political is purely contingent and, therefore, foundationless. However, these polar opposite conceptions of freedom are extremes and, therefore, cannot sustain themselves on their own. Consequently, the problem is not with the alliance between scepticism and faith, but with the nature of the mixture. In other words, Oakeshott's rejection of the 'mésalliance' is revelatory of what he deems to be the legitimate mixed form of politics.

---

[128] *WH*: 239.

[129] *Ibid.*

[130] *Ibid.*, original emphasis.

[131] *Ibid.*

[132] *WH*: 240.

[133] *Ibid.*, original emphasis.

[134] *RP*: 31–33.

Contingent Foundations:
The Legitimate Alliance of Permanence and Change

Why does the alliance between scepticism and natural rights pose a problem for Oakeshott, while the mixture represented by the principle of the mean in action is deemed to be legitimate? Is this not simply another form a complex style of politics can take? For the answer to this question we must turn to the essay 'Tower of Babel' which forms part of the collection *Rationalism in Politics*. There, Oakeshott discusses the different mixed forms of morality inherent to modernity. He identifies two ideal conceptions of the moral life in modernity. These two ideal understandings of morality correspond to contingency and permanence and perfectionism. The first of these two forms is morality understood as a habit of affection and behaviour. Following this conception of morality, 'the current situations of a normal life are met [...] by acting in accordance with a certain habit of behaviour'.[135] For this form of morality, as Oakeshott conceives of it, the majority of current situations in life do not require judgment. On most occasions, moral behaviour is 'nothing more than the unreflective following of a tradition of conduct in which we have been brought up'.[136] Thus, moral conduct, according to this conception, is 'nearly as possible without reflection'.[137] Oakeshott is adamant that he is not describing a primitive form of morality. Rather, he contends that this is the form which moral actions take in the emergencies of life. In other words, Oakeshott here assumes that 'what is true for the emergencies of life is true of most of the occasions when human conduct is free from natural necessity'.[138] For Oakeshott, the principle strength of such a form of morality is the 'remarkable stability' which it gives to the moral life from the viewpoint of both the individual and society.[139] Its stability derives from its elasticity, Oakeshott argues, as well as from its ability to suffer change without disruption.[140] In this sense, while the change it admits is never great or small; nevertheless, nothing is absolutely fixed. Morality understood as a habit of behaviour is never at rest and is perpetually experiencing change. For Oakeshott, this continual change and adaptation explains its remarkable stability.[141]

---

[135] *RP*: 467.

[136] *RP*: 468.

[137] *Ibid.*

[138] *Ibid.*

[139] *RP*: 470.

[140] *Ibid.*

[141] *RP*: 471.

This form of morality necessarily excludes 'consciously applying to ourselves a rule of behaviour' as well as 'conduct recognized as the expression of a moral ideal'.[142] This corresponds to the second form of morality. Oakeshott argues that in this form of the moral life activity is determined by '*the reflective application of a moral criterion*'.[143] It appears in two varieties: the self-conscious pursuit of moral ideals and the reflective observance of moral rules.[144] Fundamental to this form of morality is the value attributed to self-consciousness. Moral conduct is determined by reflective thought since the moral rule, as well as its application to a situation, is the result of reflection. The rule is determined first and in the abstract. Only once moral aspirations have been expressed in words by means of a rule of life or a system of abstract ideas will they be translated into behaviour by their application to current situations of life.[145] Consequently, in this form of the moral life 'action will spring from a judgement concerning the rule or end to be applied and the determination to apply it'.[146] Behaviour is here determined by 'reference to a vision of perfection'.[147] Contrary to the morality of a habit of behaviour, Oakeshott argues that the morality he terms the reflective application of a moral criterion has little power of self-modification.[148] This is the source of its weakness and failing as a form of morality. It derives its stability from 'its inelasticity and its imperviousness to change'.[149] However, when its capacity for resistance breaks down what occurs is not change, but instead revolution, rejection and replacement.[150] A further problem this form of moral life is confronted with, according to Oakeshott, is its potential obsession with one moral ideal. He maintains that 'too often the excessive pursuit of one ideal leads to the exclusion of others, perhaps all others'.[151] Finally, Oakeshott observes that this form of morality places a distracting burden on those who share the moral life. For these reasons, Oakeshott judges that this form of morality is untenable. He argues that 'this is a form of the moral life which is dangerous in an individual and disastrous in a society [...] for a society it is mere folly'.[152]

---

142 *RP*: 467.
143 *RP*: 472, original emphasis.
144 *RP*: 472.
145 *RP*: 472–473.
146 *RP*: 473.
147 *RP*: 475.
148 *RP*: 476.
149 *Ibid.*
150 *Ibid.*
151 *Ibid.*
152 *RP*: 476–477.

These forms of the moral life, like their political counterparts, faith and scepticism, are ideal extremes. One is all habit and the other is all reflection and, as such, they cannot stand alone. Hence, morality is necessarily a mixed form of these two ideal extremes. It may either consist of a mixture where habit dominates, or it may take the form of a mixture dominated by reflection. For his part, Oakeshott holds that the mixed form of morality where habit dominates is preferable to the one dominated by reflection, which, he holds, is untenable. The mixture where habit is dominant is judged to be preferable by Oakeshott since it benefits from the advantages inherent to each extreme form of morality. Thus, in the mixture dominated by habit, action will retain its primacy. The moral life's confidence in action will remain unshaken.[153] For Oakeshott, this means that 'conduct itself will never become problematical, inhibited by the hesitations of ideal speculation or the felt necessity of bringing philosophic talent and the fruits of philosophic education to bear upon the situation'.[154] However, this mixed form of morality will benefit from the advantages which belong to reflective morality. Most notably, it will enjoy the power to criticize, reform and explain itself, and it will also benefit from the intellectual confidence in its moral standards and purposes.[155] Since habit dominates the mixture, this mixed form of morality will benefit from the advantages of reflection 'without the danger of moral criticism usurping the place of a habit of moral behaviour, or of moral speculation bringing disintegration to moral life'.[156]

As regards the mixed form of morality dominated by reflection, Oakeshott argues that it is defective because the dominant extreme is itself defective. To this end, he contends that 'the radical defect of this form is the radical defect of its dominant extreme — its denial of the poetic character of all human activity'.[157] Oakeshott means several things by this. First and foremost, he is referring to the common assumption that moral activity consists in the translation of the idea of what ought to be into a practical reality. That is, the transformation of an ideal into concrete existence.[158] This view of moral activity is mistaken, Oakeshott argues. He is adamant that moral ideals are not the product of reflective thought. Rather, moral ideals are 'the products of human behaviour, of human practical activity, to which reflective

---

153 *RP*: 477.
154 *Ibid.*
155 *Ibid.*
156 *Ibid.*
157 *RP*: 479.
158 *Ibid.*

thought gives subsequent, partial and abstract expression in words'.[159] In this sense, in the mixture where habit of behaviour is subordinate to the pursuit of ideals, reflection takes charge and has a 'disintegrating effect upon habit of behaviour', thereby denying the poetic character of human activity.[160] Consequently, Oakeshott contends that when action is required speculation or criticism will supervene. Furthermore, moral behaviour will tend to be problematic since it will seek its self-confidence in the coherence of an ideology.[161] In short, for Oakeshott, the mixed form of morality dominated by reflection is untenable because 'the pursuit of perfection will get in the way of a stable and flexible moral tradition, the naive coherence of which will be prized less than the unity which springs from selfconscious analysis and syn-thesis'.[162] Therefore, Oakeshott concludes that the mixed form of morality, and by extension of the political, where habit (contingency) dominates is preferable to the mixture where reflection is dominant since it benefits from the advantages and positive elements inherent to the two ideal extremes.

Both politics and morality are mixtures of contingency and perma-nence and perfection: that is, of the two ideal extremes. If we refer to the two examples previously outlined regarding the mixed forms of politics, it must be concluded that Oakeshott is favourable to the prin-ciple of the mean in action since contingency dominates the mixture, and, by the same token, that he rejects the alliance of the politics of scepticism and natural rights because it is dominated by reflection, the pursuit of perfection, the self-conscious pursuit of an ideal as well as by the reflective application of a criterion. Consequently, modern politics for Oakeshott is a mixture of contingency and permanence and per-fection where the contingent element must be dominant. The implica-tion for Oakeshott's political thought is not that the political is free of foundations or antifoundational. On the contrary, what his conception of modern politics implies is that it possesses foundational elements. This, in itself, is not problematic so long as the contingent element remains dominant. In other words, Oakeshott implicitly argues for a type of contingent foundations.

Contingency and Permanence United by Poetry

There is, consequently, a foundational element to Oakeshott's con-ception of the political. It remains to determine what kind of founda-

---

159 *RP*: 479–480.
160 *RP*: 478.
161 *Ibid.*
162 *Ibid.*

tions satisfies the criteria he establishes. Following Seery's framework, I have distinguished between two different kinds of foundations: Edenic and constructivist. It is my position that Oakeshott does not belong to the Edenic tradition of foundations. He rejects any sort of prior grounding claim about unquestionable, sacred or natural premises. Oakeshott commentators agree that his conception of the political is devoid of such foundations. His conception of authority does not rest on a social purpose, on approved moral ideals, a common good, a general interest or an abstract idea of justice. Rather, the tie of civil association is continuous assent by *cives* to civil authority. Put another way, what relates *cives* to one another is the acknowledgment of the authority of *respublica* and the continued recognition of the rules of association as rules. Moreover, as regards political activity, its persuasive and argumentative character excludes Edenic foundations. Conclusions about the desirability of civil prescriptions cannot be deduced from theorems about the natural conditions of human life, from a moral rule, a law of reason, a law of nature, a principle of utility, a categorical imperative or a Golden Rule. Nor can they be established by connecting it inferentially with a superior norm of unquestionable or acknowledged desirability. The discussion of the mixed form of politics reinforces this point. The alliance of scepticism and natural rights, the mixture of contingency and permanence adopted by the American Founding Fathers, is deemed to be an illegitimate mixed form of politics by Oakeshott because the foundational element it incorporates is Edenic. Therefore, if the foundational element his conception of the political postulates cannot be Edenic, it must, consequently, be constructivist. In this sense, Oakeshott does not argue for the kind of contingent foundations Butler proposes. He is not a proponent of grounding claims which remain 'ungrounded' and 'open' in that they may always be redefined, reconceived and reinterpreted. There simply are no such grounding claims in Oakeshott's conception of the political and commentators in this regard are correct in their analysis of his political thought.

What, then, is the constructivist foundational element present in Oakeshott's conception of the political? What has thus far been overlooked by commentators is the central role played by imagination in founding the political in Oakeshott's thought. If attention is solely paid to Oakeshott's discussion of authority and politics in *On Human Conduct*, then it would naturally be concluded that the tie of civil association is simply the continued recognition of the rules as rules by *cives*. However, what this analysis ignores is the fundamental importance of identity for Oakeshott's political thought. As I argue in chapters 4 and 5, at the heart of his conception of conservatism is his concern for an individual's as well as for a political society's identity. A political society simply cannot exist, cannot function without a sense of identity, of self-consciousness and of self-understanding. There is more to human living-together for Oakeshott than the recognition of the rules as rules. This tie is insufficient to sustain a political society. More is required to ensure social cohesion and this is precisely the foundational role played by the political imagination. It is the political imagination, an indispensable ingredient of an articulate civilized life, which, by means of its construct, a legend of political life, founds a political society's identity. Political legends are thus foundational constructs in the Arendtian constructivist tradition. More than this, they are also contingent foundations. By this, I mean that in political legends, contingency and permanence are united. I posit that it is poetry, a constitutive element of legends of political life, which unites contingency and permanence and thus gives these foundational constructs their contingent character. Poetry in relation to human activity is, thus, at once contingent and foundational.

Poetry's contingency relates to Oakeshott's phrase concerning the 'poetic character of all human activity'.[163] Oakeshott's principal criticism of morality understood as the reflective application of a moral criterion is that it denies the poetic character of all human activity.[164] He holds that we have come to think of poetic activity as first having an idea and then expressing it. Put another way, an abstract aesthetic idea is subsequently translated into words. This view, Oakeshott contends, is mistaken.[165] It misunderstands poetry in that it superimposes upon art 'an inappropriate didactic form'.[166] By this, he means that a poem is not the 'translation into words of a state of mind'.[167] For Oakeshott, what the poet says and what he wants to say are not two different things; rather, 'they are the same thing'.[168] It follows, then, that the poet 'does not know what he wants to say until he has said it'.[169] In other words, nothing exists ahead of the poem itself, nothing except for 'poetic passion'.[170] He claims that what is true of poetic activity is true of all human moral activity. That is, moral ideals are not first abstract ideas which are subsequently translated into moral action.[171] When this is the case, the poetic character of human activity has been denied. For

---

[163] *RP*: 479.
[164] *Ibid.*
[165] *Ibid.*
[166] *Ibid.*
[167] *Ibid.*
[168] *Ibid.*
[169] *Ibid.*
[170] *Ibid.*
[171] *Ibid.*

Oakeshott, then, human activity is poetic in so far as it creates practices, traditions and habits of behaviour. These are the result of human action and creativity and, as such, are poetic in character.

Legends of political life are also the result of human action and creativity and, therefore, deeply poetic. As the example of Rome illustrates, legends are a form of intellectual organization in which the events and fortunes of a people are endowed with universal significance by being made to compose a work of art. Legends are artistic creations, the work of poets, historians and lawyers, but are also poetic in character in that they are not overly reflective. While legends are stabilizing constructs which endow a society with its sense of self-consciousness and self-understanding, poets do not set out with the intention of founding their societies. They do not first establish that their society needs stabilizing constructs or that it needs to be endowed with a sense of identity and then proceed to determine what that identity will be and how they will fashion its foundational narrative. In other words, poets do not first dream up a list of abstract ideals that they then turn into a story. Rather, by means of memory, they recall to mind a past event and create a narrative. There is never the reflective intention to create a foundational narrative, as this is simply impossible. In sum, just as nothing exists ahead of the poem itself, a political society's legend of political life, and consequently its identity, is not an abstract aesthetic idea which poets subsequently translate into words. A legend of political life comes into being when the poet creates it and he cannot know what the narrative will be until he has created it. Thus, poetry is not overly reflective or rationalistic. Poetry creates and recreates a political society's identity contingently. In this sense, political legends contingently found a political society's identity.

However, when a political society is in a state of crisis, it will become increasingly difficult for it to poetically found its identity. Such a society will struggle to create and recreate its identity. It is at this point that a society in crisis or in difficulty will lose its 'poetic character'. It will try to shore up its threatened sense of self-consciousness and self-understanding by translating its identity into abstract principles and attempt to represent it to its members and to transmit it in an overly reflective manner. Moreover, this rationalistic representation of a society's identity and culture generates a false sense of reassurance and security since it gives the impression that they are safeguarded. Although Oakeshott never explicitly puts forward the preceding argument, it does nevertheless respect his thought regarding the poetic character of all human activity.

Finally, as we will also see in Chapter 5 in regards to the Roman political experience, legends of political life also respect the criterion of dominant contingency established by Oakeshott in so far as the exploration of their intimations leads to change which allows for a political society's identity to be augmented. As for poetry's foundational element, I show in Chapter 4 how it radically guards a political society against the corruption of its consciousness by creating and recreating its values. Furthermore, poetry also achieves its foundational purpose by ensuring that a society is knowledgeable of itself and is self-critical. Poetry ensures that a society does not become unrecognizable to itself. Poetry, then, unites contingency and permanence. While it safeguards a political society's identity, it first endows it with its sense of self-consciousness and of self-knowledge in a contingent manner and ensures that its sense of self-understanding may be augmented over time, thereby reflecting its experiences.

Oakeshott, therefore, is a constructivist in the tradition of Hannah Arendt. In his discussion of the constructivist tradition of foundations, Seery emphasizes the 'poetic' approach favoured by constructivist theorists. He asserts that they are found 'building cities in words or imagining elaborate poetic underworlds'.[172] Among the 'poetically creative' accounts of the political constructivist theorists admire most is Virgil's *The Aeneid*. Seery notes that the best known theorist to have been influenced by Virgil is undoubtedly Arendt as is demonstrated by her writings on foundations in *On Revolution*. He also declares himself to be an admirer of Virgilian political thought and this influence is most notable in his own conception of foundations. He states that his 'preferred architectural model is [...] Virgil's nether world, a fictive necropolis'.[173] We will see in Chapter 5 that Oakeshott is also an admirer of the Romans and that his thought on foundations is also deeply marked by their political experience.

Furthermore, Richard Rorty, who counts Oakeshott among the contemporary thinkers who, like himself, 'wanted to retain Enlightenment liberalism while dropping Enlightenment rationalism', argues that moral progress ought to be understood as 'the history of making rather than finding, of poetic achievement by "radically situated" individuals and communities, rather than as the gradual unveiling, through the use of "reason", of "principles" or "rights" or "values"'.[174] [175] Here, Rorty points to the central role played by building and the poetic in the moral life. There are no 'reasons', 'rights', 'principles' or 'grounding claims' to

---

172 J. Seery 1999: 472.
173 *Ibid.*: 485.
174 R. Rorty 1989: 57.
175 R. Rorty 1988: 267.

be discovered, only worlds of sense and understanding to be built by means of the poetic.

The phrase 'the poetic character of all human activity' is one that has been noted and remarked upon by numerous commentators interested in Oakeshott's aesthetics and, more particularly, in its relationship with practice and the moral life. What precisely does Oakeshott mean by this phrase? For Elizabeth Campbell Corey, this phrase means that Oakeshott conceives of poetry or aesthetics as the most satisfying and least incomplete kind of human experience. This is the case since, in poetry, manner and motive are united. In this sense, poetic experience differs from practical experience (which includes politics and morality) where what 'is' and what 'ought' to be can never be fully reconciled.[176] Poetry, however, is perfectly unified since its character is that of 'wholly self-sufficient experience in which images are delighted in *for their own sake*'.[177] Campbell Corey explains that, for Oakeshott, contemplating and delighting do not follow from the enjoyment of poetic images. Rather, contemplating and delighting constitute poetic experience itself. In this sense, 'the activity of imagining poetically *is* contemplative activity'.[178] Thus, when engaged in poetic activity, humans are living wholly in the present.[179] Consequently, Campbell Corey posits that, for Oakeshott, 'poetry [...] may serve as a kind of model for what all experience hints at but cannot achieve'.[180] She argues that poetry offers a model of ideal unity which morality may approximate while still retaining its practical character. Put another way, when moral conduct is united in manner and motive it may be said to be 'poetic'. This occurs when moral conduct is valued for itself.[181] For Campbell Corey, then, poetry 'stands as the model for a certain kind of moral activity, and yet they are not the same activity'.[182]

Campbell Corey contends that Oakeshott's principle argument in 'Tower of Babel' is that of the two forms of morality he identifies only one strives to model itself upon poetry. This lies at the heart of Oakeshott's critique of rationalist or reflective morality as well as of the mixed form of morality dominated by the reflective application of a moral criterion. According to Campbell Corey, the problem with what she terms 'servile' morality is that it 'does not approach any kind of

---

176 E. Campbell Corey 2006: 114, 117.
177 *Ibid.*: 112, original emphasis.
178 *Ibid.*: 110, original emphasis.
179 *Ibid.*: 116.
180 *Ibid.*: 117.
181 *Ibid.*: 118.
182 *Ibid.*: 119.

aesthetic unity at all'.[183] Rather, reflective morality is prosaic in character. She argues that, in Oakeshott's view, moral ideals are prosaic because 'they require "translation" of an abstract idea into a practical reality'.[184] The translation of an abstract ideal into an action is 'the very opposite of poetry'.[185] In effect, reflective morality denies the 'spontaneity and creativity that is natural to poetry'.[186] Poetry is spontaneous and fully engaged in the present. It does not look towards the future and devise means for achieving human perfection. As Campbell Corey understands it, it is Oakeshott's view that 'the radical defect of this prosaic morality of ideals is that it denies the "poetic character of all human activity" and instead turns to "the easily translatable prose of a moral ideal"'.[187] For Oakeshott, a better form of morality is one that is 'fundamentally creative', Campbell Corey argues.[188] The morality of a habit of behaviour, or 'liberal' morality as she terms it, is the form of the moral life which models itself upon poetry. She contends that 'this view of morality depends upon an idea of unified conduct that takes its bearings from Oakeshott's aesthetic theory'.[189] Moral conduct is unified in so far as it is fully engaged with the present. Campbell Corey argues that such a view entails 'taking the world as it is given and accepting it [...] with a graceful humility' and, consequently, 'delighting in what is before us'.[190] In other words, a morality dominated by habit and affection is poetic in character since it is 'disposed toward present enjoyment rather than the constant quest to achieve'.[191] Such a form of the moral life is not overly intellectual since abstract ideals of human perfection have no place in it and justification by principles is confined to a secondary role. For Campbell Corey, the morality of a habit of behaviour is 'natural, creative, and habitual. At its highest reaches, it may almost be called aesthetic'.[192] This, for her, is what Oakeshott understands by the phrase 'the poetic character of all human activity'.

Wendell John Coats, Jr., in three separate essays, also attempts to elucidate the meaning of the phrase 'the poetic character of all human activity'.[193] Coats, Jr. contends that implied in the phrase is the idea that

---

[183] *Ibid.*: 127.
[184] *Ibid.*: 148.
[185] *Ibid.*
[186] *Ibid.*
[187] *Ibid.*: 149.
[188] *Ibid.*: 153.
[189] *Ibid.*: 128.
[190] *Ibid.*: 135.
[191] *Ibid.*: 139.
[192] *Ibid.*: 128.
[193] See W.J. Coats, Jr. 2000, 2003 and 2005.

the structure of all mediated human activity is creative.[194] For Coats, Jr., Oakeshott's view is that the form and content of human activity evolve simultaneously and are inseparable.[195] Put another way, what is experienced and how arise simultaneously or 'poetically'.[196] Although this sort of unity is most apparent in poetry where '*what* is said or done, and *how* it is said or done, are for fleeting moments completely unified', Coats, Jr. believes that Oakeshott's point is that the form and content of all human activity evolve simultaneously.[197] [198] Thus, for Coats, Jr., this insight into the character of human activity becomes the basis for Oakeshott's critique of Rationalism.[199] He argues that 'the attempt to abstract a moral code or political ideology from an historically evolved, concrete activity and then woodenly use it to initiate and govern that and other activities denies "the poetic character of human conduct" [...] which is to say virtually all human experience for Oakeshott'.[200] Rationalism is guilty of overestimating the role of conscious intellect in activity.[201] As a consequence, the fluidity of action of not only morality and politics, but all human activity, is mechanically broken down 'into discrete, accessible steps'.[202] In other words, action that ought to be spontaneous and unreflective, that is, poetic, becomes prosaic. For Coats, Jr., then, Oakeshott's critique of Rationalism is:

> based upon an argument or insight into the fluid and creative character of all human experience and activity, a character which Rationalism is seen to deny in its prosaic and wooden approach to organizing and originating human action, in its denial of the poetic character of human activity and conduct.[203]

Glenn Worthington pursues a similar train of thought to Coats, Jr. and Campbell Corey. He discusses the phrase 'the poetic character of all human activity' in two articles where he argues that the phrase indicates the 'importance of a poetic quality in the moral life of a society' for Oakeshott.[204] Like Coats, Jr. and Campbell Corey, he also points out that of the two ideal forms of the moral life present in modernity only one, the morality of a habit of behaviour, possesses a poetic quality.

---

194 W.J. Coats, Jr. 2003: 101.
195 W.J. Coats, Jr. 2000: 104.
196 W.J. Coats, Jr. 2005: 309.
197 W.J. Coats, Jr. 2000: 104, original emphasis.
198 W.J. Coats, Jr. 2000: 105; W.J. Coats, Jr. 2003: 107; W.J. Coats, Jr. 2005: 309, 312.
199 W.J. Coats, Jr. 2003: 101, 107; W.J. Coats, Jr. 2005: 306.
200 W.J. Coats, Jr. 2005: 314.
201 *Ibid.*
202 *Ibid.*
203 *Ibid.*: 315.
204 G. Worthington, 2005: 63.

The other, the morality of the reflective application of a moral criterion, denies the poetic character of all human activity.[205] For Worthington, Oakeshott refers to the inadequacies of this form of the moral life in terms of 'a poetic shortcoming'.[206] In this form of morality, abstract moral ideals 'usurp the primacy of the habits of behaviour from which they are derived' and, in so doing, robs the moral life of its creative spontaneity and flexibility.[207] Thus, morality is 'robbed of its poetic dimension'.[208] In sum, in 'Tower of Babel', according to Worthington, Oakeshott restates the thesis of *Rationalism in Politics*, that is, the critique of the dominance of Rationalism and technique in politics and the moral life, in terms of a 'poetic shortcoming'.[209]

For his part, J.G. Blumler's interpretation of Oakeshott's phrase differs considerably from that of the other commentators. Blumler claims that the phrase 'the poetic character of human activity' reveals the foundations of Oakeshott's political philosophy. He contends that these foundations 'express an *aesthetic* preference for the preservation of historical continuity'.[210] In answer to the question why should social and political arrangements be preserved, or, put differently, why should traditional authority be accepted, Blumler argues that, for Oakeshott, the decisive consideration lies in the 'denial of the poetic character of all human activity'.[211] He maintains that, in Oakeshott's view, traditionalism is the only style of politics which should appeal to a cultured person. Blumler acknowledges that Oakeshott places politics within the world of practical activity and not poetry.[212] However, he points out that, in 'On Being Conservative', Oakeshott speaks of the conservative disposition in terms of what conservatives delight in. Conservatives 'delight in what is present'.[213] Therefore, conservatism, which is applicable to politics, is akin to poetry. Blumler concludes from this that Oakeshott 'must regard politics as an activity to which aesthetic responses are appropriate'.[214] Politics is thus a complex activity. It belongs to practice and, yet, its intimations are poetic.[215] For Blumler, this means that politics must 'gratify practical needs and

---

[205] G. Worthington, 2002: 308.
[206] *Ibid.*: 307.
[207] G. Worthington, 2005: 63.
[208] *Ibid.*
[209] G. Worthington, 2002: 307.
[210] J.G. Blumler 1964: 355, original emphasis.
[211] *Ibid.*: 358.
[212] *Ibid.*
[213] *Ibid.*
[214] *Ibid.*
[215] *Ibid.*

aesthetic inclinations at one and the same time'.[216] Rationalism's radical defect is that it denies the 'poetic character of all human activity' and, hence, only recognizes the practical element inherent in politics.[217] Blumler's contention is that Oakeshott finds traditionalism a more aesthetically pleasing form of politics than Rationalism since it provides the opportunity 'for delighting in the perpetuation of our customary arrangements'.[218] For Blumler, then, Oakeshott's political philosophy rests on an aesthetic preference for traditionalism.

In all of the preceding interpretations, the phrase the 'poetic character of all human activity' is essentially understood as a restatement of Oakeshott's dichotomy between Rationalism and practice/tradition/contingency which, he claims, characterizes political modernity. The fact that the question of foundations resurfaces once more is proof of this. For Campbell Corey, a morality that denies the 'poetic character' of human activity arises in response to uneasiness about the contingency of the world and uncertainty about the future. Moral ideals and rules offer stability. Consequently, a morality of the reflective application of a moral criterion, which is essentially made up of ideals and rules, promises substantial security and stability.[219] However, this is a false view since 'it is founded on a desire not to be reconciled to the human condition (which is by nature uncertain and contingent), but to overcome it'.[220] In other words, this form of morality attempts to 'build an unshakeable rational foundation'.[221] For Oakeshott, according to Campbell Corey, this view is false and simply untenable since rational rules cannot be postulated ahead of moral activity.[222] Put another way, although moral ideals and rules may in fact exist, they had to originate in the actual experience of moral conduct. That is, they 'cannot be said to be the absolutely rational, *a priori* foundations of activity'.[223] Furthermore, Campbell Corey argues that there is an element of creativity inherent to subscribing to rules. By this, she means that although a rule may tell us what to do, it cannot tell us how to do it. Individuals choose how to act creatively and spontaneously.[224] This creative element, which is inherent to all human activity, 'defies the Rationalist desire for certain knowledge of how to

---

216   *Ibid.*: 359.
217   *Ibid.*
218   *Ibid.*
219   E. Campbell Corey 2006: 140.
220   *Ibid.*
221   *Ibid.*
222   *Ibid.*
223   *Ibid.*: 141.
224   *Ibid.*: 142.

act'.[225] Thus, unshakeable stability and security is simply impossible to achieve in morality.

Coats, Jr. argues that, for Oakeshott, the form and content of all human activity evolve simultaneously and that this unity is best exemplified in poetic activity. Hence, all mediated human experience is creative. Rationalism's principle defect is 'mistaking its origins for "nature" or "truth" or "reason", rather than some historically evolved way of living'.[226] Put another way, Rationalism erroneously believes that it can 'self-consciously and successfully recreate its own political and moral life from new beginnings'.[227] That is, it wrongly thinks that it can completely separate form from content, which is untenable since it denies the creativity and spontaneity inherent to human activity and experience.

The discussion of the 'poetic character' of human activity in Oakeshott's thought does not move beyond the dichotomy between Rationalism, permanence and perfection and contingency and practice. Foundations are here again understood solely in Edenic terms. I wish to make the case that poetry allows us to move beyond this dichotomy. I argue that poetry reconciles both sides of the dichotomy, uniting permanence and contingency and thereby providing constructivist, contingent foundations for the political. It is my position that stabilizing constructs are constructed for practices and traditions and that these take the form of political narratives. The question of aesthetics, or poetry, is complex, as is its relation to practice and politics. This will be discussed fully in Chapter 4. At this stage, I simply wish to point out that Oakeshott's understanding of poetry is more expansive than the relation between poetry and morality outlined so far might suggest. For now, I will simply suggest what contingent foundations might consist in for Oakeshott and the role poetry might play in founding the contingent. I take a different approach from commentators, who focus on the relation between the moral life and poetry, and will focus on the role the poetic plays in relation to the political. I posit that the key to the problem of contingent foundations is to be found in Oakeshott's interpretation of the Roman political experience. Like Hannah Arendt and John Seery, Oakeshott greatly admires the ancient Romans. This fact is aptly demonstrated by David Boucher in his article 'Oakeshott, Freedom and Republicanism'.[228] He lauded the Romans as 'a remarkable people' whose 'political experience is one of the most memorable

---

[225] *Ibid.*

[226] W.J. Coats, Jr. 2003: 103; W.J. Coats, Jr. 2005: 308.

[227] W.J. Coats, Jr. 2003: 103; W.J. Coats, Jr. 2005: 308.

[228] D. Boucher 2005a.

of all the political experiences of European peoples'.[229] As I discussed in chapters 1 and 2, Oakeshott claims that the Roman political experience, or tradition of political behaviour, was never turned into a rationalist system of abstract ideals or into an ideology. Rather, its intellectual organization took the form of a legend of political life, a work of art, a drama, a story. That is, it is their legend which allowed the Romans to translate their political experience into the idiom of general ideas and to be endowed with universal significance.[230] Here we find the solution to the problem of contingent foundations. While the Roman political society was not founded upon abstract principles or prior grounding claims about unquestionable or sacred premises; nevertheless, Roman politics was not purely contingent, Oakeshott contends. The legend of Roman politics, a poetic construct, provides an element of permanence and stability to the political. For Oakeshott, their political legend constitutes the Romans' political self-consciousness and therefore endows them with a political identity.[231] Nevertheless, in spite of this element of permanence and stability, contingency remains dominant. A way of life, political experience, or, put another way, a tradition of political behaviour is founded contingently by means of a poetic legend. This is the role Oakeshott attributes to poetry in relation to the political and foundations. Poetry unites contingency and permanence and by means of its creations, political legends, it contingently founds a political society's identity. The present chapter explored poetry's contingent element. Chapter 4 examines the permanence and stability poetry provides political societies.

Conclusion

Oakeshott, then, as a philosopher of the political imagination, conceives of constructed foundations for the political. Here I draw on the distinction made by Seery between Edenic and constructed foundations. While I agree with commentators that Oakeshott's understanding of politics and authority in *On Human Conduct* is devoid of foundations defined as prior grounding claims about unquestionable, sacred or natural premises, I argue that the mixed form of politics he defends implies some sort of foundations for the political. What Oakeshott implicitly argues for is a mixed form of foundations, one where permanence and change are united, but where contingency dominates the mixture. In other words, Oakeshott espouses the concept of contingent foundations. It is my position that what has thus far been overlooked

---

[229] *LHPT*: 176.
[230] *LHPT*: 208.
[231] *LHPT*: 177.

by commentators in regards to the question of foundations in Oakeshott's political thought is the matter of a political society's identity and the central role played in its foundation by the political imagination. When attention is paid to Oakeshott's writings on the political imagination, it becomes evident that, for him, human living-together requires more than the continued recognition of rules as rules by *cives*. This is simply insufficient to sustain social cohesion. Of central importance to Oakeshott's political thought is a person's and a political society's identity. A political society's identity needs to be founded. I claim that this is the function served by the political imagination which, by means of legends of political life, founds a political society's identity. Thus, far from being devoid of foundations, in Oakeshott's conception of the political a poetic, imaginative construction endows a political society with its identity and stabilizes its present-future. These constructed foundations, legends of political life, are a very specific sort of foundation in that they combine permanence and change. I contend that it is poetry, one of legend's constitutive elements, which unites permanence and change, thus allowing for contingent foundations. Political legends are creations of poetry. Poets create legends in a manner which is not overly reflective and thereby endow a society with its identity contingently. Contingency and creativity are bound together. What is more, as we will see, political legends are constantly recreated and redeployed which means that a political society's identity is augmented. However, this is not done at any cost. It is also poetry which guards a society from the corruption of its consciousness. This is the subject of Chapter 4. Thus, in poetry, change and permanence are united. Legends of political life, then, fulfil the criteria established by Oakeshott in regards to foundations: they are a construction and, while a society is safeguarded, it is contingency which dominates the mixture.

Chapter Four

Legends of Political Life and Poetry

Introduction

Poetry, Oakeshott asserts, characterizes human activity. Just as nothing exists ahead of the poem itself, human activity is poetic in that it is not the translation of abstract ideals into behaviour, but, rather, the creation of practices, traditions and habits of behaviour. In this sense, the poetic character of human activity refers to its contingency. Humans also act poetically in making themselves at home in the world. By means of imagination, humans construct a world of meaning and sense and thus abate the inherent menace and mystery of the universe. Humans, in effect, construct narratives, create works of art and produce signs and symbols, all of which belong to poetry, in order to make sense of the world that surrounds them. For political purposes, societies construct legends of political life which stabilize the problematic practical present. Events recalled from the practical past form the basis of these political narratives. As such, the practical past is a constitutive element of legends of political life. In the present chapter, I argue that poetry is also a constitutive element of political legends and therefore serves a foundational purpose. I show that, for Oakeshott, poetry at once endows a society with its sense of identity and self-consciousness and guards against the corruption of its consciousness by creating and recreating its values. While a society may undergo change, it never becomes unrecognizable to itself since it is perpetually being created and recreated by poetry. In so far as legends are poetic constructs or creations, they found a society's identity and guard against the corruption of its consciousness. The concept of the poetic character of human activity, then, has two meanings. The first meaning refers to the contingency of human activity, which I discussed in the previous chapter, while the second meaning refers to the element of permanence present in poetical activity which I explore here.

The relationship between legend and poetry is far more difficult to establish than its relationship to philosophy and history. This is due to the fact that the relationship between poetry and practice is more ambiguous than is practice's relationship with philosophy and history. Whereas Oakeshott remains steadfast throughout his writings and maintains a strict division between practice and philosophy and practice and history, he is not as definitive in regards to poetry. As the discussion has clearly demonstrated so far, legends have an undeniable practical purpose, particularly in relation to the political. Moreover, Oakeshott claims on at least two occasions that legends are poetic creations.[1] Since the relationship between practice and poetry is ambiguous and complex, it therefore cannot be excluded that legends are poetry. The relationship between poetry and practice in Oakeshott's thought has been thoroughly studied by commentators interested in his aesthetics, in particular by Glenn Worthington, Elizabeth Campbell Corey and Efraim Podoksik. Two positions emerge in the debates concerned with the relationship between poetry and practice in Oakeshott's thought. The first contends that Oakeshott's conception of poetry clearly evolved towards a strict division between poetry and practice. Elizabeth Campbell Corey is representative of this position. The second position argues that Oakeshott's conception of poetry, and specifically the relationship between poetry and practice, remains ambiguous throughout his writings. Glenn Worthington forcefully defends this position as does Efraim Podoksik, although more moderately. I will present Oakeshott's conception of poetry with reference to the debate between Campbell Corey, Worthington and Podoksik on the matter of the relationship between poetry and practice. Following this discussion, I defend the position that the relationship between poetry and practice remains ambiguous and, as a consequence, legends of political life may legitimately be said to be poetry. The argument I develop emphasizes the point that the difficulty poetry has had in emancipating itself from practice is indicative of the deep human need for meaning, sense and stability. Finally, I argue that Oakeshott's conservative disposition is deeply poetic since only poetry can guard a society's sense of self-consciousness and protect its values against the threat posed by change.

Oakeshott's Conception of Poetry

The most detailed account of Oakeshott's conception of poetry, or aesthetics, is found in his 1959 essay 'The Voice of Poetry in the Conversation of Mankind'. In Chapter 2, it was noted that Oakeshott intended this essay to be a retraction of a statement, or of a 'foolish sentence' as he puts it, he made in *Experience and its Modes* regarding

---

[1]   *WP*: 347; *LHPT*: 208.

poetry. There, he argued that poetry belongs to the mode of practice. More specifically, he asserts that 'in them [science, history and philosophy] we hope to find a more radical and more complete escape from life than that which art, music and poetry can offer. For in these, in the end, we are wholly taken up with practical life'.[2] This earlier conception of poetry differs considerably from the one he defends in 'The Voice of Poetry in the Conversation of Mankind'. There, he identifies poetry as a mode or idiom in its own right, completely divorced from practical considerations. Oakeshott defines activity in poetry as contemplating and delighting.[3] Contemplating, he specifies, is a specific mode of imagining and moving among images. It is the activity of making and entertaining mere images. Poetic imagining, then, is contemplative activity. The voice of contemplation is the voice of poetry.[4] Delighting, for its part, is not a reward which follows from the activity of making and moving among mere images. Rather, delighting is another name for contemplation. It is the activity of making and entertaining mere images.[5] In other words, delighting is aesthetic experience. The mode of poetry is distinguished from the other modes in that it imagines and makes mere images, that is, non-symbolic images.[6] This is central to Oakeshott's conception of aesthetics in 'The Voice of Poetry in the Conversation of Mankind'. Poetic images are not recognized as 'fact' or 'not-fact', or as 'events'. They do not attract either moral approval or disapproval.[7] Mere images are not signs or symbols of something else, nor are they the causes, effects or means to ulterior ends.[8] In this sense, poetry is not didactic: it has nothing to teach about how to live.[9] In other words, poetic images are not useful or useless. Rather, Oakeshott asserts that 'contemplation does not use, or use-up or wear-out its images, or induce change in them: it rests in them, looking neither backwards nor forwards'.[10] Poetry rests in its images. It is non-laborious activity.[11]

It is important to emphasize that Oakeshott's contention is that the relationship between symbol (language) and meaning (thought) is different in poetry from the relationship in the idiom of practice. He

---

2   *EM*: 297.
3   *RP*: 509.
4   *RP*: 513–514.
5   *Ibid.*
6   *RP*: 512.
7   *RP*: 509–510, 514.
8   *RP*: 512, 514.
9   *RP*: 540.
10 *RP*: 510.
11 *RP*: 514.

argues that the business of practical life is conducted in a symbolic language. If it is possible to engage in confident communication with other selves, it is because the words and expressions which compose the symbolic language, the medium of communication, are agreed signs with fixed and precise usages. Signs, gestures or movements are also symbols and they may be substituted for words and serve the same purpose of communication between selves. When we use these words and signs, Oakeshott argues, we do not seek to enlarge their meaning. We are not trying to give a novel nuance to a symbol. Rather, we are trying to be understood in a settled language and, to this end, the more fixed and invariable the meanings of the symbols which compose it are, the better we are able to understand one another. In other words, when we use a symbol in a practical manner, we evoke an image, we do not create one.[12] For Oakeshott, then, 'speaking here is expressing or conveying images and is not itself image-making'.[13] As a consequence, in symbolic, practical language meaning and symbol are distinct. By this, Oakeshott means that a practical image symbolizes something outside of itself. However, meaning and symbol are not radically separable because in the mode of practice 'every word has its proper reference or signification'.[14] It is in this sense that Oakeshott argues that practical images are laborious. By symbolizing something outside of itself, a symbolic language allows for confident communication between selves. In the idiom of poetry, there is no separation of symbol and meaning. This idea is at the heart of Oakeshott's conception of poetry in 'The Voice of Poetry in the Conversation of Mankind'. A poetic image is its meaning; it symbolizes nothing outside of itself. He holds that in poetry 'words are themselves images and not signs for other images; imagining is itself utterance, and without utterance there is no image'.[15] Hence, it is a 'mere' image. It is not a symbol for something else as is the case for images which compose the symbolic language of practice. As we will see, the question of the ambiguous relationship between poetry and practice in Oakeshott's thought centres on whether he maintains the different relationship between symbol and meaning in poetry in his works which follow 'The Voice of Poetry in the Conversation of Mankind'.

Poetry is clearly distinguished from the mode of practice which is composed of symbolic images recognized as 'fact' and 'not fact'. The laborious activity in practice is expressing and conveying images of

---

12   *RP*: 503.
13   *Ibid*.
14   *RP*: 504.
15   *RP*: 527.

desire and aversion and of approval and disapproval.[16] In this essay, Oakeshott is adamant that the images of one mode are not available to a different mode of imagining.[17] Hence, poetic images, which are mere images, are not available to the mode of practice which is composed of symbolic images. Efraim Podoksik astutely summarizes the conception of aesthetics Oakeshott elaborates in 'The Voice of Poetry in the Conversation of Mankind' when he argues that he 'presents a radical view of the nature of aesthetic experience, which he sharply distinguishes from other forms of experience. He unequivocally argues in favor of an independent character of aesthetic activity and advocates the view of art for art's sake'.[18] However, although the modes are independent of one another, they do engage in what Oakeshott terms 'conversation', which necessarily implies some sort of interaction between them. By conversation, Oakeshott means a meeting-place for the idioms which compose current human intercourse.[19] As we will see, this leaves Oakeshott open to charges of ambiguity in regards to the relationship between poetry and practice. Nevertheless, Oakeshott's thought on aesthetics changes significantly between *Experience and its Modes* and 'The Voice of Poetry in the Conversation of Mankind'. I propose to examine the evolution of Oakeshott's conception of aesthetics by analysing Campbell Corey's, Worthington's and Podoksik's interpretations of the relationship between poetry and practice in his thought. Following this, I will attempt to elucidate Oakeshott's understanding of aesthetics with reference to legends. In this regard, I will examine the texts on aesthetics which are key for the understanding of legends. This will allow me to stake my claim in the debate on aesthetics as well as better determine the character and function of legends in relation to the political.

Elizabeth Campbell Corey, Glenn Worthington and Efraim Podoksik agree that Oakeshott's thought on aesthetics undergoes a significant transformation between his early and mature writings on the subject. Where their interpretations diverge is as to whether this transformation is a steady development of his thought in one direction culminating in 'The Voice of Poetry in the Conversation of Mankind' and the strict division of poetry and practice (this is Campbell Corey's position), or whether, despite this perceived evolution, Oakeshott's conception of aesthetics remains ambiguous on the question of the relationship between poetry and practice throughout all of his writings

---

16 *RP*: 503, 504.
17 *RP*: 514.
18 E. Podoksik 2002: 727–728.
19 *RP*: 489.

(this is Worthington's position). Podoksik, for his part, contends that Oakeshott's thinking on aesthetics at once reflects a steady development and stipulates the division of poetry and practice and, yet, at the same time, maintains a certain ambiguity in relation to practice. Campbell Corey and Worthington both agree that Oakeshott's thought on aesthetics developed in three distinct stages. I will adopt their framework and integrate Podoksik's interpretation of the texts in question to the discussion. The first stage consists of Oakeshott's earliest writings on aesthetics ('Shylock the Jew: An Essay in Villainy' and 'Religion and the World') and culminates in *Experience and its Modes*. The second stage includes Oakeshott's review of R.G. Collingwood's *The Principles of Art*, 'The Claims of Politics', 'Work and Play' and '*Leviathan*: A Myth'. These writings are essentially preludes to 'The Voice of Poetry in the Conversation of Mankind', the third stage in the development of Oakeshott's conception of aesthetics.

For Worthington, Oakeshott at first 'includes poetry as an idiom wholly taken up with the world of conduct. This is the position announced in *Experience and its Modes*'.[20] He maintains that this position is confirmed by a number of references in earlier essays, including 'Shylock the Jew: An Essay in Villainy'. He argues that although Oakeshott distinguishes poetic appreciation from moral judgment, they nevertheless refer to a common scale and thus belong to a common idiom.[21] Hence, Worthington contends that in Oakeshott's works, up to and including *Experience and its Modes*, poetry is 'significant primarily as an exemplar of moral and religious experience'.[22] Campbell Corey, for her part, perceives in the aforementioned essay 'the germ of a central idea expressed years later in "The Voice of Poetry", namely, that moral considerations have no place in the pure poetic experience'.[23] Moreover, although she acknowledges that Oakeshott understands poetry to be a part of the practical mode in *Experience and its Modes*, she nevertheless insists on the fact that his conception of practice in this work is 'both more expansive as well as more inclusive' and, therefore, goes beyond concern with desires and encompasses 'all that we mean by beauty'.[24] For her, Oakeshott's early essays on aesthetics express one of the central tenets of his later view of poetry, that is, 'that moral considerations positively stand in the way of the full poetic experience'.[25] In other words, Oakeshott's mature conception of aesthetics is clearly

---

[20] G. Worthington 2002: 300.
[21] *Ibid.*: 292–293.
[22] *Ibid.*: 297.
[23] E. Campbell Corey 2006: 105.
[24] *Ibid.*: 106
[25] *Ibid.*: 105.

intimated in his early essays, according to Campbell Corey. For Podoksik, *Experience and its Modes* expresses the idea that 'an artist is independent of society, but also involved in it up to his neck', thereby confirming his view that Oakeshott's conception of aesthetics stipulates the autonomy of poetry, but, nevertheless, implies a relationship between poetry and practice.[26]

In the second stage of the development of his thought on aesthetics, all three commentators concur that Oakeshott begins to distinguish poetry more fully from the other modes of experience. For the purposes of my argument, I will focus primarily on their respective analyses of two texts from this middle period: 'The Claims of Politics' and 'Leviathan: A Myth' since they support my argument concerning the foundational role of legends. For Campbell Corey, 'The Claims of Politics' represents the first signal that Oakeshott has 'begun to question the appropriateness of placing the poet and artist unambiguously within practice'.[27] Both Campbell Corey and Podoksik point out that, in this essay, Oakeshott argues that politics is only one way of participating in the life of a society. Moreover, as an expression of social sensibility it is relatively unimportant.[28] Campbell Corey points out that, for Oakeshott, the more profound contributions are made by those engaged in the activities of literature, art and philosophy. Podoksik explains that this is the case for only they have the ability to 'contribute to the permanent recreation of a society'.[29] Both Campbell Corey and Podoksik assert that, for Oakeshott, the role of poets, artists and philosophers is to create and recreate the values of a society. This is of vital importance as the 'last corruption that can visit a society is a corruption of its consciousness'.[30] They fulfil their role by making a society 'conscious and critical of itself', thereby mitigating its ignorance of itself.[31] However, Campbell Corey wonders exactly how poets and artists create and recreate the values of a society.[32] R.G. Collingwood's influence on Oakeshott's thought is remarked upon by Campbell Corey and Worthington. Of particular importance is the reference to Collingwood's idea of the 'corruption of consciousness' which he develops in *The Principles of Art*. I will discuss Collingwood's idea of the 'corruption of consciousness' later on in the chapter. Campbell Corey and Podoksik both stress that, for Oakeshott, artists, poets and philosophers, in order

---

26 E. Podoksik, 2002: 722.
27 E. Campbell Corey 2006: 108.
28 E. Campbell Corey 2006: 108; E. Podoksik 2002: 723.
29 E. Podoksik 2002: 723.
30 *RPML*: 95.
31 *RPML*: 95–96.
32 E. Campbell Corey 2006: 108.

to make their profound contributions, 'should abstain from any political activity'.[33] However, in this essay, the relationship between poetry and practice as a whole remains ambiguous. Both commentators argue that it is not clear where poets and philosophers are situated. Campbell Corey concludes that they clearly have a connection with society, but that the nature of this connection is difficult to specify. While their activity is not altogether removed from practice, it does not wholly take place there either. It appears that the activity of poets, artists and philosophers takes place in a deeper sphere of consciousness.[34] Podoksik, for his part, believes that Oakeshott suggests that an artist does in fact play an important social role, but that this role can only be fulfilled at the price of retreating from participation in the public life. What is truly important for Oakeshott, he contends, is that 'these activities render service to the society on a deeper level as they affect society's understanding of itself'.[35] While poetry plays a social role in 'The Claims of Politics', for both Campbell Corey and Podoksik, it is clear that it is not political in nature. This view is shared by Worthington who concludes that in this essay Oakeshott makes it abundantly clear that art excludes considerations of politics. The nature of the relationship between poetry and society as well as between poetry and practice, however, remains ambiguous.[36]

In the essay '*Leviathan*: A Myth', Oakeshott reads and interprets Hobbes's work as a work of art and not of philosophy. For him, *Leviathan* represents one of the masterpieces of literature. He argues that a civilization is a collective dream. Put another way, a people dreams its civilization and the substance of this dream is a myth or 'an imaginative interpretation of human existence, the perception (not the solution) of the mystery of human life'.[37] The role of art and literature in relation to the dream of civilization is 'perpetually to recall it, to recreate it in each generation'.[38] The artist derives his ability from his power to dream more profoundly.[39] Hence, *Leviathan*, as a work of literature, possesses all of these poetic qualities. However, because it is a book of philosophy which has reached the level of literature, it possesses the additional ability, or gift, to increase the knowledge a civilization has of itself. Thus, the gift of such a work of art is 'an increase in knowledge; it will prompt and it will instruct. In it we shall

---

33 E. Podoksik 2002: 723.
34 E. Campbell Corey 2006: 108.
35 E. Podoksik 2002: 723.
36 G. Worthington 2002: 296, 303; 2005: 59.
37 *HCA*: 159–160.
38 *HCA*: 160.
39 *Ibid.*

be reminded of the common dream that binds the generations together, and the myth will be made more intelligible to us'.[40] Both Worthington and Campbell Corey assert that in this essay Oakeshott specifies the character of poetry as a unique mode of experience. Worthington contends that in '*Leviathan*: A Myth' Oakeshott 'provides his most detailed account of the distinctively creative character of poetic imagining'.[41] Although he argues that poetry's character becomes more distinctive in this essay; nevertheless, as we will see later on, Worthington claims that, here, Oakeshott characterizes poetry in terms of the social whole.[42] This forms part of the basis for his argument that Oakeshott's conception of aesthetics remains ambiguous throughout his writings. Campbell Corey's interpretation of the text reflects her position that Oakeshott's thought on aesthetics develops steadily in a single direction. In this sense, she contends that he is 'gradually singling out poetry as a unique type of experience — one whose function is only to enlighten, not to instruct. As such it becomes less and less practical'.[43] For her, Oakeshott makes the distinction between poetry and practice clear in this essay.

Campbell Corey and Podoksik would concur with Worthington's statement that the works of the second stage are preludes to 'The Voice of Poetry in the Conversation of Mankind' where Oakeshott 'demonstrates the explicit philosophical grounds for his distinction between poetry and other worlds of experience'.[44] For Campbell Corey, the essay represents 'the natural outcome of a progression in Oakeshott's thought'.[45] It sets out the distinct nature of poetry, which, she insists, is neither ambiguous nor paradoxical. Rather, poetry constitutes a mode of its own and, as such, acquires 'a kind of purity that it did not have for Oakeshott in the 1920s and 1930s'.[46] Worthington, for his part, acknowledges that Oakeshott distinguishes the non-symbolic character of poetic images from the symbolic images that constitute the idioms of practice and science.[47] However, he points out that, for Oakeshott, the voice of poetry has to be understood by the other voices with which it is in conversation. This suggestion, he claims, 'brings to the fore areas of ambiguity in the voices that he distinguished between so clearly in

40   *Ibid.*
41   G. Worthington, 2002: 300.
42   *Ibid.*: 297, 306.
43   E. Campbell Corey 2006: 109.
44   G. Worthington 2002: 300.
45   E. Campbell Corey 2006: 110.
46   *Ibid.*
47   G. Worthington 2002: 290.

the opening sections of "The Voice of Poetry"'.[48] Podoksik makes the same observation and draws a similar conclusion relative to the idea of conversation. He claims that Oakeshott defends a view of aesthetics in which art is irrelevant to practical considerations and, thus, aligns himself with 'the respectable modern philosophical tradition which sees in "disinterestedness" the central feature of aesthetic experience'.[49] The metaphor of conversation allows him to say that the idioms of each voice are irrelevant to the arguments of other voices, thereby supporting the argument of the disinterested nature of aesthetics. However, the voices are able to recognize each other and understand the medium in which they are conversing.[50] This leads Podoksik to conclude that 'although practice and poetry are strictly speaking irrelevant to each other, there are still in practical activity "intimations of contemplative imagining capable of responding to the voice of poetry"'.[51] Consequently, while both Podoksik and Worthington acknowledge that Oakeshott rejects a straightforward relationship between poetry and practice, they both contend that the relationship is not as clear-cut as it may seem since 'he still thinks that there are some intimations of poetry in the practical life'.[52]

In spite of the differences in their interpretations of Oakeshott's thought on aesthetics, up to and including 'The Voice of Poetry in the Conversation of Mankind', Campbell Corey, Worthington and Podoksik agree that his conception of aesthetics undergoes a radical transformation. The crux of the debate revolves around Oakeshott's post-'Voice' essays. At issue are the 'intimations of poetry in the practical life'.[53] Worthington argues that if the thesis which stipulates that Oakeshott's thought on aesthetics developed steadily in one direction is correct, then all of his references to poetry following 'The Voice of Poetry in the Conversation of Mankind' should 'maintain the view of poetry as an autonomous voice'.[54] Worthington contends that this is not the case. In fact, he claims that Oakeshott's writings after 'The Voice of Poetry in the Conversation of Mankind' and, in particular, *On Human Conduct*, show that 'poetic imagining occurs as an idiom of the moral life'.[55] More specifically, Worthington asserts that 'the poetic dimension of the moral life is the realization of this life in its most comprehensive

48   *Ibid.*: 291.
49   E. Podoksik, 2002: 726.
50   *Ibid.*: 730.
51   *Ibid.*
52   *Ibid.*
53   *Ibid.*
54   G. Worthington 2002: 301.
55   *Ibid.*: 305.

terms; it is a condition in which the moral character of an individual and a society is experienced at its most intense level'.[56] While Campbell Corey acknowledges that poetry appears to be related to moral conduct, she maintains that this does not mean that morality becomes poetry. Rather, poetry is a model practice may strive to emulate.[57] In this sense, the mode of poetry offers 'an ideal unity that morality may sometimes approximate'.[58] Podoksik, for his part, finds merit in both positions and defends a view which can be described as the middle ground between Campbell Corey and Worthington. As concerns Campbell Corey's argument, Podoksik writes that, in his opinion, she 'performs brilliantly' in overcoming the obstacles facing any scholar who emphasizes the significance of religion and poetry in Oakeshott.[59]

Worthington defends the position that the moral personality and social value are poetic creations. He bases his first assertion on the concept of self-enactment Oakeshott develops in *On Human Conduct*. Worthington notes that in this work Oakeshott characterizes moral conduct as self-enactment. By this, he means that a self is created in its enactments. In other words, no self exists prior to its enactment. Enactments refer to the motives in which a self acts. Every performance enacts a self and every self is responsible for the self it becomes.[60] Worthington establishes a parallel between moral conduct understood as the creation of a self and poetry. He contends that 'the enactments of a self are poetic in that the enacted self is not a representation of its moral qualities'.[61] That is, Worthington argues that 'just as in poetic imagining nothing exists prior to the poetic image (the image is not a symbol or representation of some pre-extant meaning), so in self-enactment the self is created in its enactments'.[62] Put another way, every individual in enacting its self is a poet.[63]

Worthington refers to works of the second stage in order to support his claim that social value is a poetic creation. He gives particular importance to the essays 'The Claims of Politics' and '*Leviathan*: A Myth'. Oakeshott's concern in these essays, he claims, is the poetic dimension in the moral life of a society.[64] In them, he characterizes the

---

56   *Ibid.*
57   E. Campbell Corey 2006: 118.
58   *Ibid.*
59   E. Podoksik 2009: 224.
60   G. Worthington 2002: 305–306.
61   G. Worthington 2005: 60.
62   *Ibid.*
63   G. Worthington 2002: 306.
64   *Ibid.*

activity of the poet in terms of the social whole.[65] Worthington argues that the poetic experience moves beyond the creation of the moral self and becomes involved in the 'creation of the values in terms of which moral selves are created'.[66] That is, it is the poet who is the creator of the values of a society. This, Worthington argues, is the essence of Oakeshott's argument in 'Leviathan: A Myth'. He asserts that Oakeshott's characterization of the poetic creation of value in this essay 'presents this activity as creating the tapestry in which moral characters are situated as well as the creation of these selves'.[67] Poetic insight expresses what a society knows itself to be. If a society loses this insight, that is, if it fails to appreciate the poetic dimension of the moral life, it becomes deluded about what it is. Put another way, members of a society become deluded about their way of life. In short, it suffers what Oakeshott terms a corruption of consciousness.[68] For Worthington, poetry plays a significant role in the moral life since it possesses the ability to 'protect the moral life against the corruption of consciousness'.[69] Poetry, then, according to Worthington's view, is part and parcel of practice. His views on the role played by poetry in Oakeshott's thought are controversial and he acknowledges this himself. He goes so far as to claim that the poetic imagination:

> encompasses all aspects of Oakeshott's characterization of human conduct. Human conduct, whether it be in the realm of morality and religious experience or theoretical endeavours to understand the world historically, scientifically or philosophically, expresses an inescapably creative character.[70]

This is the case because the human world is created by humans both individually and collectively.[71] It follows, then, for Worthington that the voice of poetry refers to the power to create oneself as a moral entity and to the common way of life which emerges between individuals.[72]

Campbell Corey takes issue with Worthington's argument that the poetic imagination encompasses all aspects of Oakeshott's characterization of human conduct. She argues that this is an overstatement of the case.[73] However, she acknowledges that Oakeshott provides intima-

---

[65]   *Ibid.*

[66]   G. Worthington 2005: 61.

[67]   *Ibid.*: 62.

[68]   *Ibid.*: 64.

[69]   *Ibid.*

[70]   G. Worthington 2002: 310.

[71]   *Ibid.*

[72]   *Ibid.*

[73]   E. Campbell Corey 2006: 153.

tions that something about the poetic experience does in fact relate to conduct. She asserts that Oakeshott conceives of poetry as fully present and, thus, as a consequence, it is a complete and satisfactory form of human experience. Such perfect completion is impossible in the other modes of experience and, most especially, in practical experience where what 'is' and what 'ought' to be can never be fully reconciled.[74] Poetry overcomes the irreconcilability inherent to practice, Campbell Corey argues, because in poetic activity 'the desiring self is sublimated or temporarily lost, and what emerges is a self that engages images as fully present'.[75] As experience that is both complete and satisfactory, poetry may serve as a model for what all experience hints at but cannot achieve, Campbell Corey contends.[76] Thus, for her, this does not mean that morality becomes poetry, but only that 'it is very much *like* poetry'.[77] She uses the Aristotelian language of essence and accident to argue her point. She contends that morality's relationship to poetry can only be accidental. By this, she means that while a moral action may be perceived from a poetic standpoint and delighted in, this is in fact accidental to its essential character as a moral act concerned with fulfilling a desire.[78] Thus, although there are intimations of poetry present in practical activity, at most, poetry 'offers an ideal unity that morality may sometimes approximate'.[79] In other words, when moral conduct exhibits a unity of manner and motive it may be said to partake of a poetic character. Nevertheless, even at its most poetic, morality is distinct from poetry and the two idioms remain theoretically and modally distinct.[80] Contrary to Worthington, she maintains that the distinction between the two modes remains intact in *On Human Conduct*. She observes that throughout this work, Oakeshott 'repeatedly likens moral conduct to various kinds of art'.[81] However, she argues that this is evidence of the thesis that his 'aesthetic sensibility lies just behind his characterization of moral conduct — indeed, that poetry [...] stands as a model for what moral conduct can sometimes approximate'.[82] Hence, Campbell Corey defends the position that Oakeshott's thought on aesthetics develops in a steady direction. It culminates with the specification of poetry in 'The Voice of Poetry in the Conversation

---

74   *Ibid.*: 117.
75   *Ibid.*
76   *Ibid.*
77   *Ibid.*: 118, original emphasis.
78   *Ibid.*: 117–118.
79   *Ibid.*: 118.
80   *Ibid.*
81   *Ibid.*: 149.
82   *Ibid.*: 149–150.

of Mankind' as an autonomous mode of activity, separate from all others. Oakeshott's conception of poetry and its relationship to practice is unambiguous if it is understood as the ideal of activity, a model to be emulated.

Podoksik's position represents the middle ground between Worthington and Campbell Corey. He argues that Oakeshott never repudiated the conception of aesthetics presented in 'The Voice of Poetry in the Conversation of Mankind', which understands poetry as an autonomous human activity; he notes in that regard that in *On Human Conduct* poetry remains irrelevant to practical conduct.[83] Nevertheless, Podoksik maintains that his views on the relationship between poetry and practice still remained ambivalent in so far as he 'did not abandon completely the view that life could have aesthetic overtones, which endowed it with a unique value'.[84] However, contrary to Worthington, for whom the poetic imagination encompasses all aspects of Oakeshott's characterization of human conduct, Podoksik stresses that Oakeshott realized that these overtones could only ever be 'a brief enchantment' and, thus, transitory.[85]

Of the three interpretations of Oakeshott's thought on aesthetics, I largely concur with Worthington's. I agree that Oakeshott's conception of poetry is ambiguous and remains so throughout all of his writings on the subject. I am also in agreement with his conclusion that poetry plays a vital role in the practical world, specifically in the creation of value and in guarding against the corruption of a society's consciousness. However, I make the case differently from Worthington. I attempt to show that poetry is actively engaged in practice by referring to the case of legends. Moreover, I argue that legends, and Oakeshott's particular use of poetry in this instance, constitute a kind of foundation for the political and society. Legends of political life effectively found a political society's identity. I should note that by the political and society I understand what Hannah Arendt refers to as 'human living-together'.[86] A society, a people, a community, or, more broadly, a civilization, Oakeshott uses all of these terms, needs common references and stabilizing constructs in order to avoid the corruption of its consciousness. This, I posit, is the purpose legends, a kind of poetical activity, serve in relation to practice and its modulation politics. Thus, the relationship between poetry and practice goes beyond poetry serving as a

---

83 E. Podoksik 2002: 732.
84 *Ibid.*: 733.
85 *Ibid.*
86 H. Arendt 1993: 141.

model for practice to emulate, or practice having intermittent aesthetic overtones.

Poetry: Guardian of a Political Society's Identity

Oakeshott's concern in 'The Claims of Politics' is to refute the claim that there is an obligation to take an extended and active part in politics; that is, that it is a 'universal duty'.[87] For this to be true, he argues, politics would either have to be 'the only adequate expression of a sensibility for the communal interests of a society', or it would have to be shown that it is 'incomparably the most important and most effective expression of such a sensibility'.[88] Oakeshott rejects the first assertion by arguing that no activity is unconnected with the life of a society. In this sense, he maintains that 'the activity of a music-hall artist is no less certainly connected with the common life of his society than that of a Prime Minister'.[89] As Timothy Fuller notes, Oakeshott's position differentiates him from Leo Strauss and Hannah Arendt, both of whom locate the heroic in the political realm.[90]

His refutation of the second claim is both more detailed and more complex. Oakeshott's argument centres on the distinction he draws between creation and protection. Political activity is not of superior importance for the following reasons. It constitutes a highly specialized and abstract form of communal activity. It is conducted on the surface of the life of a society and only very rarely makes an impression below the surface.[91] In other words, it might aptly be described as a 'superficial' activity. As such, it is not involved in the fundamental and profound aspects of the life of a society. This is due to the fact that its function is not one of creation, but one of protection. Rather than create, politics protects. A political system, Oakeshott asserts, presupposes a civilization and its function is to protect and modify as required its recognized legal and social order. A political system is not self-explanatory in that its end and meaning cannot be understood without reference to the social whole to which it belongs.[92] This social whole is already determined by law, custom and tradition, none of which, Oakeshott maintains, 'is the creation of political activity'.[93] Politics is a superficial activity in that it protects a legal and social order, which is the result of the interactions between the law, custom and tradition.

---

[87] *RPML*: 91.
[88] *Ibid.*
[89] *RPML*: 92.
[90] T. Fuller 1993: 10, note 6.
[91] *RPML*: 93.
[92] *Ibid.*
[93] *Ibid.*

Together, these determine the social whole. In this sense, while political activity did produce Magna Carta and the American Bill of Rights, two 'protective' documents, it is not responsible for their contents, which, Oakeshott claims, 'came from a stratum of social thought far too deep to be influenced by the actions of politicians'.[94] Hence, political activity is unable to reach the deeper strata of social thought. For this reason, politics is not the 'continuous consideration and reconsideration of the life and order of a society from the bottom upwards' since its activity is conducted on the surface of this life.[95] Moreover, since the impression it makes below the surface is negligible, politics cannot be involved in the 'continuous recreation of the communal life'.[96] Oakeshott establishes a clear distinction between creation and protection. Politics plays the significant, yet superficial, role of protecting the legal and social order. As such, it never delves deep into the recesses of the social whole, but remains on the surface.

The function of protection, Oakeshott contends, is never of primary importance. In times of political crisis it may appear to be so, but this is due to the absence, or poverty, of creative activity.[97] Society may effectively survive and be preserved by means of political action, but when this occurs, Oakeshott asserts, 'protection has usurped the place of recreation'.[98] Thus, in relation to a society, the political function of protection is not what is most valuable. Oakeshott argues that it is necessary to move beyond mere protection in order to 'make' a society 'live'. He is emphatic on this point and maintains that 'to make it [a society] live requires a social activity of a different and more radical character'.[99] For a society to be alive, it needs not only for its civilization to be guarded, but also for it to be recreated.[100] In this respect, Fuller notes that 'Oakeshott proposes that the strength of a civilization derives from the capacity for continual self-recreation or renewal'.[101] The radical activity required is creative or poetical activity. This essential activity is performed by those 'whose genius and interest lies in literature, in art and in philosophy'.[102] The genius of the poet, artist and, to a lesser extent, the philosopher is their ability to 'create and recreate the

---

94   *Ibid.*
95   *Ibid.*
96   *Ibid.*
97   *RPML*: 94.
98   *Ibid.*
99   *Ibid.*
100 *RPML*: 95.
101 Fuller 2001: xxx.
102 *RPML*: 95.

values of their society'.[103] These values are the 'real life and character of
a society'.[104] Consequently, Oakeshott attributes an essential and highly
important role to poetry since it is by means of the genius of the poet,
artist and philosopher, he argues, that a society 'becomes conscious and
critical of itself, its whole self'.[105] Poetry makes a society conscious of its
character and, therefore, of its values. In sum, poetry mitigates a little a
society's ignorance of itself.[106] As Fuller succinctly puts it, 'politics
maintains and defends social life [...] but seldom rejuvenates or
recreates it. The latter task falls to poets, artists, philosophers and to the
imaginative use of their resources by countless individuals'.[107]

For Oakeshott, then, in order for a society to live it must be conscious of itself. Also, society must know itself and it must have the
power of recreating itself. Otherwise, it will be threatened with the
corruption of its consciousness. Oakeshott contends that the 'last
corruption that can visit a society is a corruption of its consciousness,
and from this the politically active cannot protect it'.[108] Although he
distinguishes between the political function of protection and the
poetical activity of creation, and, hence, argues that poets 'are not [...]
the guardians of the values of society', I posit that poetry does in fact
guard and protect society and that it does so in a more radical and
fundamental way than politics.[109] Oakeshott asserts that politics cannot
protect society from the corruption of its consciousness. In fact, political
activity 'involves a corruption of consciousness from which a society
has continuously to be saved'.[110] He is adamant that only poetry is able
to save a society from the corruption of its consciousness. In this sense,
he argues that 'if a society is to be saved from a corrupt consciousness it
will be saved not by having its values and its civilization protected, but
by knowing itself and having its values recreated'.[111] In other words,
poetry both creates and recreates the values of a society and thereby
guards its very identity and its consciousness. This, I argue, is part of
the foundational role played by poetry in regards to society. While it
does not protect a society in the superficial manner of politics, it does
guard it in a more profound and significant way. In sum, poetry pro-

---

[103] *Ibid.*
[104] *Ibid.*
[105] *Ibid.*
[106] *RPML*: 96.
[107] T. Fuller 1993: 9.
[108] *RPML*: 95.
[109] *Ibid.*
[110] *Ibid.*
[111] *Ibid.*

vides an 'actual remedy for more fundamental defects by making a society conscious of its own character'.[112]

In her analysis of 'The Claims of Politics', Campbell Corey asks in regards to poets', artists' and philosophers' function of creating and recreating the values of a society 'exactly *how* do they do this?'[113] I posit that they do this by means of legends. I will develop my argument in greater detail later on. At this point, I wish to point out that in this essay Oakeshott provides valuable insight into how poetry and legends work. He argues that what poetry provides is action itself, but 'in another and deeper sphere of consciousness'.[114] This other and deeper sphere of consciousness, I argue, is the deep stratum of social thought which, Oakeshott claims, is responsible for the contents of Magna Carta and of the American Bill of Rights. That is, poetry is able to access and act upon the deep stratum of social thought which politics cannot reach. The contents of these documents are values such as conceptions of rights, liberty and freedom which emerge contingently in a society's consciousness. Poetic action taps into the deep stratum of social thought and, by means of legends and myths, creates and recreates the values of a society, thereby ensuring that it is conscious of its own character and critical of its whole self. Values, such as freedom, emerge contingently as a result of poetry's action on the deeper sphere of consciousness. A society thus knows itself and knows that these are its values and will seek to protect or found them. Magna Carta and the American Bill of Rights are examples of 'protective' documents produced by politics, the purpose of which is to protect recognized rights and freedom. However, politics can only ever provide a superficial protection of the values of a society. Documents such as Magna Carta and the American Bill of Rights contain principles and ideals abstracted from the deeper stratum of social thought. Since politics is a highly abstract form of activity, it remains on the surface of the social whole, which is itself determined by law, custom and tradition. When political understanding is abstracted to the point where it becomes ideology or rationalist, a society's consciousness has become corrupted. The problem lies in the erroneous belief that politics is self-explanatory when its meaning lies beyond itself in the social whole to which it belongs.[115] Politics, then, offers a superficial protection and foundation of the values of a society.

---

[112] *Ibid.*

[113] E. Campbell Corey 2006: 108, original emphasis.

[114] *RPML*: 95.

[115] *RPML*: 93.

A more profound, fundamental and radical sort of protection and foundation for the values of a society is that provided by poetry. Poetical activity guards a society against the corruption of its consciousness by making it conscious of itself and recreating its values. Poetry guards a society's very identity, or as Oakeshott puts it, makes it live.[116] In this sense, while Magna Carta and the American Bill of Rights may be understood on one level as the superficial protection of values, they are also key components of the English and American political legends. As symbolic images, they are fully integrated into their respective legends. Moreover, they also represent the emergence of their societies' values as well as of their societies' consciousness of those values. They are continually referred to as symbols of their societies' respective conceptions of rights and freedom. Any change or expansion to either of these societies' values must be tied back to their legends and, in particular, to these components. As elements of legends, Magna Carta and the American Bill of Rights guard their societies in a more fundamental and radical way by protecting them from the corruption of their consciousness. What Oakeshott posits in 'The Claims of Politics', I argue, is the contingent and poetical foundation of a society's identity.

As the argument will show, the idea of the corruption of consciousness is central to Oakeshott's thought. It is the key to understanding the poetic role legends play in guarding a society's identity and sense of self-consciousness. As such, it is fundamental to my argument which posits contingent foundations for the political in Oakeshott's thought. Oakeshott undoubtedly finds the inspiration for his concept of the corruption of consciousness in R.G. Collingwood's *The Principles of Art*, which he reviewed for the *Cambridge Review* in 1938. In that review, Oakeshott explains that it 'would be stupid here to attempt any exposition of the doctrine, and worse to offer any criticism of matters of detail'.[117] For him, the value of Collingwood's contribution 'does not depend upon our being convinced by the doctrine (though I myself find it singularly convincing); it lies in the experience it offers of following a masterly discussion of all the fundamental questions which any doctrine must consider'.[118] Oakeshott's essay 'The Claims of Politics', where he first introduces the concept, was written in 1939. While the two concepts are not identical, they share a definite kinship in terms of the knowledge a society must have of itself and the role played by art in providing that knowledge. Consciousness, for Collingwood, is the

---

[116] *RPML*: 94.
[117] *CPJ*: 185.
[118] *Ibid*.

level of thought between pure psychical experience, that is, feeling or emotion, and intellection. The activity of consciousness converts feeling into idea. Put another way, the activity of consciousness converts sensation into imagination. Imagination, then, is 'the new form which feeling takes when transformed by the activity of consciousness'.[119] While consciousness is nothing other than thought, it is not yet intellect.[120] However, consciousness is 'thought in its absolutely fundamental and original shape'.[121] Consciousness is fundamental because it is the basis for every further development of thought. That is, intellect deals with feeling converted into imagination. In other words, consciousness prepares the ground for intellection by attending to a present feeling and thus perpetuating it, though at the cost of turning it into something new: domesticated feeling or imagination.[122] For Collingwood, a true consciousness is 'the confession to ourselves of our feelings'; subsequently, a false consciousness is 'disowning them'.[123] A feeling is disowned when, in the process of becoming conscious of it, we 'take fright at what we have recognized: not because the feeling, as an impression, is an alarming impression, but because the idea into which we are converting it proves an alarming idea'.[124] The problem being that it is thought that the idea cannot be dominated or domesticated. For Collingwood, when this occurs, as humans we 'give it up, and turn our attention to something less intimidating'.[125] This is what he calls the 'corruption' of consciousness. Consciousness becomes corrupted because, in disowning a feeling which it is thought cannot be domesticated or converted into imagination, it 'permits itself to be bribed or corrupted in the discharge of its function, being distracted from a formidable task towards an easier one'.[126] Since consciousness is the basis for every further development of thought, a corrupt consciousness necessarily 'infects the imaginations which it constructs. When consciousness is corrupted, imagination shares the corruption'.[127] That is, when an element of experience is disowned by consciousness, any other element which it claims as its own also becomes corrupted. The claimed element does genuinely belong to consciousness, that is, consciousness is being truthful. However, the disowned element infects

---

[119] R.G. Collingwood 1945: 215.
[120] *Ibid.*
[121] *Ibid.*: 216.
[122] *Ibid.*: 223.
[123] *Ibid.*: 216.
[124] *Ibid.*: 217.
[125] *Ibid.*
[126] *Ibid.*
[127] *Ibid.*: 218.

this truth with error.[128] In short, the picture which consciousness paints of itself is 'not only a selected picture [...] it is a bowdlerized picture, or one whose omissions are falsifications'.[129]

Consciousness and truthfulness are fundamental concepts of any theory of art, Collingwood claims, as they define good art. In a work of art an agent is trying to express a given emotion. Artistic activity, therefore, is conscious activity in that not only is the agent trying to do something definite, but he also knows what it is he is trying to do.[130] That is, a work of art may either be good or bad and an agent, because he is conscious, 'knows which it is. Or rather, he necessarily knows this so far as his consciousness in respect of this work of art is uncorrupted'.[131] For Collingwood, to express an emotion and to express it well 'are the same thing'.[132] Good art is the successful artistic expression of an emotion; whereas to express an emotion badly is to fail to express it at all. Consequently, the unsuccessful expression of an emotion is what defines bad art. In this sense, Collingwood writes that 'a bad work of art is an activity in which the agent tries to express a given emotion, but fails'.[133] Collingwood argues that expressing an emotion and becoming conscious of it are the same thing. Thus, since a bad work of art is the failure to express a given emotion, it follows that it is the unsuccessful attempt to become conscious of that emotion. For Collingwood, a consciousness which 'thus fails to grasp its own emotions is a corrupt or untruthful consciousness'.[134] In short, Collingwood maintains that bad art arises when we disown certain of our emotions.[135]

When we express emotions and become conscious of them, we become conscious of who we are. For Collingwood, this is of fundamental importance for 'to know ourselves is the foundation of all life that develops beyond the merely psychical level of experience'.[136] That is, Collingwood argues, if consciousness does not successfully convert feeling into imagination, 'the only things upon which intellect can build its fabric of thought, are false from the beginning'.[137] In other words, 'a truthful consciousness gives intellect a firm foundation upon which to

---

128 *Ibid.*
129 *Ibid.*
130 *Ibid.*: 280–282.
131 *Ibid.*: 281.
132 *Ibid.*: 282.
133 *Ibid.*
134 *Ibid.*
135 *Ibid.*: 284.
136 *Ibid.*
137 *Ibid.*

build; a corrupt consciousness forces intellect to build on a quick-sand'.[138] Since a truthful consciousness is the foundation for all thought, the consequences of a corrupt consciousness are severe for a society. In this sense, Collingwood contends that in so far as consciousness is corrupted 'the very wells of truth are poisoned. Intellect can build nothing firm. Moral ideals are castles in the air. Political and economic systems are mere cobwebs'.[139] As for remedying a society's untruthful consciousness, Collingwood claims that 'art is the community's medicine for the worst disease of mind, the corruption of consciousness'.[140] Art, Collingwood maintains, must be prophetic. The artist must prophecy 'in the sense that he tells his audience, at risk of their displeasure, the secrets of their own hearts. His business as an artist is to speak out, to make a clean breast'.[141] Since the artist is the spokesman for his community, what he expresses are not his own secrets, but rather the secrets of the community. A community needs the artist because 'no community altogether knows its own heart; and by failing in this knowledge a community deceives itself on the one subject concerning which ignorance means death'.[142] The artist does not suggest a remedy for the evils which stem from a society's ignorance of itself since he has already given one: 'the remedy', Collingwood maintains, 'is the poem itself'.[143] The life of the artist, Collingwood asserts, is one of constant warfare against the corruption of consciousness.[144] However, the effort to overcome the corruption of consciousness must not only be made by specialists, but by everyone who uses language since 'every utterance and every gesture that each one of us makes is a work of art'.[145]

The purpose of the preceding discussion is to put the concept 'corruption of consciousness' in context and show how it evolved within the British idealist tradition. The concept originated in Collingwood's thought and was adopted by Oakeshott with modifications. Therefore, while not identical, similarities may be drawn between the manner in which the two thinkers conceive of the corruption of a society's consciousness, most significantly as regards the connection to aesthetics. Oakeshott, like Collingwood, is adamant that 'the last

---

138 *Ibid.*
139 *Ibid.*
140 *Ibid.*: 336.
141 *Ibid.*
142 *Ibid.*
143 *Ibid.*
144 *Ibid.*: 284.
145 *Ibid.*: 285.

corruption that can visit a society is a corruption of its consciousness'.[146] That is, a society's ignorance of itself, its failure to know its own heart, means its death. A corrupt consciousness forces the intellect to build morality and the political on falsehoods which the intellect can never correct. A truthful consciousness, therefore, one that does not disown emotions and thereby provides a complete representation of experience, is the foundation for all life. It should be noted that Collingwood and Oakeshott hold divergent views on the question of art and emotion. In this respect, in the essay 'The Voice of Poetry in the Conversation of Mankind', Oakeshott explicitly rejects the idea that art is the expression of emotion which is Collingwood's thesis. Oakeshott denies that poetry is the expression of emotion designed to evoke the same emotion in the audience.[147] However, Collingwood unequivocally rules out a means–ends relationship in art. He holds that emotion is only discovered in its expression. The criterion of good art is the ability to evoke that same emotion in others. For his part, Oakeshott argues that although the idea that art is the expression of emotion is commonly held, it rests on the mistaken view that poetry must be informative and instructive. In this sense, the poet must have undergone the emotion from which the poetic image derives.[148] This view is mistaken, Oakeshott contends, in that it 'makes a necessity of what is no more than an unlikely possibility'.[149] In sum, in the essay 'The Voice of Poetry in the Conversation of Mankind', Oakeshott holds that art has nothing to do with the expression of emotion, whereas for Collingwood the corruption of consciousness is inseparable from the expression of emotion since it is the result of failing to express emotion.

In spite of Oakeshott's and Collingwood's divergent views on art and emotion, the point I wish to make is that, for both thinkers, it is imperative that a society know itself. Moreover, as regards the role of art in relation to society's consciousness, Oakeshott concurs with Collingwood's argument that art is the remedy for a corrupt consciousness. It cures society of its disease by telling it what it is. For Collingwood, the artist accomplishes this by means of a poem in which he discloses its secrets; for Oakeshott, the poet guards society against the corruption of its consciousness by creating and recreating its values. I argue that the concept of consciousness and of its corruption is central to Oakeshott's political thought, in particular for understanding his conservatism as well as the role played by legends, understood as

---

[146] *RPML*: 95.
[147] *RP*: 521 and 524–526.
[148] *RP*: 524.
[149] *Ibid.*

stabilizing poetic constructs, in relation to the political. Oakeshott refers to the concept of consciousness throughout his writings, alternatively as self-consciousness, identity, as being recognizable to ourselves or as being in sympathy with ourselves. The fundamental point, however, is that for Oakeshott a society must have knowledge of itself. It is one of the functions of poetry to endow a society with its sense of self-consciousness and to protect it from being corrupted. A society whose consciousness is corrupt finds itself threatened since 'ignorance means death'.[150] My objective, then, in the present chapter, is to show that legends of political life, poetic constructs, are informative and instructive and that this is also true for poetry under certain circumstances. I make the case that this is due to the difficult emancipation of poetry from the mode of practice. Emancipation made difficult by the primordial human need to inhabit a world of sense and meaning, that is, a world fit for human living.

Oakeshott pursues his exploration of the relationship between poetry and practice in the essay '*Leviathan*: A Myth'. In particular, he addresses the question of how philosophy may play a creative role in relation to society, an argument he made in 'The Claims of Politics'. In the essay, Oakeshott makes the unusual and surprising claim that Hobbes's *Leviathan* is best understood as a work of art. The book, he asserts, is 'one of the masterpieces of literature of our language and civilization'.[151] What makes *Leviathan* a masterpiece of what Oakeshott terms 'philosophical literature' is 'the profound logic of Hobbes's imagination, his power as an artist'.[152] It is a claim he also makes in his 'Introduction to *Leviathan*' where he states that philosophy knows two styles of writing: the contemplative and the didactic.[153] Oakeshott maintains that Hobbes's way of writing is an example of the didactic style of writing.[154] Moreover, he emphasizes that Hobbes's style is imaginative. Oakeshott does not say this merely on account of Hobbes's use of imagery nor because it requires imagination to create a system. More than this, for Oakeshott, Hobbes's imagination 'appears also as the power to create a myth'.[155] He argues that the power of Hobbes's imagination created the myth of *Leviathan* which he defines as 'the transposition of an abstract argument into the world of the imagination'.[156] In the myth, Oakeshott explains, 'we are made aware at a

---

[150] R.G. Collingwood 1945: 336.

[151] *HCA*: 159.

[152] *HCA*: 163.

[153] *RP*: 234.

[154] *Ibid.*

[155] *Ibid.*

[156] *Ibid.*

glance of the fixed and simple centre of a universe of complex and changing relationships'.[157] Although Oakeshott observes that Hobbes's argument 'may not be the better for this transposition' and that 'what it gains in vividness it may pay for in illusion'; nevertheless, he is adamant that *Leviathan* is an accomplishment of art that Hobbes, in the history of political philosophy, shares only with Plato.[158]

In order to appreciate his unorthodox interpretation of this work, it is necessary to understand Oakeshott's conception of civilization and literature's function in regards to it. I argue that an idea akin to the one of the 'deep stratum of social thought' forms the basis for his view of civilization. He defines civilization as a 'collective dream'.[159] To specify his meaning, he quotes Plotinus who said that 'insofar as the soul is in the body, it lies in deep sleep'.[160] For Oakeshott, 'a people' is akin to the soul and, consequently, it lies in deep sleep. He contends that what 'a people' dreams in its deep, earthly sleep 'is its civilization'.[161] The substance of this dream, he asserts, is 'a myth, an imaginative interpretation of human existence, the perception (not the solution) of the mystery of human life'.[162] For Oakeshott, 'a people' dreams its civilization and this dream is a myth. He is clear: a people understands itself and the world by means of a myth. The terms 'collective dream' and 'deep sleep' correspond to the idea expressed by the concepts 'deep stratum of social thought' and 'deep consciousness' which Oakeshott develops in 'The Claims of Politics'. The civilizational myth, or imaginative interpretation of human life, originates in this state of deep sleep and dreaming. Similarly to 'The Claims of Politics', Oakeshott argues that not every form of human activity can act upon the dream or myth, that is, the deep stratum of social thought. In fact, he even goes so far as to assert that most persons are 'slaves' to the dream. To this end, he argues that 'we, whose participation in the dream is imperfect and largely passive, are, in a sense, its slaves'.[163] Put another way, the average person engaged in the practical world receives the dream 'passively', as Worthington observes.[164] The power to affect the dream belongs to the mode of poetry. In this sense, Oakeshott argues that literature is able to 'make more articulate the dream-powers of a

---

[157] *Ibid.*

[158] *RP*: 234, 234–235.

[159] *HCA*: 159.

[160] *Ibid.*, Plotinus cited by Oakeshott.

[161] *Ibid.*

[162] *HCA*: 159–160.

[163] *HCA*: 160.

[164] G. Worthington 2002: 298–299.

people'.[165] In other words, by the gift of imagination, literature expands a people's faculty of dreaming.[166] As Bruce Frohnen aptly puts it, 'the task and the genius of an artist such as Oakeshott's Hobbes lies in his ability to enrich the dream which is our civilization [...] the artist may actually comprehend the dream, may go beyond the surface of limited modes to the moral essence of a people, their non-rational, spiritual being'.[167] This ability stems from the artist's power to dream more profoundly and from his genius to 'dream that he is dreaming'.[168] Specifically, literature acts upon the myth of civilization by perpetually recalling it and recreating it in each generation.[169] Once more, we find the idea that the office of aesthetics, in this case literature, is to recall and recreate a people's civilization, that is, its identity. Oakeshott describes in considerable detail how literature, and poetry in particular, recreates the myth:

> Under its inspiration the familiar outlines of the common dream fade, new perceptions, and emotions hitherto unfelt are excited within us, the till-now settled fact dissolves once more into infinite possibility, and we become aware that the myth (which is the substance of the dream) has acquired a new quality, without our needing to detect the precise character of the change.[170]

Thus, while literature and poetry do not create the myth as such, it is dreamt by a people in its earthly sleep by an access of imaginative power, they nevertheless act upon it by perpetually recalling it and recreating it, thereby keeping the myth of civilization alive.

However, in addition to literature and poetry, Oakeshott also identifies philosophical literature as an activity which acts upon the myth of civilization. He contends that books of philosophy may sometimes reach the level of literature and, when they do, they affect the dream more significantly than literature does.[171] Rather than expanding a people's imaginative power, the gift of philosophical literature is 'an increase of knowledge; it will prompt and it will instruct'.[172] Philosophical literature prompts and instructs by reminding a people of 'the common dream that binds the generations together' and by making the myth more intelligible.[173] It achieves this by the vision of the myth it

---

[165] *HCA*: 160.
[166] *Ibid.*
[167] B. Frohnen 1990: 801.
[168] *HCA*: 160.
[169] *Ibid.*
[170] *Ibid.*
[171] *Ibid.*
[172] *Ibid.*
[173] *Ibid.*

presents.[174] For Oakeshott, this is the meaning of a book of philosophy which has reached the level of literature. It serves a didactic purpose in that it increases the knowledge a people has of itself; it prompts by reminding them of the common dream that binds the generations (that is, it reminds the society of its foundation) and it instructs by making the myth, hence their identity, more intelligible to present generations.

What is striking is how differently Oakeshott conceives of literature, poetry and philosophical literature in comparison to both philosophy and poetry. In particular, they do not respect the criterion of autonomy Oakeshott specifically establishes in regards to the mode of practice. Furthermore, literature and philosophical literature differ considerably from Oakeshott's conception of aesthetics presented in 'The Voice of Poetry in the Conversation of Mankind'. These two literary forms are not composed of mere images which provoke contemplation and delight. The dream or myth is composed of symbolic images which tell the story of a people's civilization and, in so doing, it binds the generations. Literature and philosophical literature act upon the myth in the following manner: they perpetually remind society of it, they recreate it and, in instructing a people about it, they increase the knowledge of it and, thereby, make it more intelligible. The understanding of poetry here is very different from the one Oakeshott offers in 'The Voice of Poetry in the Conversation of Mankind' and which is considered by many commentators to represent the culmination of his thought on aesthetics. Poetry in this instance is laborious in the sense that its images are made available to the mode of practice and, as such, are read as signs and symbols. Literature in '*Leviathan*: A Myth' is not contemplation. It does not rest in its images 'looking neither backwards nor forwards'.[175] In order to bind the generations, the myth, and its literary recollection and recreation, tells the story of a 'legendary' past as well as offers a vision of the present and of the future. Literature does in fact teach and instruct a people about its civilization and, consequently, about how to live. The mode of poetry such as it is presented in '*Leviathan*: A Myth' is clearly not divorced from practice such as Oakeshott stipulates it should be in 'The Voice of Poetry in the Conversation of Mankind'.

Oakeshott's conception of philosophical literature also differs markedly from his understanding of philosophy. The most blatant difference is the fact that philosophical literature does not respect the strict division Oakeshott establishes between philosophy and practice. Philosophical literature, such as it is portrayed in '*Leviathan*: A Myth',

---

[174] *Ibid.*
[175] *RP*: 510.

serves a definite didactic purpose and is thus fully engaged with practice. In so far as it prompts by reminding a people of the myth of civilization, or that it instructs by making the myth more intelligible, philosophical literature is not philosophical activity sought for its own sake. It is not independent from the extraneous interests of practice, and, hence, it is not activity which is critical throughout. In short, philosophical literature disregards the criteria Oakeshott establishes for philosophy in all of his writings on the subject.

Thus, literature, poetry and philosophical literature are clearly engaged with practice in the essay '*Leviathan*: A Myth'. The myth, while it is dreamt by a people, is nevertheless acted upon by poetry through the faculty of the imagination. It is literature which recalls and recreates the myth and it is its counterpart, philosophical literature, which increases a people's knowledge of it and, therefore, of their very identity. Poetry plays a foundational role in that it reminds a people of the common dream that binds the generations. In so doing, it serves a stabilizing function and ensures humans inhabit a world of sense. Thus, we find once more the idea that poetry radically guards a people's civilization and, consequently, its identity and self-knowledge by recalling, recreating and increasing the knowledge it has of its civilization myth.

The Difficult Emancipation of Poetry
from the Authority of Practice

Poetry in the essays 'The Claims of Politics' and '*Leviathan*: A Myth' engages with practice in order to create and recreate a society's values and ensure that it knows itself in order to guard its identity. Its images here are not mere images since meaning and symbol are distinct. That is, the image created by poetry symbolizes something outside of itself. It may be argued that the image evoked by a legend of political life symbolizes a political society's identity. If we recall, in the essay 'The Voice of Poetry in the Conversation of Mankind', Oakeshott argues that the relationship between meaning and symbol in poetry is unique in that they are not distinct. A poetic image is its meaning and it therefore symbolizes nothing outside of itself. In short, in 'The Voice of Poetry in the Conversation of Mankind', Oakeshott clearly states that in poetry meaning and symbol are not distinct whereas they are in the mode of practice. The question is whether Oakeshott maintains this distinction in his works which follow that essay. This is the question which is at the heart of the debates on the ambiguous relationship between poetry and practice in Oakeshott's thought. Following the more conventional interpretation represented by Campbell Corey, he clearly distinguishes between mere poetic images and symbolic, practical images in 'The

Voice of Poetry in the Conversation of Mankind' and all other works thereafter. According to this position, there is no ambiguity between poetry and practice in Oakeshott's thought. The claim here is that if an image is not a mere image, if it is symbolic, then it is not a poetic image. Oakeshott does not suggest that poets only contemplate and delight in images. His contention is only that if and when they do anything else, it is not poetry. Thus, in the case of legends of political life, exponents of this interpretation would argue that they cannot be poetry since the story they tell is a symbol for a political society's identity. However, I concur with Worthington who argues that the relationship between poetry and practice remains ambiguous. I claim that the ambiguous nature of the relationship is illustrated in two essays written after 'The Voice of Poetry in the Conversation of Mankind'. As we will see, in both instances, the ambiguity relates to legends of political life. Oakeshott makes it clear that it is poetry which creates or constructs these foundational narratives. In other words, poetry creates symbolic, laborious images and not only mere images. I argue that this is in large part due to the difficult emancipation of poetry from the authority of practice. Oakeshott is adamant that humans' primordial activity is to make themselves at home in the world. There is a deep human need to live in a world of sense and meaning. This is the role of poetry, to create and recreate symbolic narratives which endow political societies with their sense of identity, thereby allowing humans to know who they are and where they are in the world. Although poetry, on rare occasions, is able to emancipate itself from the authority of practice and create mere images, this remains a difficult achievement. More often than not, poetry is joined with practice in the endeavour to create a world fit for human life. As regards politics, poetry creates legends of political life which found political societies' identities. This is the argument I make and develop in the following section.

***

'The Voice of Poetry in the Conversation of Mankind' is considered by many commentators to be Oakeshott's definitive statement on aesthetics. Commentators, such as Campbell Corey, argue that the essays 'The Claims of Politics' and '*Leviathan*: A Myth' are stages in the development of Oakeshott's thought on aesthetics and, as such, do not present a fully worked out and comprehensive view of the mode of poetry. According to this interpretation, 'The Voice of Poetry in the Conversation of Mankind' represents the culmination of Oakeshott's thinking on aesthetics and presents a complete and unambiguous conception of aesthetics since he clearly distinguishes between the idioms of poetry and practice. Therefore, while Oakeshott's earlier writings on aesthetics may be ambiguous and, consequently, open to interpretation, any such ambiguity is resolved with 'The Voice of Poetry in the Conservation of Mankind'.

Oakeshott does effectively conceive of poetry, practice, history and science as four distinct idioms in the conversation of mankind. In this respect, he argues that 'the images of one universe of discourse are not available [...] to a different mode of imagining'.[176] Consequently, Oakeshott is insistent that poetry is 'a unique utterance, not to be assimilated to any other'.[177] It follows that an apology for poetry in the idiom of practice is 'misconceived'.[178] However, given the fact that it is now commonly believed that 'practical enterprise and moral endeavour are the pre-eminently proper occupations of mankind', Oakeshott recognizes that the most common apology for poetry is a vindication of it in respect of practice.[179] To this end, it is said that the office of poetry is:

> to tell us how we ought to live or to provide us with a particular kind of criticism of our conduct; it is to record and disseminate a scale of moral values; it is to give a special kind of moral education in which good emotions are not merely described and recommended but actually awakened in us; it is to promote emotional health and sanity; it is to cure a corrupt consciousness and to 'attune us to existence'; it is to reflect the structure and operation of the 'society' in which it appears; it is to comfort the miserable, to strike terror into sinners, or merely to provide 'music while you work'.[180]

Oakeshott here appears to repudiate his earlier position regarding the role of poetry in relation to society which he elaborated in 'The Claims of Politics' and '*Leviathan*: A Myth'. In this essay, the office of poetry is to cure a corrupt consciousness only when it is justified in terms of practice and therefore misconceived. Oakeshott argues that although some of these observations are not necessarily untrue, their enquiry is concerned only with the subordinate relationship of poetry to practice.[181] Consequently, whereas earlier the guarding of society against the corruption of its consciousness was the office of poetry, in 'The Voice of Poetry in the Conversation of Mankind', Oakeshott identifies such a relationship between poetry and society as the subordination of poetry to practice and, hence, inherently 'unpoetic'. As far as I am aware, this is the only work where Oakeshott makes such an assertion

---

[176] *RP*: 514.
[177] *RP*: 539.
[178] *RP*: 534.
[179] *RP*: 532–533.
[180] *RP*: 533.
[181] *RP*: 534.

in regards to the relationship between poetry and society. In so far as 'The Voice of Poetry in the Conversation of Mankind' represents his definitive statement on aesthetics, a position he never repudiated according to Podoksik, it would seem that his earlier writings on poetry ought to be disregarded. However, I argue further on that in two essays written after 'The Voice of Poetry in the Conversation of Mankind', Oakeshott returns to the position he developed in 'The Claims of Politics' and '*Leviathan*: A Myth'. In other words, I contend that Oakeshott's thought on aesthetics remains ambiguous.

Moreover, although it would appear that Oakeshott's position in 'The Voice of Poetry in the Conversation of Mankind' is unequivocal; nevertheless, as Podoksik and Worthington both observe, the fact that poetry finds itself in conversation with the other idioms of experience implies some kind of relationship between poetry and practice.[182] The dynamics of the conversation leave room for ambiguity as to the precise nature of the relationship between poetry and practice. I concur with Podoksik's and Worthington's respective assessments. I agree that the relationship between poetry and practice remains ambiguous. However, I wish to focus on a different aspect of Oakeshott's argument in 'The Voice of Poetry in the Conversation of Mankind' to support my contention that poetry, in certain circumstances, is engaged with practice. The element which, I think, explains Oakeshott's ambiguity relative to the relationship between poetry and practice relates to legends and myths.

An important argument made by Oakeshott, and which is touched upon by Podoksik, is the difficult emancipation of poetic images from the authority of the symbolic language of practical activity. Oakeshott makes it clear in his discussion on the practical apology for poetry that he believes that practical activity is 'the commonest manner of imagining'.[183] A consequence of practical imagining's domination, Oakeshott claims, is the fact that 'we absolve ourselves from it with difficulty and we easily relapse into it'.[184] Put another way, Oakeshott asserts that 'the symbolic language of practical activity offers a strong and continuous resistance to the appearance of poetry'.[185] The appearance of poetry is possible only when practical imagining has lost its authority. Thus, while he reasserts the idea that no image can survive outside its own universe of discourse, Oakeshott argues that 'diminished or interrupted activity in one mode may generate an

---

[182] E. Podoksik 2002: 730; G. Worthington 2002: 291.
[183] *RP*: 497.
[184] *Ibid.*
[185] *RP*: 529.

opportunity for the appearance of another'.[186] In the case of practical activity, Oakeshott states that:

> any occasion which interrupts the affirmative flow of practical activity, any lessening of the urgency of desire, any softening of the wilfulness of ambitions, or anything that blunts the edge of moral appraisal offers an invitation to contemplative activity to make its appearance.[187]

Consequently, a practical image cannot forcibly be converted into a contemplated image. In order for the passage from practice to contemplation to occur, one must be ready to seize upon every chance or opportunity that may lead to poetry.[188] For Oakeshott, departures from practical activity 'have always the appearance of excursions into a foreign country; and this is pre-eminently so with contemplation, which can never be expected to be more than an intermittent activity'.[189]

Oakeshott claims that the intermittent nature of poetic activity, that is, of its difficult emancipation from practice, is undeniable from an historical viewpoint. To this end, he argues that although there undoubtedly were persons for whom the 'myth and magical spell and the cryptic utterances of the seer were not images of power or wisdom but of delight', the event of the emancipation of poetic imagining from practical imagining 'may only rarely be detected'.[190] He asserts that it 'never took place in ancient Greece; a glimpse of it is to be found among the Romans; and subsequently in Europe it has been slowly and uncertainly achieved'.[191] Therefore, the emancipation of poetry from the authority of practice is an historical achievement, but one which has only been uncertainly achieved in modernity. Oakeshott argues that only a few centuries ago what are now recognized as works of art were then recognized:

> primarily as the servants of practical activity. Their office was understood to be decorative and illustrative [...] They were prized as expressions or evocations of [...] respect for justice and deference to authority; as the means whereby the memory of notable persons and events were preserved.[192]

The recognition of these images as mere images, that is, as contemplative or poetic images, Oakeshott contends, sprang from circumstantial

---

186 *RP*: 516.
187 *RP*: 515.
188 *RP*: 516.
189 *RP*: 515.
190 *RP*: 530.
191 *RP*: 530–531.
192 *RP*: 531.

changes. Most notable among these circumstantial changes are the passing of time and ordinary forgetfulness which are responsible for:

> the survival of stories whose messages had been lost and of images whose 'meaning' has been forgotten, and the encounter with images (both verbal and plastic) from elsewhere whose symbolism was unknown. In the *Midsummer Night's Dream* and in the *Tempest* [...] there are spells which do not bind, images which have lost their emotive power and figures who, having lost their place in both history and myth, acquire poetic character.[193]

Oakeshott draws a net distinction between poetry, which is composed of mere images, and myth and legends which carry a meaning and a message and, thus, embody the symbolic language of practice. This is the distinction Oakeshott makes in 'The Activity of Being an Historian' between the 'contemplative past' and the 'practical past'. There he argues that:

> To remember, and to contemplate a memory, are two different experiences; in the one past and present are distinguished, in the other no such distinction is made. In short, just as when an object of use [...] is 'contemplated' its usefulness is neglected, so when what in another attitude would be recognized as a past event is 'contemplated', its pastness is ignored.[194]

Poetry, then, only emerges once the symbolism, message and meaning of myths and legends have been forgotten. The emancipation of poetry from the authority of practice is a recent, but uncertain, achievement. For Oakeshott, whatever in the modern attitude runs counter to the emancipation of poetry may be understood as 'a survival from bygone times before poetry had emerged and had been recognized, or as a revulsion from what is for us, historically, a comparatively new and still imperfectly assimilated experience'.[195]

Oakeshott acknowledges that throughout history the emancipation of poetry from the authority of practice has been rarely achieved and only with great difficulty. In modernity we are always at risk of 'relapsing' into practice since poetry is an uncertainly achieved and imperfectly assimilated experience. But why is the emancipation of poetry so difficult to achieve? Why does practice have such a powerful hold over creative images? I posit that it is because humans need stabilizing constructs such as 'unemancipated' symbolic stories like myths and legends. The meanings and messages myths and legends transmit allow persons, as well as societies, to understand themselves

---

[193] *Ibid.*

[194] *RP*: 164.

[195] *RP*: 532.

and the world around them. I suggest that Oakeshott is fully aware of the necessity for this 'indispensable ingredient' of civilization, which is why he recognizes the importance of the role of poetry for practice in two works written after 'The Voice of Poetry in the Conversation of Mankind'. Those two works are the lecture on 'Roman Political Thought (1)' which has been dated to the late 1960s and 'The Emergence of the History of Thought', which Oakeshott wrote in 1967. I have referred to these texts in the preceding discussions on the idea of legend. In 'The Emergence of the History of Thought', Oakeshott defines the legendary past, or the evoked past, as 'a work of art, a legend of past which has to be created, learned, cared for and culti- vated'.[196] It is poetry which constructs the 'epic story of the past in which an individual or an association of individuals identifies itself'.[197] Recall that, for Oakeshott, the intelligibility and value of the legendary past 'lies in the messages it delivers, the lessons it teaches and the authority and confidence it gives to current engagements'.[198] Poetry thus constructs a society's sense of identity, its self-consciousness and self-awareness. It also endows it with authority and confidence. This also holds true for a society's intellectual organization. Oakeshott argues that if:

> a whole generation of associates appeared disposed to self-recognition in what may generally be called intellectual terms, then it may be expected that such persons will seek the confirmation of their identity in a past of corresponding character, a legendary intellectual past.[199]

This view of poetry is confirmed in Oakeshott's lecture 'Roman Politi- cal Thought (1)'. As I explained in the previous chapters, he claims that the knowledge the Romans had of their manner of governing was not turned into a system of abstract ideals, rather, it was transformed into a legend. Put another way, Roman society ensured its intellectual organization and confirmed its identity by means of a legendary intellectual past 'in which the events and the fortunes of this remark- able people was endowed with a universal significance by being made to compose a work of art—a drama, or a story, whose moral was always being made explicit in events'.[200] A legend is clearly understood by Oakeshott to be a work of art. It takes the form of a drama or a story. The function of poetry is to organize the intellectual life of a people or of a society by constructing a legend endowed with universal signifi-

---

196   *WH*: 347.
197   *WH*: 348.
198   *WH*: 347.
199   *WH*: 352.
200   *LHPT*: 208.

cance and an explicit moral. It may be argued by some that while poetry did play such a role during Roman times that this no longer holds true in modernity, where the passage from practice to poetry has been realized. However, it must be remembered that the emancipation of poetry from the authority of practice is difficult to achieve and that it is easy to relapse into practice. Moreover, Oakeshott contends that the Romans did in fact have a glimpse of an emancipated and autonomous mode of poetry, but it may be assumed that just as it is uncertainly achieved in modernity, so it was difficult for them to maintain a strict division between poetry and practice because of the need for sense and meaning.[201]

These two works show that although for the purposes of his theory Oakeshott might argue for the autonomy of poetry, he nevertheless recognizes that, in 'practice' as it were, it is difficult to achieve because of the very basic need humans have for stabilizing constructs. These constructs endow a society with its identity, its sense of self-consciousness and knowledge of itself. Hence, legends ensure that persons and associations of persons are at home in a mysterious and menacing universe.[202] It belongs to poetry to create the legends, myths, dramas, stories or totem poles that serve as stabilizing constructs. This, I posit, explains the ambiguity of Oakeshott's thought on aesthetics.

The emancipation of poetry from the authority of practice is a difficult and rare achievement, even in modernity where poetry remains a 'brief enchantment'.[203] This does not mean that there is no poetry; only that it is engaged with practice, most notably to create myths and legends which serve as stabilizing constructs for the political and society. In the lecture entitled 'The Political Experience of the Ancient Greeks', which forms part of *Lectures in the History of Political Thought*, Oakeshott discusses the function of legends and myths in relation to the political. He asserts that 'every people awakened to political self-consciousness constructs a myth, an imaginative interpretation of how this came about'.[204] Clearly, then, this type of poetic creation is an 'indispensable ingredient' of civilized life and it is still very much present in modernity. Oakeshott cites as an example the myth of modern English politics which, he claims, 'began to be constructed in the seventeenth century, and it is something to which our current political arguments and attitudes are always returning, and which is

---

[201] *RP*: 530.
[202] *WH*: 347.
[203] *RP*: 540.
[204] *LHPT*: 46.

always in a process of enlargement and revision'.[205] The fact that current political arguments derive their authority from myths and that a people turns to it in search of their society's identity shows the indispensable nature of myths for society. Moreover, the myth and, consequently, the identity of a society is never established once and for all. It is perpetually being revisited and enlarged. Hence, legends and myths may be thought of as a kind of contingent foundation for the political. They create and guard a society's consciousness and values, but they are always being recreated in an attempt to protect a society against the corruption of its consciousness. I will return to the idea Oakeshott introduces here of augmentation and preservation of the legend or contingent foundation in Chapter 5. In sum, the reason the passage from practice to poetry is so difficult to make is because the political and society need stabilizing constructs, such as legends and myths, which are the creations of poetry.

To conclude, the question of whether legend and myth are a form of poetry cannot be addressed without placing it within the context of the debates regarding the relationship between the modes of poetry and practice in Oakeshott's thought on aesthetics. It is my position that the relationship between poetry and practice remains ambiguous throughout all of his writings and that legend and myth illustrate the complex relationship between the two modes. The relationship between poetry and practice remains ambiguous because of the difficult emancipation of poetic images from the authority of practice. The emancipation of poetry is rarely achieved. Oakeshott refers to such 'pure' poetic moments as a 'brief enchantment'. I argue that the reason the passage from practice to poetry is so difficult is because humans and societies need stabilizing constructs in order to make sense of the world and to understand their place in it. Legend is just such a stabilizing construct. It is a mixture of poetry and practice. It performs a practical, prescriptive and didactic function poetically. It is the poet who, by means of legend and myth, creates and recreates the values of a society and guards it from the corruption of its consciousness by ensuring that it is both knowledgeable and critical of itself. Only poetry is able to reach and act upon the deepest stratum of social thought. Therefore, legend and myth, a mixture of poetry and practice, serve as contingent foundations for the political since they create the values of a society and guard its consciousness. Yet, by acting upon the deep strata of social thought, they *recreate* a society's values and, thus, its self-consciousness. A society's identity and values are thereby protected, but they never become moribund.

---

[205] *Ibid.*

Oakeshott's Poetic Conservatism

'The Masai, when they were moved from their old country to the present Masai reserve in Kenya, took with them the names of their hills and plains and rivers and gave them to the hills and plains and rivers of the new country. And it is by some such subterfuge of conservatism that every man or people compelled to suffer a notable change avoids the shame of extinction'.[206] Here, neatly summarized, is Oakeshott's conception of conservatism. We find expressed in the story of the Masai people the constitutive elements of his conservatism. Identity, whether a person's or a society's, is central to Oakeshott's conservatism. Forced to suffer change, the Masai people avoided the shame of extinction, that is, the corruption of their consciousness, by having recourse to a subterfuge of conservatism: imagination, creativity and the construction of a symbolic imaginary. By means of imagination or poetry, the Masai people were able to protect their identity and culture from extinction. Oakeshott, therefore, makes a direct association between poetry (imagination) and conservatism. The discussion on poetry has revealed that it is the only human activity which can guard or protect a society from the corruption of its consciousness. In other words, despite the best political care, a society's identity inevitably finds itself corrupted by political activity. For this reason, I argue that Oakeshott's conservative disposition is deeply poetic since only poetry can guard a society's sense of self-consciousness and protect its values against the threat posed by change.

Oakeshott sets out his conception of the conservative disposition in the essay 'On Being Conservative'. For him, to be conservative is to be 'disposed to think and behave in certain manners; it is to prefer certain conditions of human circumstances to others; it is to be disposed to make certain kinds of choices'.[207] The certain manners of thinking and of behaviour, the certain conditions of human circumstances and the kinds of choices which characterize the conservative disposition all relate to change and innovation. To be conservative is to be aware of having something to lose, something which has been cared for and nurtured.[208] What is at risk of being lost is the identity and self-consciousness of an individual or of a community. For this reason, the conservative disposition is 'averse from change'.[209] Change, Oakeshott argues, represents a 'threat to identity, and every change is an emblem

---

[206] *RP*: 410.

[207] *RP*: 407.

[208] *RP*: 408.

[209] *RP*: 409.

of extinction'.[210] Change, then, is something which must be suffered and a person of conservative disposition, understood as 'one strongly disposed to preserve his identity', cannot be indifferent to it.[211] However, to be conservative is not merely to be averse from change. Conservatism also implies a manner of accommodation to change. A political society must find a way to assimilate change without 'becoming unrecognizable' to itself, in other words, without corrupting its consciousness.[212]

The question, then, is how can a society guard its identity and sense of self-consciousness while still allowing for change and innovation? Put another way, how can change and permanence be tied together? Oakeshott argues that a community's identity is 'not a fortress into which we may retire'.[213] The only means of defending identity is by 'throwing our weight upon the foot which for the time being is most firmly placed, by cleaving to whatever familiarities are not immediately threatened and thus assimilating what is new without becoming unrecognizable to ourselves'.[214] Not all of the elements which compose a society's identity undergo change at once; thus, by 'cleaving' to those familiar elements, a society may assimilate change without suffering the corruption of its consciousness. Familiarity is closely linked to the idea that humans' primordial activity is building a world fit to live in, an idea which is central to Oakeshott's thought. Humans need to live in a world which has sense and meaning in order to know who they are and where they are in time and space.

Thus, change remains a threat to a society's identity, and, in so far as change is an integral part of political activity, politics constitutes a threat to identity and self-consciousness. As we have seen, a society's self-consciousness will be saved from corruption by 'knowing itself and having its values recreated'.[215] While Oakeshott acknowledges that a society's tradition of behaviour is 'a tricky thing to get to know', the difficulty in gaining knowledge of a political tradition in all its detail and all its intricateness is overcome by means of a legend.[216] [217] Hidden within the legend is its own understanding of its political experience.[218] A political legend, then, transmits knowledge of the tradition of

---

[210] *RP*: 410.
[211] *Ibid.*
[212] *Ibid.*
[213] *Ibid.*
[214] *Ibid.*
[215] *RPML*: 95.
[216] *RP*: 61.
[217] *RP*: 62.
[218] *RP*: 63.

behaviour. Consequently, a legend is a 'pre-eminent part of a political education'.[219] Poetry, by means of a legend or myth, endows a society with its self-consciousness and, by creating and recreating its values, guards against the corruption of its consciousness. The identity of a society is thereby at once preserved and augmented. Thus, Oakeshott's understanding of the conservative disposition is profoundly poetic.

Conclusion

Oakeshott's writings on legend and myth are sporadic; he never devotes himself to a systematic discussion or analysis of the subject. Whenever he introduces the subject, it is always within the context of discussions about one of the modes of experience or philosophy where myth and legend serve as a comparison or as a methodological technique in order to distinguish the modes and philosophy from what they are not. The purpose of my concluding remarks is to pull the various threads together to form a coherent understanding of Oakeshott's thought on legend and myth and its function as a contingent foundation for the political. Since Oakeshott does not offer a systematic treatment of the question, there are contradictions and confusions, in particular in regards to the relationship between poetry and practice, as is to be expected.

First, following Oakeshott's discussion of 'legenda', I posit that legends are fragments or objects which are alleged to have survived from the past. Although these fragments are purported to be survivals from the past, Oakeshott maintains that in actuality they are not survivals but objects which have merely survived and which are stored in the practical present. As such, artefacts which have survived are part of the present-future of practical engagement. Legends form a part of the present contents of an ever increasing deposit or storehouse into which are emptied the lives, utterances, achievements and sufferings of mankind.[220] Consequently, legends belong to the practical present. Moreover, the survived fragments and artefacts may be actual or imaginary and may, therefore, be products of the poetic imagination. However, the provenance of survived fragments, whether in the past or present or whether they be actual or imaginary, is not what is of importance. What is of importance is the function they serve in relation to the practical present, that is, in what they may be made to mean for society. Legends are recalled to mind in a process of recollection from where they lie in the present in order to stabilize the present-future of practical engagement. The practical present is a mysterious, menacing,

---

[219] *Ibid.*
[220] *OH:* 43.

puzzling and intractable world. The process of recollection joins a problematic present with a known and unproblematic past, such as it is portrayed in a legend, in order to compose a less puzzling and more manageable present.[221] In other words, legends stabilize the present for humans by making sense of the world and informing them of their place in it. What is more, by means of the messages they deliver, the lessons they teach, the authority and confidence they give through the stories they tell of past events, actions, performative utterances, ideas, thoughts and beliefs, legends endow persons and associations of persons with a sense of identity, self-consciousness and self-understanding.[222] Thus, the legendary past is a past 'constituted in interested recollection'.[223] A legend is remembered and not contemplated.

The fragments of the past which are recalled in order to stabilize the practical present, among them legend and myth, are not products of the past nor history since they are not really past at all. They are only alleged to be from the past and this identity is constructed into them. The recalled survived fragments, or legend and myth, are poetic constructions. However, poetical activity here is not poetry understood as a 'brief enchantment', rather, it is poetry engaged with practice. A legend is a work of art which has to be created, learned, cared for and cultivated.[224] Therefore, poetry constructs the 'epic story' to which an association of individuals identifies itself. It is important to remember, however, that poetry, when legend-making, is engaged with practice and, consequently, not acting alone. Although he appears to contradict himself in the essay 'Present, Future and Past' when he first asserts that legends are the creations of the poetical imagination and then goes on to claim that they are the products of the practical imagination, this is not in fact the case.[225] Legend and the past it evokes are imagined and they are imagined by the poetical and practical imaginations. This accounts for the symbolic images that compose legends and myths. It also confirms the ambiguity of poetry's relationship to practice as well as my position that legend and myth are a mixture of the two modes. Poetry is profoundly engaged with practice since one of its principle functions is the radical guarding of society. Only poetry is able to reach the deepest strata of social thought and, by acting upon it, create the values of a society, such as freedom, by means of a legend or myth. The creation of poetry, a legend or myth, provides an association of persons

---

[221] *OH*: 18.
[222] *WH*: 345–372.
[223] *WH*: 347.
[224] *Ibid.*
[225] *OH*: 18, 48.

with knowledge of itself, that is, its self-consciousness and identity. By perpetually reminding a society of its myth of civilization or legend of politics, poetry is able to guard against the corruption of its conscious-ness. Yet poetry not only creates the values of a society and guards against the corruption of its consciousness; it also recreates its values, thus ensuring that they do not become moribund. Oakeshott confirms this when he argues that the myth of modern English politics is per-petually in a process of revision, enlargement and augmentation.[226] Moreover, as the example of Rome shows, poetry, by constructing a legend, is responsible for a society's intellectual organization. Poetry guards the Roman manner of governing by endowing it with universal significance and by ensuring that its legend contains and transmits an explicit moral. Roman society is thus protected against the corruption of its consciousness.

The intellectual organization as well as the creation and recreation of the values of a society imply reflection upon the political. In the earlier discussion on the modes of experience, I agreed with Greenleaf that, from 'The Voice of Poetry in the Conversation of Mankind' onwards, Oakeshott conceives of imagining as a form of thought. Con-sequently, legend and myth, which are the products of poetical and practical imagining, constitute a kind of reflection upon politics. Oakeshott's theory of modes excludes the possibility that the kind of reflection poetry and practice engage in is philosophical. Poetry and practice are autonomous modes of activity and philosophy has the responsibility of accounting for them and determining their characters. In regards to political activity, political philosophy is concerned with understanding the place of politics on the map of human activity and this is clearly not the kind of reflection legend and myth are engaged in. For these reasons, it is my position that the kind of reflection involved in legend and myth is what Oakeshott specifies as explana-tory and foundational reflection upon politics. The concern of legend and myth is to determine and establish the identity of a political society by fixing limits, setting up landmarks and laying out anchorages beyond which reflection will not move. In this sense, reflection here is knowledge of a familiar political world and, as is demonstrated by the fact that poetry acts upon the deep stratum of social thought of a particular society, this kind of reflection always remains tied to the political experience from which it springs.

As for the structure and content of myth and legend, they are com-posed of symbolic images, that is, of symbolic persons, actions, utter-ances, situations, ideas and beliefs. They are prescriptive in that they

---

[226] *LHPT*: 46.

carry and transmit an explicit moral and message and, as such, serve as an authority for the political. This is how poetry is able to create and recreate the values of a society and guard it against the corruption of its consciousness. The purpose of recalling these fragments which have survived from the past is to endow a society with a sense of identity, its self-consciousness and self-understanding, thereby transforming the practical present from a menacing and intractable world into an unproblematic, intelligible and manageable one. In sum, legend and myth ensure that associations of persons understand the world and know their place in it.

Clearly, then, for Oakeshott, legend and myth are an 'indispensable ingredient of an articulate civilized life'.[227] Therefore, we may conclude that they present an acceptable form of foundation for the political. Poetry constructs or creates representations of the past which stabilize the practical present. Although this approach to foundations has definite foundational elements, such as the guarding of a society against the corruption of its consciousness, it is also strongly contingent since poetry recreates the values of a society and, consequently, its political legend is perpetually enlarged and revised. Thus, it is my position that Oakeshott contingently and aesthetically founds the political.

---

[227] *OH*: 48.

Chapter Five

Legends of Political Life: Ancient Rome and Modern England

Introduction

'No people of modern times has exceeded the Romans in their self-consciousness'.[1] This quotation reveals Oakeshott's great admiration for the ancient Romans and confirms David Boucher's assertion that 'there can be no doubt that Oakeshott admired the Roman political experience above all others in European history'.[2] Oakeshott's high regard for the Romans cannot be clearer when he declares that 'it is hardly an exaggeration to say that the Romans are the only people to show a genuine genius for government and politics'.[3] The Romans, Oakeshott explains, identified human genius with man's 'procreative spirit' as well as with the 'human ability to act'.[4] Consequently, when referring to the Roman genius for politics, Oakeshott means the Roman people's ability to act and create politically. Thus, we are not surprised to find that, for Oakeshott, it is the legend of Roman politics which 'constitutes the political self-consciousness of the Romans', for, according to him, it is just such an 'imaginative construction' which endows a political society with a heightened sense of self-consciousness.[5] In other words, no other people, before or since the Romans, has constructed a legend which surpasses the Roman political legend's capacity to endow a political society with a sense of identity and self-consciousness and, consequently, stability.

I want to suggest that the Roman legend of politics, which was generated by the Roman political experience, serves as a model and

---

[1]   *LHPT*: 178.
[2]   D. Boucher 2005a: 85.
[3]   *LHPT*: 176.
[4]   *LHPT*: 248.
[5]   *LHPT*: 177 and 176.

ideal for Oakeshott's concept of myth and legend which, I posit, functions as a contingent foundation for the political. To this end, I will present Oakeshott's interpretation of the legend of Roman politics and show how it incorporates the criteria I identified previously and which are indispensable to any political legend. That is, it is a poetic construction which evokes the practical past in order to stabilize a problematic present. In so doing, the Roman legend of politics engages in an explanatory and foundational kind of reflection upon the political. Following the exploration of the theoretical aspect of the Roman legend, I will focus on its content, that is, the story it tells of symbolic events and occurrences and their meanings. As we will see, the story centres on the foundation of Rome by Romulus understood by Romans as 'the most momentous "free act" in their history'.[6] That is, it represents the foundation of Roman freedom. I argue that the free act of foundation is best understood as a survived artefact recalled from the practical past in order to stabilize the present-future of Roman society. Oakeshott maintains that, for the Romans, to be rooted in this foundation 'was the first and supreme "freedom"'.[7] Their 'mission', Oakeshott contends, 'was to explore and elaborate it and spread it through the world'.[8] It is for this reason that the Romans developed an understanding of religion conceived of as being 'bound' to the original act of foundation and a conception of authority viewed as the preservation and augmentation of the foundation. The Roman legend, then, is the story of the foundation of Rome and of the freedom of the Roman people, the exploration of the intimations of that foundation as well as its preservation and augmentation such as it is represented by symbolic persons and events. I argue that the study of the Roman legend sheds new light on Oakeshott's conception of legend and myth and reveals an important theoretical element, that is, the idea that political societies perpetually return to their legends in order to explore their intimations, preserve their meanings and augment them. It is my position that the Roman legend, that is, an imaginative construction of poets which endows the Roman political experience with 'poetic universal significance', provides strong evidence that legends serve as a contingent foundation for the political.[9] The chapter's discussion of the legend of Roman politics will focus on Oakeshott's *Lectures in the History of Political Thought*, specifically lectures 11–15. As we will see throughout the discussion, Oakeshott's and Hannah Arendt's respective interpreta-

---

6   *LHPT*: 248.
7   *Ibid.*
8   *LHPT*: 249.
9   *LHPT*: 206.

tions of the Roman political experience of foundation share numerous similarities, and, notably, what Arendt identifies as the coincidence of authority, tradition and religion, all three of which, she claims, sprang from the act of foundation and formed the backbone of Roman history.[10]

In addition to suggesting that the Roman legend of political life serves as a model for Oakeshott's concept of myth and legend, I also want to propose that the Roman political experience shapes his conservatism. To this end, I argued in Chapter 4 that a society's self-consciousness and the threat of its corruption are central to Oakeshott's conception of the conservative disposition. In this respect, the conservative disposition aims to assimilate change without corrupting a society's identity. In order to do so, Oakeshott understands political activity as the pursuit of the intimations of a tradition of behaviour. I posit that this understanding of what it means to be conservative can be found in the Roman political experience where change was understood in terms of the augmentation and amplification of the original foundation, thereby keeping the Roman identity intact.

While no other people in European history has been able to construct a legend comparable to that of the Romans, modern political societies do, nevertheless, construct legends of political life which constitute their political self-consciousness. Oakeshott cites the modern English political legend as an example of modern political societies' ability and need to act and create politically. Following the discussion of the Roman legend, I will explore the modern English legend of political life in order to show that these imaginative constructions are thoroughly modern and that political modernity cannot do without imagination and a constructed political imaginary. The discussion of the modern English legend also underscores the foundational nature of these poetic constructs.

In the final section of the chapter, I show that Oakeshott's own thought is deeply poetic. Since he defends a conservative view of the political, I posit that at times he must do so poetically. As the collection of essays which comprise *Rationalism in Politics* makes clear, Oakeshott is profoundly concerned about the fate of modern Europe's self-consciousness which he believes to be threatened with corruption by Rationalism. For this reason, I argue that the essay 'Rationalism in Politics' is best understood, not as a work of philosophy, but as a work of poetry, a poetic attempt to save Western civilization's identity and self-consciousness.

---

10   H. Arendt 1963: 202.

The Roman Legend of Political Life

As both David Boucher and Luke O'Sullivan point out, Oakeshott greatly admires the genius the ancient Romans showed for politics.[11] What he particularly admires of the Roman political experience was its ability to generate a legend which endowed Roman political society with a heightened self-consciousness, which, he claims, has never been exceeded in modernity.[12] No other people in European history, either before or since the Romans, has constructed a legend of its politics which surpasses the Roman legend in its ability to endow a political society with self-consciousness. In other words, the ancient Romans, Oakeshott contends, were the first people to create a viable political legend. While Oakeshott states that perhaps 'not even the most primitive tribe is without some traces of self-consciousness', it is something which, he believes, has grown very slowly.[13] To this end, he asserts that out of the million years of human existence, 997,000 of them were spent in relative or absolute communal unconsciousness.[14] He maintains that Egypt and Mesopotamia only ever showed the smallest signs of it. It is only in the fifth century B.C. that it appeared in a highly developed form in Greece. Although the Greeks were undeniably a people awakened to political self-consciousness; nevertheless, Oakeshott argues that the legend of political life they created to represent their own awareness of their politics did not match the Roman legend.[15] For Oakeshott, while the legend the Greeks constructed of their political fortunes was one of the most notable achievements of their political thought, it was, however, 'remarkably thin and unelaborate'.[16] This is due to the fact that the Greeks gave 'remarkably little thought to their past' and were unimpressed by precedent.[17] Oakeshott contends that 'they rarely looked to the past for the authority for current conduct. They never thought of themselves [...] as borne along on a stream of

---

11   Both David Boucher (2005a) and Luke O'Sullivan (2000 and 2003) have written about Oakeshott's interpretation of the Roman political experience and Roman political thought. O'Sullivan does so in the context of his discussion of Oakeshott's views on European political history, while Boucher refers to the Romans to contend that Oakeshott 'belongs to the Roman form of republicanism, exemplified by Cicero, in which freedom is equated with the rule of law' (Boucher 2005a: 81). Neither treats the question of the Roman political imagination which is the concern of the present chapter.

12   *LHPT*: 176–178.

13   *WH*: 150.

14   *Ibid.*

15   *LHPT*: 45–46.

16   *LHPT*: 46.

17   *Ibid.*

events which flowed towards a better condition of things'.[18] The reason the Greeks did not seek for the authority for current political conduct in the past is because their experience did not lead them to the conclusion that political change is progressive and has a direction. On the contrary, the Greek political experience was one of 'frequent, often revolutionary, change'.[19] Consequently, their experience of perpetual change led to the belief that every political community must endure an 'endless cycle of constitutional change'.[20] This core belief was interpreted imaginatively and, subsequently, reflected symbolically in the Greek legend of politics in the idea that political forms and beliefs are essentially unstable.[21] The principle difficulty, then, with the Greek legend of politics is that it fails to recognize the past. Since the Greek legend does not look to the past for the authority for current political conduct, I contend that it does not respect a criterion indispensable to all political legends and which I identified in the second chapter; that is, it does not recall a survived artefact from the practical past in order to stabilize the problematic present-future. In other words, the Greek legend does not have recourse to the practical past in order to provide authority and stability. Thus, the Greek political experience was in fact profoundly unstable and prone to frequent change. Oakeshott concludes that Greek politics was the politics of perpetual revolution and, therefore, the product of an 'all too lively political imagination'.[22]

For Oakeshott, the Roman legend of politics is an advancement over the Greek legend. The principle difference with the Greeks is that the Romans recognized the function the practical past serves in stabilizing current political conduct. As the discussion will show, while the Roman political experience did undergo considerable change over the course of its history, all change was bound back to a past artefact, the foundation of Rome and its freedom, thus lending Roman political life greater stability and continuity. However, before broaching the legend of Roman politics itself, it is important to understand how Oakeshott conceives of and theorizes it. Most significantly, the Roman legend, such as he understands it, respects the criteria I identified as being constitutive of a political legend. That is, it is a foundational kind of reflection upon politics, it is a poetic construction and, finally, as I asserted earlier, it looks to the practical past as the source of authority for current political conduct.

---

18 *Ibid.*
19 *LHPT*: 58.
20 *Ibid.*
21 *Ibid.*
22 *LHPT*: 177.

In his first of three lectures on the political experience of Ancient Rome entitled 'The Political Experience of the Ancient Romans (1)', Oakeshott reasserts the view he first establishes in 'Political Philosophy' that there are three levels of political thought. At its most practical level, political thought is concerned with deliberation about policy and about the institutions and instruments of government.[23] However, when political thought reaches a certain level of abstraction, Oakeshott claims that it may branch out into an 'imaginative construction of a legend of political life which endows the aspirations and fortunes of a political society with a heightened self-consciousness; or into a philosophical examination of the conditions of political life'.[24] The concept of a legend of political life which endows a society with a heightened self-consciousness corresponds to the kind of reflection upon the political which Oakeshott terms explanatory and qualifies as foundational. This kind of political thought remains tied to the political experience from which it emerges and establishes firm points of anchorage beyond which reflection cannot move. The Romans, Oakeshott claims, were not given to intellectual adventures. That is, they were not a philosophical people and, as a consequence, they appear to be a 'remarkably "unintellectual" people, whose thoughts never reached the level of their deeds. It is conceded that there were Roman poets; there were historians and lawyers; but we look in vain for a philosopher'.[25] However, Oakeshott stresses that their powers of thought should not be underestimated, for, while the Romans did not develop a philosophy of politics of the order of the Greeks, they did, nevertheless, have a 'remarkably firm and profound intellectual organization'.[26] That is, although the Roman political experience did not generate a philosophy of politics, it did generate a legend of political life which allowed the Romans to understand their political experience in the idiom of general ideas.[27] For Oakeshott, the central core of this intellectual organization of political ideas was 'the beliefs the Romans had about the sort of community they believed themselves to constitute'.[28] In short, the legend generated by the Roman political experience endowed Roman society with its self-consciousness.

The legend of Roman politics, Oakeshott states, appears in the writings of Livy, Tacitus, Polybius, Cicero and Virgil.[29] That is, it is the

---

23 *LHPT*: 176.
24 *Ibid.*
25 *LHPT*: 208.
26 *Ibid.*
27 *LHPT*: 206–207.
28 *LHPT*: 209.
29 *LHPT*: 177.

work of historians, poets and lawyers and not philosophers. For Oakeshott, it is these writers who endowed the Romans with political self-consciousness.[30] As I pointed out in the previous chapters, Oakeshott claims that the manner in which the Romans governed and were governed was never turned into a coherent system of abstract ideas.[31] Rather, Roman historians, poets and lawyers constructed a legend in which 'the events and the fortunes of this remarkable people was endowed with a universal significance by being made to compose a work of art—a drama, or a story, whose moral was always being made explicit in events'.[32] The Roman legend of politics, then, is an imaginative interpretation of the political experience of the Roman people in which 'actions and events acquired poetically universal significance'.[33] Clearly, for Oakeshott, a legend of political life is a poetic construction, that is, a work of art, more precisely a drama or a story, which endows fortunes, events and actions with poetically universal significance. The chief '*dramatis persona*' of the drama or story of Roman politics was the *populus Romanus*, the Roman people.[34] Oakeshott asserts that 'this legend is the story of a hero and the vicissitudes of his life in the world. The hero of this legend is the Roman people, the *populus Romanus*'.[35] The drama of Roman politics centres upon the Roman people and the beliefs they had about their beginnings, that is, the foundation of Rome and their freedom, and 'the interpretations they imposed upon their fortunes'.[36] As the discussion will show, the interpretation the Roman people imposed upon their fortunes was that every event, action and circumstance was the exploration, the preservation and the augmentation of the political foundation. This is the story the legend of Roman politics tells. Oakeshott underscores the idea that in this legend of political life everything that happened happened to the Roman people. To this end, Oakeshott argues that 'every actor who appeared upon the stage was recognized as a representative of the Roman people'.[37] In other words, the whole of the Roman political experience is a drama, or a story. All actions are those of actors who represent the Roman people and all events happen to them. This is very important. The dramatic, and hence poetic, character of the Roman political experience cannot be underestimated. Oakeshott writes that

---

[30] *LHPT*: 208.
[31] *Ibid.*
[32] *Ibid.*
[33] *LHPT*: 206.
[34] *LHPT*: 209.
[35] *LHPT*: 178.
[36] *LHPT*: 177.
[37] *LHPT*: 209.

the Romans '"saw" themselves, as an actor might "see" himself, play-ing a part on the stage; and they were fascinated in the part they under-stood themselves to be playing'.[38] It is the legend of Roman politics, understood as a work of art, that is, as a drama or a story, which endows the Roman people and their political experience with poetically universal significance.

The event at the core of the legend of Roman politics is the founda-tion of the city of Rome. For Oakeshott, in the Roman legend this 'was, and remained, the most momentous event' of Roman history.[39] Accord-ing to the legend, Rome, the *civitas Romana*, was founded by Romulus, the son of Mars and of a vestal virgin, a niece of a king of the Latin settlement of *Alba Longa*. The act of foundation is the origin of the *popu-lus Romanus*, the Roman people. The momentousness of the event, that is, the impact the legendary foundation had on the Roman psyche, is reflected in part in the fact that every subsequent event of Roman his-tory was dated from the year of the foundation. Traditionally, the foundation of Rome is said to have taken place in 753 B.C. The Romans called that year, the year of the foundation of the *civitas Romana*, or *anno urbis constitution*, year 1.[40] Thus, every event and action in Roman his-tory is directly tied to the act of foundation. Oakeshott stresses the importance of the original foundation, and therefore of past, for Roman political experience and thought when he asserts that 'the Romans might, at some period in their history, look forward, but they never failed to look back with wonder and pride to the foundation of their *civitas*'.[41] The magnitude of the importance of the story of the founda-tion of Rome by Romulus for Roman politics should not be under-estimated. Following Oakeshott's understanding of the practical past, I posit that the legend of the foundation of Rome is a survived artefact recalled from the past in order to stabilize the present-future of Roman politics. Moreover, every action and event as well as every thought con-cerning the political, which together compose the drama of Roman politics, are directly tied to or bound to the foundation. As the dis-cussion will show, the legend of Roman politics is the story of the foundation of Rome and of its preservation and augmentation.

The extent to which the legend of Roman politics structures Roman thought is made abundantly clear in the manner in which the Roman people thought about themselves. Oakeshott claims that in the expression '*populus Romanus*' can be found 'the notion of the Romans as

---

38   *LHPT*: 178.
39   *LHPT*: 181.
40   *LHPT*: 180–181, 225.
41   *LHPT*: 181.

composing a single family — both literally and metaphorically'.[42] The idea that the Roman people compose a single family is directly related to the foundation of Rome. A family is founded by an 'original progenitor', a father. Thus, in order to understand the Roman people as composing a single family required them to have a 'father', Oakeshott argues, more specifically, a 'founding father'. For him, the ancient Romans did indeed have a 'father figure' since they thought of Romulus, not only as the founder of the Roman *civitas*, but, just as significantly, as the 'original parent' or the 'father' of the Roman people.[43] Oakeshott contends that the Romans took this idea of the 'founding father' quite literally. He claims that '*Romulus parens*, the Romulus who was the first *pater patriae*, was a figure looked back upon even after centuries of Roman history'.[44] Here again, we find the idea of the ancient Romans looking back to their legendary past, in this case to Romulus, a symbol of the foundation of Rome as well as a representative of the Roman people themselves, in order to find a sense of who they are and how they came into the world. The idea of paternity, which allowed the Roman people to think of themselves as composing a family, was symbolically maintained throughout Roman history. To this end, Oakeshott argues that the supreme figures of Roman politics were thought of 'not merely as honorary "founders" or "refounders" of the Roman *civitas*, but as honorary progenitors of the *populus Romanus*'.[45] Consequently, the *populus Romanus* did not compose just a family, rather, they composed a 'perpetual family'.[46] In sum, then, Oakeshott posits that the concept of 'the family' was 'a compelling analogy by which to understand the *communitas* composed by the Roman people'.[47]

For Oakeshott, however, the analogy of the family was not the only manner in which the Roman people thought of themselves. While the word *familia* represented the 'poetic unity of the Roman people', he adds that the word *foedus* represented the 'practical operation of this unity'.[48] In other words, if the family is the poetic representation of how the Roman people think of themselves, *foedus*, that is, the idea of a contractual partnership, is the practical representation of their unity. Like the family, the idea of *foedus* also finds its symbolic origin in the original act of foundation. Oakeshott explains that the notion of the

---

42   *LHPT*: 209.
43   *Ibid.*
44   *LHPT*: 210.
45   *Ibid.*
46   *LHPT*: 211.
47   *LHPT*: 210.
48   *LHPT*: 212.

Roman political community, being based upon an agreement, was very ancient since it originates in the foundation and 'might be taken to represent the facts of the case about the founding of the city of Rome'.[49] What was symbolically founded by Romulus, then, was a partnership, and the character of this unity was represented by the idea of 'treaty' or 'alliance'.[50] That the Roman people thought of their political community as being based upon an agreement is undeniable, Oakeshott maintains, and is confirmed by the fact that on the two notable occasions in Roman history when the *communitas Romanorum* was disrupted 'unity was restored by the renewal of the "treaty" which was believed to be its foundation'.[51] For Oakeshott, the idea that the *populus Romanus* was founded upon and held together by a treaty had 'one supremely important entailment'.[52] Since the Roman political community was held together by a treaty, Oakeshott argues that the notion of *fides*, or 'keeping faith' in the observance of the terms of the treaty, 'was of unmistakable importance'.[53] Otherwise, the partnership would be dissolved. It is for this reason that *fides*, or keeping faith between partners, was 'a constantly operative idea in the conduct of Roman politics'.[54] The idea that the Roman political community was a contractual partnership held together by partners keeping faith in the observance of the terms of the treaty leads Oakeshott to claim that the Romans composed a 'civil association'.[55] Here, Oakeshott distinguishes between two polar opposite conceptions of association: civil association and purposive or enterprise association. The conceptualization of these two types of association is what he devotes himself to in *On Human Conduct*. For the purpose of my argument, I simply want to point out that Oakeshott contends that the Roman people think of themselves as composing a civil association and that he considers this form of association to constitute significant progress in relation to the Greek political experience. He claims that what united the Romans was '*not* engagement in a common enterprise, but respect for the *mos majorem*, ancient customs, and respect for the *law*. And this law was *not* thought of as the organization of an enterprise, but as the terms in which they kept faith with one another. And this is what I mean by civil association'.[56]

---

49   *Ibid.*
50   *Ibid.*
51   *Ibid.*
52   *Ibid.*
53   *Ibid.*
54   *Ibid.*
55   *Ibid.*
56   *Ibid.*, original emphasis.

Moreover, the partnership which constituted the *populus Romanus* was a 'sacred' partnership – a *communio sacrorum*, according to Oakeshott.[57] It was a partnership 'in the performance of sacred rites' relating to the foundation of Rome.[58] Oakeshott's view that the Roman people were held together by a sacred partnership related to the original foundation echoes Hannah Arendt's position regarding the 'sacredness of foundation' for the Romans.[59] Arendt maintains that the aura of sacredness of the Roman foundation derives from the fact that this unique event, this unrepeatable beginning, remains binding for future generations.[60] As we will see, Arendt, like Oakeshott, argues that the foundation of Rome was understood to be a religious event, and that its preservation was not only a political, but, importantly, a religious duty.[61] For Oakeshott, as well, the Roman understanding and practice of religion were intertwined and inseparable from the original foundation. In this sense, the Romans were a deeply religious people. Furthermore, it may be argued that their politics were profoundly marked by religion since, as we will see, the concepts of authority and freedom were also derived from the foundation and were characterized by the performance of sacred rites.

Just as he explains Arendt does, Oakeshott draws upon the popular meanings of words in order to understand how the Romans thought of authority, religion and freedom.[62] Oakeshott begins by determining the etymology of the words. He begins with the concept of religion. He explains that the Latin word *religio* was understood by the Roman historian Cicero to be connected with the verb *ligare* which means to 'tie' or to 'bind'.[63] Religion, consequently, signified 'the condition of being "bound" or "obliged", and the activities which belong to this condition'.[64] To be religious, then, meant to recognize and celebrate a sacred 'bond'.[65] For the Romans, Oakeshott asserts, this sacred bond was 'the obligation which tied a present generation to its forebears'.[66] As was discussed earlier, in Rome, the term 'forebears' referred to the ancestors of the family as well as to progenitors and founders of the larger family of the *populus Romanus*. Thus, religious activity centred at

---

57 *LHPT*: 213.
58 *Ibid.*
59 H. Arendt 1993: 120.
60 *Ibid.*: 121.
61 *Ibid.*
62 *WH*: 317.
63 *LHPT*: 214.
64 *Ibid.*
65 *Ibid.*
66 *LHPT*: 215.

once upon the family and upon the Roman *civitas* and its gods and ancestors.[67] *Religio*, then, stood for the obligations which 'bound' the Romans to their gods and ancestors.[68]

Politically, Oakeshott explains, *religio* meant to be bound to the foundation of Rome. This is also Arendt's understanding of the Roman word religion, which, she asserts, literally meant *re-ligare*, that is, to be tied back or obligated to the original foundation.[69] Oakeshott, for his part, writes that *religio* stood for a 'profound, pious and "binding" attachment to the great event in which the *populus Romanus* itself emerged, namely the foundation of the city of Rome and the Roman state by Romulus'.[70] It was the religious duty of the Roman people to preserve the original foundation, or, as Oakeshott puts it, to preserve 'what Romulus had founded'.[71] (It is important to note that throughout the discussion Oakeshott continually returns to Romulus and what he was 'reputed' to have done. Romulus is understood by Oakeshott to be 'an actor who appeared upon the stage', that is, in the drama of the legend of Roman politics, and, as such, was a representative of the Roman people.[72] In other words, by constantly referring to Romulus, the 'founding father' of the city of Rome, Oakeshott ceaselessly underscores the fact that it was a legend which endowed the Roman people with their self-consciousness and their identity.) The Romans were religiously bound to preserve the original foundation because there was only one Rome. In the Roman world there were no new independent foundations.[73] For this reason, it was 'the "destiny", the "mission" of the *populus Romanus* […] to make Rome immortal'.[74] It was all the more important to preserve the integrity of the beginning since the Roman people 'sought the authority for every enterprise in this original sacred foundation'.[75] The Romans, then, were bound to the event of foundation and the founding father Romulus in *pietas*, piety, and *fides*, fidelity.[76] Oakeshott's interpretation of Roman *pietas* recalls Arendt's who states that the idea of being 'tied back to the beginning of the ancestors in pious remembrance and conservation' corresponded to the

---

67   *Ibid.*
68   *LHPT*: 217.
69   H. Arendt 1993: 121.
70   *LHPT*: 217.
71   *Ibid.*
72   *LHPT*: 209.
73   *LHPT*: 218.
74   *Ibid.*
75   *Ibid.*
76   *Ibid.*

Roman concept of *pietas*.[77] In so far as religion, which for the Romans meant being bound to the foundation, was at the centre of their self-identity, Oakeshott asserts that the Romans were a deeply religious people. Moreover, since religion was so profoundly connected to the *civitas*, indeed its very purpose was its preservation, religion and politics were inseparable activities in Rome.[78] Oakeshott concludes that 'the Roman religion was the energy of Roman politics; and Roman politics was the reflection of Roman religion'.[79]

The Roman concept of authority, like religion, is also closely tied to the original act of foundation. Oakeshott asserts that the word *auctoritas*, authority, stood for the qualities which belonged to an *auctor*, an author.[80] An *auctor* was 'a man who originated something – an author, a creator, a founder, or a progenitor'.[81] Arendt also argues that the word *auctor*, when its root meant the same thing as the English word 'author', referred to the person who inspired an enterprise.[82] To be in authority, or to have *auctoritas*, then, meant to be the creator, or the cause, or the origin of something. Those who possessed *auctoritas* were inventive and showed initiative.[83] Oakeshott explains that both the words *auctor* and *auctoritas* derived etymologically from the verb *augere* which meant to 'increase', to 'enlarge', to 'augment' or 'to add luster to'.[84] Oakeshott is most interested in the concept as it relates to human activities, specifically politics. Again, his focus on the Roman legend of politics and its principal protagonist, Romulus, cannot be ignored. The founding father of Rome was Romulus and, as such, he was the creator or progenitor of the *populus Romanus*, the Roman people, as well as of the city of Rome. In other words, Romulus was the *auctor* and, consequently, was 'the possessor of a natural *auctoritas*'.[85] Romulus, as the founder of Rome and, thus, as its *auctor*, possessed political authority. Therefore, throughout Roman history, whoever was understood to have authority was thought to have derived it from Romulus and his original foundation.[86] That is, they were themselves understood to be an *auctor* and, as possessors of authority, it was their role to create, found and originate something. For Arendt also, the

77 H. Arendt 1963: 202.
78 *LHPT*: 218.
79 *Ibid.*
80 *LHPT*: 224.
81 *Ibid.*
82 H. Arendt 1993: 122.
83 *LHPT*: 224.
84 *LHPT*: 225.
85 *Ibid.*
86 *Ibid.*

authority of the living was always derivative and depended upon the authority of the founders.[87] More specifically, authority was maintained by means of tradition, by which the Romans understood 'the handing down, through an unbroken line of successors, of the principle established in the beginning'.[88] Thus, for authority to be inviolable tradition had to be uninterrupted.[89] For Oakeshott, since Rome had been founded and there could only be one Rome, that is, it was a unique, unrepeatable event, it fell to the Romans to 'increase', to 'enlarge', to 'augment' or to 'add luster to' Romulus's original foundation.[90] Thus, authority in the living always derived from the original *auctor*, Romulus, the founder of Rome.[91] Arendt also traces back the origin of the word *auctoritas* to the verb *augere*.[92] For her, what Roman authority augmented was the foundation laid down by the ancestors.[93] That is, the Roman concept of authority tied permanence and change together.[94] In this sense, Arendt speaks of 'the miracle of permanence' in that because change could only mean the increase and enlargement of the old, Roman political structures were endowed with durability and continuity.[95] Thus, to be in authority meant to conserve and augment. Arendt insists that this understanding of authority was one of the most important contributions the Roman political experience made to Western thought.[96] To put it in Oakeshottian terms, authority derives from a recalled artefact which stabilizes the present-future of society. The foundation of Rome by Romulus is an imaginary construct where Romulus represents the Roman people. Since to be in authority meant to be an *auctor*, that is, an author or a creator, the activity of every subsequent *auctor*, then, was to increase or augment the legend of Roman politics.

As for the nature of the relationship of *auctoritas* to *res publica* and the *populus Romanus*, Oakeshott argues that it was a tutorial relationship. To be an *auctor* and to exercise *auctoritas* was 'to advise, to give guidance, and to educate'.[97] More precisely, in relation to *res publica*, those who were recognized to have *auctoritas* were expected to provide

---

87   H. Arendt 1993: 122.
88   H. Arendt 1963: 202.
89   H. Arendt 1993: 124.
90   *LHPT*: 225.
91   *Ibid.*
92   H. Arendt 1993: 121–122; 1963: 202.
93   H. Arendt 1993: 122; 1963: 202.
94   H. Arendt 1963: 202.
95   H. Arendt 1963: 202; 1993: 127.
96   H. Arendt 1963: 202.
97   *LHPT*: 226.

reflective advice and initiative in policy-making. This kind of advice and reflection could only be offered by men who were 'steeped in the *traditio* which joined the present generation to its roots in the original foundation'.⁹⁸ *Auctoritas*, as the Romans understood it, was a spring of political initiative, according to Oakeshott. Thus understood, authority was clearly distinguished from *potestas*, power. Oakeshott explains that *auctoritas* 'was, precisely, *not* to have power [...] it was to be a teacher, not a commander'.⁹⁹ Consequently, a state without *auctoritas* would still retain an apparatus of power, Oakeshott maintains. However, it would be devoid of a sense of direction since it would be 'cut off from the "tradition" which flowed from its "foundation"'.¹⁰⁰ In the case of Rome and of the Roman people, the loss of *auctoritas* would have meant the loss of what it meant to be Roman. That is, it would have meant the loss of Roman identity and self-consciousness since for there to be no contemporary representative of *auctoritas* would have been recognized as a break with the original foundation which would be 'the equivalent of the destruction of everything that belonged to *res Romana*'.¹⁰¹

As for who possessed *auctoritas*, Oakeshott returns to the legend of the foundation of Rome in order to ascertain the answer. For the Romans, whoever had *auctoritas* acquired it through an historical connection he had with Romulus, who was the original *auctor* of the Roman *civitas*.¹⁰² The nature of this connection is 'notional-historical', as Oakeshott puts it.¹⁰³ By this, we can conclude that he means legendary since, in order to explain the notional-historical connection in question, he relates the story of how Romulus was reputed to have chosen 'a hundred of the heads of the most distinguished families of early Rome to be his counselors, and this was the reputed origin of the senate'.¹⁰⁴ It was the senate which, during the republic, was the 'preeminent possessor of *auctoritas*'.¹⁰⁵ As such, it was the right of the senate to give advice and initiate policy-making. Moreover, given its structure and composition, the senate never died and was perpetually in session; hence, *auctoritas* was perpetually available to the Romans.¹⁰⁶ Consequently, if we understand the attribution of *auctoritas* to the senate according to how Oakeshott theorizes the function of legend in relation

---

⁹⁸ *Ibid.*
⁹⁹ *Ibid.*, original emphasis.
¹⁰⁰ *Ibid.*
¹⁰¹ *Ibid.*
¹⁰² *Ibid.*
¹⁰³ *LHPT*: 227.
¹⁰⁴ *Ibid.*
¹⁰⁵ *Ibid.*
¹⁰⁶ *Ibid.*

to the political, it is an imaginary construct, specifically, the legend of Roman politics, which endows the senate with *auctoritas*. The Romans, then, translated what they believed to be an indispensable feature of political activity, that is, the necessity for reflection about the conduct of public affairs, into the idiom of a general idea.[107] However, the necessity for reflection about the conduct of public affairs was not transformed into an abstract ideal or a doctrine. Rather, it was translated into a legend.

Oakeshott understands Roman politics to be 'the exploration of the intimations of an original foundation'.[108] This exploration, Oakeshott argues, required 'an understood and an unbroken connection with that foundation and its *auctor*'.[109] It was *auctoritas* which ensured the connection between the present of Roman politics and the original foundation and its *auctoritas*. Those in possession of *auctoritas*, the senate during the republic and the *princeps* under the empire, were recognized to be the custodian of the *mos maiores* of the Roman people, that is, of 'the ancient customs of the original foundation to which the *populus Romanus* belongs'.[110] In Rome, political decisions, change and policy had to be congruent with the *mos maiores*. Therefore, as the custodian of the *mos maiores*, the bearer of *auctoritas* was the guardian of 'the unchanging standards of conduct which should guide political activity', hence, their role as adviser, teacher, guide and counsellor.[111] However, those who had *auctoritas* did not merely provide counsel in regards to political activity. More important for Oakeshott was the insight they provided into the '*fortuna*, the destiny and the traditions of the Roman people'.[112]

The word *auctor* was not only connected with the concept of *auctoritas* in Roman political thought; Oakeshott asserts that it was also connected with the Roman understanding of freedom or *libertas*. This was an important word in the Roman political vocabulary. Oakeshott explains that for the early Romans the concept of freedom was understood as the characteristic of a man's *genius*. *Genius* was identified by the Romans as a man's immortal part and they also regarded it as his procreative spirit.[113] *Libertas*, Oakeshott claims, was 'a condition in which a man's *genius* could fulfil itself and demonstrate its immor-

---

[107] *LHPT*: 228.
[108] *Ibid*.
[109] *LHPT*: 228–229.
[110] *LHPT*: 229.
[111] *Ibid*.
[112] *Ibid*.
[113] *LHPT*: 248.

tality'.[114] Consequently, freedom was the defining characteristic of an *auctor*, that is, of the creator, founder, progenitor or author. Freedom was connected with the human ability to act and this was also recognized by the Romans as the work of the human *genius*.[115] In Rome, history was understood to be composed of the *res gestae*, that is, the 'things done' by humans which 'demonstrated their freedom to act, their capacity to be an *auctor*'.[116] Politically, the idea of *libertas* was the recognition that Rome began in a free act.[117] That is, Romulus, the ultimate *auctor*, demonstrated his freedom to act and his *genius* completely fulfilled itself and demonstrated its immortality in the act of founding Rome. Oakeshott argues that this idea was of fundamental importance to the Romans and that all other ideas about freedom were tied to and found their meaning in the original foundation. He writes that:

> the fundamental beliefs of the Romans, the belief to which all other beliefs about freedom were connected, was that the foundation of the city of Rome represented the most momentous 'free act' in their history.[118]

Freedom, then, like religion, authority and tradition was tied to the foundation of the city of Rome. As Oakeshott points out, 'from almost every point of view, Roman political thought began *ad urbe condita*, from the foundation of the city'.[119] In regards to freedom, the act of foundation was the original act of freedom. For the Romans, Oakeshott asserts, to be rooted in the foundation of Rome was 'the first and supreme "freedom"'.[120] It was their profound belief that it was their mission to explore and elaborate that freedom, that is, the original act of foundation.[121] Therefore, the Roman concept of *libertas* fits in with and completes the broader understanding of politics. Just as it was their political mission to explore the intimations of the original foundation, likewise the Romans had as their mission the exploration of the most momentous free act: the first and supreme freedom. *Libertas* is also intimately related to *auctoritas*. Both concepts are related to the word *auctor* and both aim to augment the original act of freedom, the foundation of Rome by Romulus. For Oakeshott, '*auctoritas* indicated the path you must, as a Roman, tread; and *libertas* was to walk in that path'.[122]

---

[114] *Ibid.*, original emphasis.
[115] *Ibid.*
[116] *Ibid.*
[117] *Ibid.*
[118] *Ibid.*
[119] *Ibid.*
[120] *Ibid.*
[121] *LHPT*: 249.
[122] *Ibid.*

Freedom for the Romans was an inheritance and that inheritance was the outcome of 'an act of freedom, an act of the free, "generative" spirit, the *genius* of Romulus'.[123] Arendt concurs with Oakeshott that the Roman concept of freedom springs from the act of foundation. She claims that freedom for the Romans was 'an accessory of doing and acting'.[124] For the Romans, Arendt argues, action occurred when something new came into the world.[125] It follows, then, that the beginning of Roman history 'contained the authentic element of Roman freedom'.[126] Moreover, in order for freedom to be sustained it also meant that the permanence of the foundation had to be ensured by augmenting it.[127] In sum, for Arendt, the foundation of the city was the guaranty of Roman freedom.[128]

Like Arendt, Oakeshott believes in 'the human capacity for building, preserving, and caring for a world that can survive us and remain a place fit to live in for those who come after us'.[129] Oakeshott perceives the need for stabilizing constructs. His focus is primarily on the human capacity to build. How do we successfully build or rebuild a world fit for living? Oakeshott turns to the Romans, the 'master builders' and their remarkable construct, the Roman legend of political life, as a model and source of inspiration. As the discussion will show, the Roman political experience shows how a well-crafted legend, a poetic construct, endows a society with a sense of identity and self-consciousness, guards its identity and saves it from the corruption of its consciousness by combining it with preservation and augmentation. That is, Roman identity and self-consciousness are preserved and augmented, and not corrupted by change. Therefore, Oakeshott is in agreement with Arendt as to the importance of the Roman notion of preservation and augmentation for the modern ability to build stable constructs for the political.

Oakeshott has recourse to Roman political thought and experience in order to conceptualize legends of political life. He finds in the Roman narrative the first coherent and successful example of a legend of politics which endows a political community with a heightened sense of self-consciousness. In other words, the legend of Roman politics was the first to serve as a contingent foundation for the political. This legend, more precisely Oakeshott's interpretation of it, fulfils

---

[123] *Ibid.*, original emphasis.
[124] H. Arendt 1993: 165.
[125] *Ibid.*: 166.
[126] *Ibid.*
[127] *Ibid.*
[128] *Ibid.*
[129] *Ibid.*: 95.

the criteria identified as being indispensable to a political legend. First, it allowed the Romans to translate their political experience into the idiom of general ideas. While this kind of reflection upon the political is not philosophical, it does nevertheless allow for a certain level of abstraction. However, reflection at this level is not subversive since its limits are clearly defined. That is, it never moves beyond fixed points of anchorage. For this reason, it may be qualified of foundational. Secondly, the legend of Roman politics is a poetic construction. As Oakeshott points out, it was the creation of writers, specifically of Roman historians, poets and lawyers. Thirdly, the legend of Roman politics recalls a survived artefact from the practical past in order to stabilize a problematic present. In so doing, it looked to the past as a source of authority for current political conduct. The Roman legend of politics, then, was an imaginative construction of poets which endowed the Roman political experience with poetic universal significance.[130]

At the core of the legend of Roman politics is the foundation of Rome by Romulus, the most momentous 'free act' in Roman history and the ultimate instance of human *genius*. The legend about the beginning of Rome was constructed long after its foundation.[131] It is in this sense that it is an artefact recalled from the practical past. The legendary foundation of Rome by Romulus was recalled to mind in order to stabilize the problematic present of Roman politics and found the society's identity. It provides stability by virtue of the fact that it is the source of political authority and freedom and it is preserved by means of tradition and religion. The foundation of Rome by Romulus serves as the starting point for the legend of Roman politics. From this foundation flows the narrative of the political drama of Rome. The protagonist of the drama was the Roman people and every actor who appeared on the stage represented them. Furthermore, everything that happened, every action and every event, happened to the Roman people.[132] Oakeshott underscores how, throughout their history, the Romans never failed to return to the original foundation as a source of authority, but also to ensure that the unique, unrepeatable event was perpetually and unfailingly recalled to mind, or to the consciousness, of the Roman people. This was reflected in their political mission which was to care for, preserve and augment the foundation or 'free act', that is, a recalled artefact and the legend of political life it generated, by exploring its intimations. The idea that the foundation of Rome is to be preserved and augmented by means of the exploration of its intima-

---

[130] *LHPT*: 206.
[131] *LHPT*: 180.
[132] *LHPT*: 209.

tions puts an 'Oakeshottian' gloss on Roman politics. In his essay 'Political Education', Oakeshott explains that the expression 'the pursuit of intimations', which he introduces there, is meant as a description of what political activity actually is.[133] The expression summarizes Oakeshott's conception of politics. He argues that politics is the activity of attending to the arrangements, or rules, which govern an association of individuals.[134] Such an understanding of politics presupposes traditions of behaviour and enjoyed arrangements which intimate change. Without these two elements, politics would be impossible since it springs from the existing traditions of behaviour.[135] The form it takes, Oakeshott claims, is 'the amendment of existing arrangements by exploring and pursuing what is intimated in them'.[136] The arrangements which constitute a society intimate change since they are at once coherent and incoherent. In their coherence and incoherence, these arrangements compose a pattern and 'intimate a sympathy for what does not fully appear'.[137] Political activity, Oakeshott maintains, is 'the exploration of that sympathy'.[138] Relevant political reasoning, then, is the 'convincing exposure of a sympathy, present but not yet followed up, and the convincing demonstration that now is the appropriate moment for recognizing it'.[139] A tradition of behaviour, therefore, is preserved but also augmented by means of the exploration of its intimations. Thus, exploring the intimations of a tradition of behaviour is the manner in which change takes place in political societies.[140] This, Oakeshott contends, is precisely how the Romans understood political activity. Political change in Rome had to be congruent with the *mos maiores*, that is, with the ancient customs of the original foundation to which the Roman people belonged.[141] The pursuit of intimations in Rome takes the shape of a poetic construct. What is preserved and augmented is the legend of the foundation of Rome and, consequently, Roman political identity. It is historians, poets and lawyers who create the narrative of the Roman drama, a narrative which unfailingly refers to the original foundation and which is therefore bound to it. The legend of Roman politics endows the Roman people with self-consciousness and reflects their common ways of thinking. In sum, it

---

133 *RP*: 66.
134 *RP*: 56.
135 *Ibid.*
136 *Ibid.*
137 *RP*: 57.
138 *Ibid.*
139 *Ibid.*
140 *RP*: 68.
141 *LHPT*: 229.

serves as a contingent foundation for Roman society and politics since in it permanence and change are tied together.

Oakeshott's Conservatism:
The Influence of the Roman Political Experience

Given his admiration for the Romans, it should come as no surprise that we should find Oakeshott's conservative disposition in the Roman political experience. Oakeshott's interpretation of Roman political experience and thought underscores the importance of identity and self-consciousness for the Romans. The Romans, like Oakeshott, were concerned with identity and how to assimilate change without corrupting society's consciousness. The Romans, through their political experience, developed a practice of politics which ensured that Roman society could suffer change without it being detrimental to its identity. In this respect, they developed an understanding of political activity as the exploration of the intimations of the original foundation. Change was therefore intimated by the foundation itself, and, since it had to be congruent with the ancient customs of the foundation, change consequently made sense for the whole of the Roman tradition and was in no way arbitrary. But more importantly, because politics inevitably corrupts a society's consciousness, the Romans had recourse to a recalled artefact, that is, the legend of the foundation of Rome, in order to stabilize and guard Roman identity. They did so by binding every change to the legend of Roman politics. It is this legend which constitutes Roman political self-consciousness.[142] Arguably, then, the idea of augmentation could be taken to mean the creation and recreation of the values of Roman society by its poets, historians and lawyers with the intent of guarding the society against the corruption of its consciousness. Therefore, identity and self-consciousness, the exploration of intimations, congruence with ancient custom and poetry, the elements which define Oakeshott's conservative disposition, are all central to Roman political thought.

The Modern English Legend of Political Life

Legends of political life not only serve as contingent foundations for a society such as Ancient Rome, but for all political societies, including modern ones. In this sense, it is important to keep in mind Oakeshott's position that 'every people awakened to political self-consciousness constructs a myth'.[143] In this respect, I take a different view from Terry Nardin and Luke O'sullivan who maintain that:

---

[142] *LHPT*: 177.
[143] *LHPT*: 46.

in the modern world, as Oakeshott's theory of modality implicitly recognizes, an irreducible plurality of viewpoints is the norm, but this plurality precludes the shared background he believed the Roman and Christian social myths had provided in ancient and medieval times. Hence, the possibility of maintaining the practical analogue of civil association, that is, government through the rule of law, is also adversely affected insofar as this depends on the existence of such a shared background.[144]

The English, therefore, like all peoples possessed of communal self-consciousness, have constructed a legend of their political fortunes, Oakeshott argues.[145] Oakeshott contends that 'the myth of modern English politics [...] began to be constructed in the seventeenth century'.[146] The myth, he asserts, is 'something to which our current political arguments and attitudes are always returning, and which is always in a process of enlargement and revision'.[147] In other words, current political conduct is bound or tied to the myth of English politics. Change, political decisions and legislation must be congruent with the myth which is itself thereby preserved and augmented. Although Oakeshott never explicitly details what these fortunes may be, I posit that poetry constructs a legend or myth which recounts the story of English freedom. The legend awakens the English people to its political inheritance and guards its tradition of freedom by means of its message, that is, that English freedom depends upon the maintenance of rights and procedures for redress.

The survived artefact which is recalled to mind in order to stabilize the present of English political life is, arguably, Magna Carta. This means that all political change within the context of the English tradition of political life must be tied back to the legal charter. In his review of J.C. Holt's *Magna Charta* (1965), Oakeshott once again distinguishes between the historical and the practical understandings of the past. Just as he argues that poetry emancipates itself with great difficulty from practice, he makes the same argument for history. In this regard, Oakeshott specifies that the historical understanding of Magna Carta, like that of nearly every important event or occasion, 'emerged gradually out of the quite different enterprise of assigning it a significant place in the legend of English life'.[148] Oakeshott asserts that the creation of a legendary understanding of past events is indispensable in order to ensure the ties that bind members of a political society

---

144 T. Nardin and L. O'Sullivan 2006: 16.
145 *LHPT*: 46.
146 *Ibid*.
147 *Ibid*.
148 *VMES*: 194.

to one another. In this regard, Oakeshott states that the 'enterprise of constructing and confirming a social identity and consciousness by establishing a significant relationship between present moods and past events is a perennial practical necessity'.[149] This enterprise is not only practical in nature, but also political, following Oakeshott.[150] In respect of Magna Carta, Oakeshott claims that this legend-making enterprise has been pursued since the fourteenth century.[151] Oakeshott, therefore, postulates that Magna Carta forms an integral part of the English legend of political life.

Briefly, the legendary story of Magna Carta relates the tense and difficult relations between King John and the barons of England, the principal actors of the drama. Oakeshott asserts that in the context of the legend-making enterprise, the baronial opponents of King John were cast in the 'legendary role of champions of liberty'.[152] Among the episodes which compose the drama is the episode when the King was at the temple in London in January 1215 when the barons arrived armed and demanded 'the grant of a charter confirming the ancient "liberties" of the realm'.[153] Later on that year, when the barons were encamped at Staines and the King at Windsor Castle, they agreed to meet 'half way' at Runnymede on 15 June 1215 and King John made 'a formal grant of the "liberties" which he had conceded'.[154] This formal grant of liberties was Magna Carta of which copies were made for distribution throughout England.[155] As concerns the Charter, Oakeshott makes what appears to be an unusual statement when he claims that 'as a storehouse of emblems of just procedure [Magna Carta] has long been credited with almost magical authority'.[156] However, Oakeshott's claim is perfectly logical in the context of the legend-making enterprise. In this sense, it is Magna Carta's quasi-magical authority which makes it the ideal survived artefact to recall from the practical past in order to form the basis of the modern English legend of political life.

Although Oakeshott notes that 'some English writers in the seventeenth century attributed to Magna Carta or to an imaginary Ancient Constitution the character of a Fundamental Law', it is important to remember, however, that for him, Magna Carta's foundational role is

---

149 *Ibid.*
150 *Ibid.*
151 *Ibid.*
152 *Ibid.*
153 D.I. Stroud 1998: 3.
154 *Ibid.*: 4.
155 *Ibid.*
156 *OH*: 46.

not to be understood in Edenic terms.[157] In this sense, in the essay 'Power and Freedom', Oakeshott argues that Magna Carta is a charter of liberties and, as such, is a record of liberties which are already enjoyed.[158] He is adamant that it is not a bill of rights, the content of which begins with an abstract idea of freedom and ends with a list of freedoms and devices for securing these freedoms. Put another way, the exercise of freedom is not first experienced and then recorded as it is with a charter like Magna Carta. Rather, Oakeshott claims, the exercise of freedom which ends with a bill of rights proceeds from 'principles laid down in constitutional documents'.[159] Once these rights are recognized and enforced, freedom is then injected into a political practice which had previously been characterized by the exercise and submission to power.[160] In sum, the exercise of freedom which culminates in a bill of rights begins with an abstract idea of freedom and not with actual experience of freedom. For Oakeshott, then, a bill of rights is a statement of rights and freedoms which demands to be authorized by the established powers.[161]

Magna Carta, as opposed to a bill of rights, is not 'a bright idea' as Oakeshott puts it in 'Political Education'.[162] He maintains that it does not constitute an abstract ideal of freedom which serves as a foundational constitutional document as is the case with a bill of rights. While this may indeed be true, above and beyond whether Magna Carta is a record of already enjoyed liberties or is a list of abstract freedoms which need to be instituted, what is important is the function it serves in relation to the political as well as in relation to the English political imaginary and sense of self-consciousness. Oakeshott broaches the subject of the role Magna Carta plays in the *Lectures in the History of Political Thought* in the context of his discussion of Roman law. One of the most important episodes of the Roman legend of politics was when the ancient, customary and unwritten law of Rome was written down and published. In the history of Roman law, Oakeshott claims, this was the 'one great event which overshadowed all others'.[163] The demand was one of the earliest made by the *concilium plebis* who, according to Livy, wished that the law 'cease to be kept secret among the mysteries and sacraments of the immortal gods'.[164] The demand resulted in the

---

[157] *OH*: 170, note 12.
[158] *WH*: 240.
[159] *WH*: 239.
[160] *WH*: 238–239.
[161] *WH*: 238.
[162] *RP*: 54.
[163] *LHPT*: 242.
[164] *LHPT*: 243.

decemviri, a commission of ten patricians whose duty it was to reduce the law in order to write it down and publish it. What they produced was the 'famous' twelve tables of the Roman law which was 'engraved on panels of metal and set up in the forum. And it was for ever cherished as the fundamental, original, sacred law of the Romans'.[165] All subsequent laws and legislation, or *leges*, were thought of as 'additions to or amplifications of this fundamental law'.[166] Oakeshott's position is that Magna Carta is akin to the twelve tables of Roman law in that it also has been forever cherished by the English as their fundamental, original and sacred law. In this sense, Nardin and O'Sullivan, the editors of the *Lectures in the History of Political Thought*, point out that Oakeshott made a marginal note in the manuscript in relation to the sentence explaining how the Romans cherished the twelve tables of the Roman law stating 'Cp. Magna Carta'.[167] Finally, following the Roman example, all subsequent English laws and legislation are thought of as amplifications of Magna Carta.

Magna Carta, then, is the recalled artefact which stabilizes the problematic present of English politics and it is from this legal charter that the English legend flows. Although it is indeed possible to understand Magna Carta historically, Oakeshott reminds us that such an understanding emerged gradually and imperfectly from the conditions of the practical and political enterprise of legend-making.[168] He cites the 'retrospective modernism' of nineteenth-century historians in which the Charter appeared as 'the palladium of English liberty' as evidence of this.[169] Moreover, Oakeshott argues that once the task of historical understanding had been embraced, historians were at first peculiarly determined to detach Magna Carta from subsequent events and to 'interpret it severely in its thirteenth-century context'.[170] Oakeshott contends that the first version of the historical understanding of Magna Carta still contained relics of the legend-making enterprise. In this sense, the baronial opponents of King John were deposed from their legendary role of champions of liberty and merely cast for another role, 'that of self-seeking dissidents and the opponents of administrative efficiency'.[171] What the discussion reveals is that, similarly to poetry, history emancipates itself with difficulty from the authority of practice due to the profound human need to live in a world of sense and mean-

---

[165] *Ibid.*

[166] *Ibid.*

[167] *Ibid.*, note 2. Editorial note.

[168] *VMES*: 194.

[169] *Ibid.*

[170] *Ibid.*

[171] *Ibid.*

ing. In this regard, Magna Carta takes on a significant symbolic quality. This is reflected in the fact that two copies of the document are on permanent display at Salisbury and Lincoln cathedrals, thereby allowing the English people to worship their sacred law. Furthermore, sculptures and statues of the protagonists adorn cathedrals throughout England. These are elements of a legend in that they are symbolic images and not mere images and, as such, transmit a message regarding the meaning of freedom in England. The story of Magna Carta, a document which, according to the British Library, represents the 'corner-stone of liberty',[172] is therefore a poetic construct, a recalled artefact, from which springs the legend of English politics.

We find in the story of Magna Carta the idea which, I argue, for Oakeshott is at the core of the legend of English politics, that is, that English freedom depends upon the maintenance of rights and procedures for redress. It is the English parliament and the English judicial process which, Oakeshott maintains, ensure the maintenance of these rights, liberties and procedures. This is the idea which is preserved and augmented in the drama of English politics and which is tied back to Magna Carta. Put another way, parliament and the English judicial process are bound to Magna Carta. In this respect, Oakeshott notes that the assembly of tenants-in-chief (the barons of England) which met on the island of Runnymede to impose Magna Carta upon King John was called a parliament.[173] The right of vassals to extract from kings redress for the misgovernment of the realm forms part of one of the three strands from which the English parliament emerged, Oakeshott argues.[174] The other two strands are, firstly, the King's council (*curia regis*) in its capacity as a deliberative body giving advice and authoritative rulings to judges and administrators.[175] The second strand identified by Oakeshott is the work of the king's courts of justice which consisted of two related activities: first, to determine the law and, secondly, to hear complaints from people who had had duties forced upon them by their feudal superiors which they believed had no legal authority.[176] In sum, the chief business of the king's courts was 'to protect the otherwise unprotected from illegal exactions'.[177] However, for my present purpose, I will focus on the third strand from which,

---

[172] British Library, www.bl.uk/onlinegallery/themes/histtexts/magnacarta.html, accessed 26 March 2008.
[173] *LHPT*: 311.
[174] *LHPT*: 309–311.
[175] *LHPT*: 309.
[176] *LHPT*: 309–310.
[177] *LHPT*: 310.

Oakeshott posits, the English parliament emerged as this is what is symbolically represented in the story of Magna Carta.

The third strand, Oakeshott asserts, is less easily identifiable, but he believes that in some respects it is the most important.[178] The third strand reflected the duty of the king's vassals to give him *concilium*, on the one hand, but also the need of a feudal king to secure the good-will of his vassals, on the other.[179] The king did this by consulting his vassals on important matters of government and obtaining their approval.[180] In sum, vassals had both the right and the duty to deliberate with the ruler.[181] However, Oakeshott specifies that this component of a parliament had two sides to it.[182] First, Oakeshott explains that this component exhibits parliament as the 'common council of the realm' composed of the king's council reinforced by an assembly of the chief vassals of the king.[183] Secondly, Oakeshott understands the office of a feudal king to be the office of an overlord who '*must* govern according to the law and not infringe the rights of his subjects'.[184] In order to ensure this, Oakeshott claims that it is the place of his chief vassals to admonish the king and to extract from him 'a proper recognition of the promises made at his coronation' should he depart from the duties of his office.[185] This is the context of the story of Magna Carta. For Oakeshott, it is the most notable of the occasions on which the barons of England were obliged to take action of this sort by presenting a legal charter reaffirming feudal rights to King John and extracting his agreement.[186] In sum, parliament stood not only for the duty of vassals to give advice and support to kings, but also for the right of vassals to extract from kings redress for the misgovernment of the realm if it occurred.[187]

The story of Magna Carta, then, is the origin of the most important English political institution, the English parliament. In the Middle Ages, Oakeshott explains, the parliament was a periodic meeting of the English magnates which oversaw the activities of the King.[188] Progressively, over the course of the thirteenth and fourteenth centuries,

---

178 *Ibid.*
179 *Ibid.*
180 *LHPT*: 311.
181 *Ibid.*
182 *Ibid.*
183 *Ibid.*
184 *Ibid.*, original emphasis.
185 *Ibid.*
186 *Ibid.*
187 *Ibid.*
188 *Ibid.*

parliament began to be understood as a court of law.[189] Oakeshott claims that as a result of the emergence of the modern state everywhere in Europe, except for England, the medieval parliamentary institutions were 'extinguished, extinguished themselves, or made subservient to the ruler'.[190] The parliaments and councils of the Middle Ages had been judicial bodies and it is from these courts of law that legislative bodies emerged.[191] As regards the Westminster parliament, Oakeshott argues that what came to be recognized as legislation sprang from 'a small and almost imperceptible enlargement of the exercise of a judicial office'.[192] In this sense, Oakeshott asserts that parliament became a necessary partner in lawmaking.[193] He claims that the feudal principle that a man's rights may not be altered without his consent is the basis for the augmentation of the role of parliament.[194] In other words, Oakeshott maintains that it was not the emergence of a new principle which promoted the importance of parliament in respect of lawmaking; rather, the principle existed already.[195] To this end, for Oakeshott, given that the circumstances of the later middle ages called more and more for the emendation of the law, parliament gained in importance as it 'offered itself as a ready manner in which the consent of all could be presumed to have been obtained'.[196] That is, the consent of parliament came to be recognized as the consent of the whole realm.[197] Nevertheless, despite the fact that parliament's activities passed over into legislation, Oakeshott maintains that 'it never lost its original character as a court of law'.[198] In the seventeenth century, therefore, it was still largely understood as a court of law.[199] The progressive enlargements of the business handled in parliament culminated in the concept of 'parliamentary government' which emerged in England in the late eighteenth and early nineteenth centuries.[200] For Oakeshott, as regards parliamentary institutions, 'the only history that matters in this connection [is] the history of England'.[201]

---

189 *PFPS*: 77.
190 *LHPT*: 381.
191 *RP*: 369.
192 *PFPS*: 78.
193 *LHPT*: 312.
194 *Ibid.*
195 *Ibid.*
196 *Ibid.*
197 *Ibid.*
198 *LHPT*: 312, 311.
199 *PFPS*: 78.
200 *PFPS*: 78 and *RP*: 369.
201 *RPML*: 109.

As for the judicial process, Magna Carta marks the symbolic inception of English Common Law which is composed of legal precedents, decisions and procedures, such as the writ of Habeas Corpus, which maintain rights and ensure the means of redress of wrongs. For Oakeshott, the English manner of thinking about freedom is rooted, firstly, in the existence of a Common Law.[202] In this sense, Oakeshott argues that English freedom exists because courts of law have, at one time or another, 'decided that certain forms of behaviour are lawful and have the protection of law'.[203] In other words, English liberties 'are based upon decisions pronounced by judges in dealing with individual cases'.[204] Secondly, Oakeshott maintains that English freedom depends upon there being 'established and known procedures by which a man can get redress if any of his recognized rights are infringed'.[205] More specifically, Oakeshott asserts that the insistence is always, not on a defined freedom, but on the presence or absence of a procedure.[206] In this respect, the existence of a procedure for redress 'is the basis of the positive exercise of freedom' and the absence of such a procedure, that is, the fact that there is no known and legal manner of exercising power in certain directions 'is the basis of the limitation of the invitation to submit to governmental power'.[207] In sum, the Common Law is at once preserved and augmented by every judgment and judicial decision. An important part of the story of English politics, then, is how medieval liberties were transformed into the freedoms of modern England.[208]

The legend of English politics, such as Oakeshott understands it, I argue, relates the story of English freedom and of the institutions which emerged to ensure its continuity. He asserts that current political arguments and attitudes are always returning to the legend in order to understand English freedom, as well as to revise and enlarge its meaning. Put another way, the English political legend is at once preserved and augmented. Political conduct returns to the legend as a source of authority and political change is bound to the story in that it must be congruent with it. For this reason, Oakeshott emphasizes that it is the English tradition of politics, which the story of English freedom recounts, that makes the English 'peculiarly, almost unreasonably, sensitive to the introduction of new procedures or the enlargement of

---

202 *WH*: 241.
203 *Ibid.*
204 *Ibid.*
205 *Ibid.*
206 *WH*: 242.
207 *Ibid.*
208 *Ibid.*

old procedures which seem to increase the power of government'.[209] Change, then, is augmentation or amplification of the legend. Permanence and change are, consequently, tied together. What is in effect preserved and augmented is the English political identity. This is true of all legends of political life which every society creates for itself. Myth and legend endow a society with its identity and with a sense of self-consciousness. When a legend is preserved it is a society's self-consciousness and identity which are preserved. The act of augmentation or amplification of the legend is the manner in which the values of a society are recreated. Poetry guards a society against the corruption of its consciousness by creating and recreating its values, thereby ensuring that it knows itself and is critical of itself. In other words, poetry protects a society by recalling and recreating its myth of civilization. In this sense, a legend is a recalled artefact which stabilizes the problematic present of a society and guards against the corruption of its consciousness by relating the story, an imaginative interpretation, of how it came about. Consequently, the fact that political conduct is bound to the legend of the political life of a society ensures not only that political change is congruent with it, but more importantly, it ensures that change does not corrupt the consciousness of the society. In the case of England, the English understanding of freedom is founded and guarded by the legend of English politics. Thus, legend serves as a contingent foundation for the political. English freedom is contingently founded in that the legend may be augmented and amplified and, consequently, the understanding of freedom as well. However, it cannot consist in just any understanding of freedom. For instance, English freedom cannot be understood in terms of an abstract ideal. If it were, English society would have suffered a corruption of its consciousness. Thus, the legend of English political life translates poetically into the idiom of general ideas the English tradition, or practice, of freedom.

'Rationalism in Politics': A Work of Poetry

For Oakeshott, the English tradition of politics is the ultimate representation of European politics conceived of as a traditional manner of politics. This understanding of politics has been discussed throughout the book; I will only briefly summarize it here. Politics, Oakeshott maintains, springs from existing traditions of behaviour. Political activity is the pursuit of intimations understood as the exploration of a society's arrangements in order to detect incoherencies and, consequently, identify and implement the changes they intimate in order

---

[209] *Ibid.*

that the arrangements correspond with the present circumstances, values and beliefs of society. Political change is not arbitrary since it must make sense for the whole of tradition. Political activity thus aims to augment the coherence of a political tradition of behaviour. A political tradition is never fixed nor finished, Oakeshott argues. It is always in movement, constantly changing and adapting itself. However, in his seminal essay 'Rationalism in Politics', Oakeshott contends that this manner of politics has been threatened by Rationalism since the seventeenth century. As will be examined in further detail, Rationalism arguably constitutes a counter-legend of European politics, one which, according to Oakeshott, conceives of politics as ideology. Thus, the seventeenth century saw the emergence of both the English legend of political life, which best symbolizes European politics understood as a tradition of behaviour, and the counter-legend of Rationalism. This is a grave state of affairs, Oakeshott stresses. Rationalism is undermining the ability of the legend of politics understood as a tradition of behaviour to endow modern Europe with its identity and sense of self-consciousness. Put another way, modern Europe's consciousness risks being corrupted. The idea that it is poetry which, by means of legend-making, guards the identity and self-consciousness of a society leads me to reconsider how Oakeshott's thought is understood. That is, given his deep concern for the fate of Western civilization, is he always philosophizing or is he at times engaged in legend-making?

Oakeshott is deeply concerned about the identity and self-consciousness of modern Europe. His works, and in particular *Rationalism in Politics*, are a testament to this. The essays which compose that collection, and most notably the title essay, are an unequivocal condemnation of what he perceives to be the 'infection' or 'invasion' of politics, understood as a tradition of behaviour, by Rationalism. In other words, the identity and self-consciousness of Western civilization is threatened of being corrupted by Rationalism. It may be argued that Oakeshott oversteps the limits of his narrow definition of legitimate philosophical activity. Indeed, at many times throughout *Rationalism in Politics* he goes beyond considering the place of politics on the map of human experience and engages in prescription and recommendation, both of which belong to the mode of practice. Numerous commentators have remarked upon this discrepancy or tension in his thought, in regards to both *Rationalism in Politics* and *On Human Conduct*. Although Oakeshott wishes to define political philosophy narrowly and to exclude practice from it, he himself has difficulty respecting the strict division he establishes between philosophy and practice. Commentators, including Pitkin (1976), Spitz (1976), Parekh (1979 and 1995) and Auspitz (1976), have noted that in *On Human Conduct* Oakeshott shows a marked preference for, and is an outright proponent of, civil association. Oakeshott claims to merely be contending that the modern European political consciousness is polarized between two polar opposite conceptions of the state: civil association and enterprise association. He characterizes the former as the state understood 'in terms of the common acknowledgement of the authority of civil (not instrumental) law specifying conditions to be subscribed to in making choices and in performing self-chosen actions', and the latter as the state understood to be 'composed of persons related in terms of a specified common purpose or interest and who recognize one another in terms of their common engagement to pursue or to promote it'.[210] [211] Despite his claims that his sole concern is to understand theoretically how the state has been characterized in modern Europe, Bhikhu Parekh convincingly argues that Oakeshott's theorizing is not purely explanatory. Rather, he engages in both explicit and implicit condemnation and recommendation. First, Parekh asserts, he explicitly condemns enterprise association. He writes that Oakeshott's:

> attack on the 'servile state', 'slavish concern for benefit', the 'shame' and 'guilt' of the modern European, 'half-men', the *canaille*, the individual *manqué* characterized by 'spiritual indigence', 'natural submissiveness', 'feeling rather than thoughts' and 'impulses rather than opinions' is ferocious and uncompromising. And he also says that the preoccupation with common purposes has 'corrupted', 'degraded', 'devalued', and 'infected' political vocabulary and discourse.[212]

Secondly, Parekh observes that Oakeshott explicitly recommends civil association. He notes that:

> he talks of the 'superior desirability' of the civil association and says that it is 'as rare as it is excellent'. He also says that only a civil association is consistent with human dignity and that a state pursuing a common substantive purpose is 'sordid' and commits 'moral enormity'.[213]

For Parekh, Oakeshott leaves no doubt in his theorizing that he has 'nothing but unqualified praise for the adventurous explorers of individuality' and 'nothing but unqualified contempt for the so-called individual *manqué* upon whose weary shoulders he generally places the responsibility for the "withering away of civil association"'.[214] Parekh acknowledges that Oakeshott recognizes that he often writes in a 'prescriptive mood' but that he 'rejoined that these were regrettable

---

[210] *HC*: 313.

[211] *HC*: 315.

[212] B. Parekh 1979: 501–502.

[213] *Ibid.*: 502.

[214] *Ibid.*

expressions of his personal opinions and did not belong to the philosophical part of his work'.[215]

D.D. Raphael points to similar tensions and discrepancies in
Rationalism in Politics. In his review article, he observes that while
Oakeshott 'holds firmly that the task of philosophy is explanation and
not commendation', he 'does not in fact maintain his thesis that the
proper business of philosophy is purely explanatory'.[216] [217] This leads
Raphael to conclude that *Rationalism in Politics*:

> does not conform markedly with his view of philosophy as explanation
> and not commendation (or discommendation). The tone of most of his
> essays is polemical, and while that does not make them any less philo-
> sophical for me, he really ought to do something about the incoherence
> between his profession and his practice, so as to let us know which we
> are to take as intimated by his work.[218]

Finally, Raphael not only finds fault with Oakeshott's philosophical
thinking, but also with his writing style, in particular his metaphors. He
states that 'the more flamboyant metaphors jar on me more often than
they please'.[219] For Raphael, it is Oakeshott's love of poetry which
'leads him to bestrew his philosophy with poetic imagery'.[220] There is
indeed much poetic imagery to be found in *Rationalism in Politics*. I do
not think, however, that Oakeshott's love of poetry sufficiently
accounts for its presence. There is something more going on. The question that arises is whether Oakeshott is solely engaged in political
philosophy in *Rationalism in Politics* or if he is also pursuing other kinds
of reflection upon the political. David Boucher observes that, for
Oakeshott, the three levels at which political reflection takes place,
those being policy-making, foundational reflection upon the political
and political philosophy, 'are not exclusive to particular texts. All three
may appear in the same text, and this is common enough in the literature on reflection about politics. We may find a mixture of modes of
practical and explanatory thinking'.[221] We may conclude, then, that for
Oakeshott a work of reflection about politics, such as *Rationalism in
Politics*, may incorporate all three levels of thinking about politics and
is, therefore, not exclusively a work of philosophy. What is more, we
may find the author of a book of philosophy engaged with different
modes or voices and not exclusively engaged in theorizing. An elo-

---

[215] *Ibid.*
[216] D.D. Raphael 1964: 208.
[217] *Ibid.*: 210.
[218] *Ibid.*: 215.
[219] *Ibid.*: 202.
[220] *Ibid.*: 215.
[221] D. Boucher 2006: 13.

quent example is Oakeshott's own claim that Hobbes's *Leviathan* is a work of art in the proper sense, one of the masterpieces of literature.[222] While undeniably a work of philosophy, *Leviathan* is also a work of literature since it recalls and recreates the dream of civilization. Furthermore, in *On Human Conduct*, Oakeshott emphasizes that philosophers sometimes digress from the engagement of theorizing since this highest level of reflection is difficult to sustain. He argues that digression, for instance writing in a different voice or exploring different levels of reflection, is in no way problematic since theorizing may be arrested without being denied.[223] Thus, Oakeshott acknowledges that philosophers are often engaged in other modes or with other voices of experience; consequently, it may be expected that he himself engages in reflection or imaginative activities other than philosophy as this does not pose any difficulty.

This sustains Oakeshott's claim that the prescriptive elements present in his writings do not 'belong to the philosophical part of his work'.[224] That being said, if they do not belong to the philosophical part of his work, then to what part do they belong? I posit that all of the problems relating to the division between philosophy and practice, to the quality of the philosophical thinking and to the style of writing are resolved if Oakeshott is understood to be engaged in poetic legend-making. In this sense, I argued in Chapter 2 that in regards to Rationalism and a tradition of a manner of political behaviour, Oakeshott is not engaged in the history of thought, but in constructing legends of intellectual past. It is not the use of metaphors and imagery, then, which makes this part of his reflection upon politics 'poetic'. Rather, it is his deep concern for the identity and self-consciousness of Western civilization, and, in particular, of English society. *Rationalism in Politics*, I argue, is best understood as Oakeshott's poetic attempt to save its consciousness from corruption. *Rationalism in Politics*, then, is not only a work of philosophy, but also a work of literature in which Oakeshott's aim is to recreate the values of society, ensure that it is knowledgeable of itself and recall the myth that binds the generations together. That is, by means of a story or drama, Oakeshott's intention is to recall society's legitimate identity and endow it anew with self-consciousness. That this is his intention is made clear in the title essay 'Rationalism in Politics' which will be the focus of my attention for the purpose of a textual analysis since his concern is most urgently and coherently conveyed in this essay. This restricted analysis will allow me to show that

---

[222] *HCA*: 159.

[223] *HC*: 11.

[224] B. Parekh 1995: 183.

Oakeshott is not always engaged in philosophy. Like Hobbes, whom he admires, he writes in the voice of poetry in an effort to recall the dream of Western civilization.

As Oakeshott himself points out, he is not the first modern writer to be preoccupied with the state of Western civilization. To this end, he reminds us that the central theme of Hannah Arendt's *Between Past and Future* is 'the crisis of our time'.[225] In that collection of essays, Oakeshott explains, Arendt makes the case that the crisis is political in nature and 'has been growing upon us since the sixteenth century'.[226] More precisely, the crisis 'constitutes an alienation of ourselves from this world which we have made for ourselves'.[227] This is precisely how I understand Oakeshott's concept of the corruption of consciousness in relation to Western civilization. Oakeshott specifies that, for Arendt, it is Hegel, Marx, Kierkegaard, Nietzsche and Burckhardt who began to diagnose the crisis.[228] Oakeshott also recognizes that Burckhardt and Nietzsche were among the first modern writers to diagnose 'the crisis of our time'. In Burckhardt's case, Oakeshott writes that 'what he saw was not very much to his liking: it was the destruction of almost everything he valued most highly'.[229] As for Nietzsche, Oakeshott explains that what may be found in his writings is a 'profound and imaginative diagnosis of a crisis in European culture'.[230] Oakeshott asserts that Nietzsche sounded an alarm 'for the world in which [he] detected the crisis was as insensible of its predicament as we are of the speed at which the earth is whirling through space'.[231] Oakeshott goes on to claim that in the very act of diagnosis Nietzsche should be understood as an artist. In this sense, Oakeshott argues that in art, insight or diagnosis is an end in itself.[232] He maintains that remedy is not something that follows. Rather, remedy lies in the diagnosis itself, that is, 'in the removal of the corrupt consciousness'.[233] This is how I understand Oakeshott. He is an artist, who, just as he explains Nietzsche does, is sounding the alarm, diagnosing the crisis of Western civilization and removing the corrupt consciousness.

'Rationalism in Politics', then, represents Oakeshott's attempt to radically guard Western civilization and its values against Rationalism.

---

225 *WH*: 316.
226 *Ibid.*
227 *Ibid.*
228 *Ibid.*
229 *VMES*: 67.
230 *CPJ*: 224.
231 *Ibid.*
232 *CPJ*: 225.
233 *Ibid.*

The essay expresses his deep concern for the fate of Western civilization's identity and sense of self-consciousness. The essay, or legendary narrative, recounts the drama of modern European civilization and of the 'invasion' or 'infection' of Rationalism, which began in the seventeenth century. (The terms 'invasion' and 'infection' are those employed by Oakeshott. His use of metaphors and imagery which relate to disease, war, violence, death and destruction should be noted.) In so doing, it transmits a clear and unequivocal message, that is, that modern Europe's legitimate, or authentic, identity is threatened and that it must be saved before it becomes thoroughly corrupted by Rationalism. To put it using Oakeshott's metaphors, the 'disease' of Rationalism is 'infecting' the self-consciousness and identity of modern Europe and everything must be done to ensure a full and complete 'recovery'.

The story's protagonist is the traditional manner of politics which slowly emerged over a period of centuries and which resulted in modern European political self-consciousness. As has been argued, this understanding of the political is itself a legend. In order to stabilize the problematic present of the contemporary world, that is, a politically, socially, economically, religiously complex world, Oakeshott recalls from the vast storehouse of the practical past the legend of politics understood as a tradition of behaviour. Whether politics was ever in fact truly practised in this fashion is not the question. What is important is the role it plays in the drama of modern Europe. This manner of politics finds its definitive representation in the English political tradition, for which Oakeshott has infinite admiration. It is this legend of political life which endows modern Europe with its identity and sense of self-consciousness. The story creates and recreates the values of society, ensures that it has knowledge of itself and recalls the myth that binds the generations together. It is this legend that has been undermined and threatened by Rationalism since the early seventeenth century. I will follow Oakeshott's narrative and discuss his portrayal of the aggressor.

Central to the Rationalist disposition is the belief in 'a "reason" common to all mankind'.[234] This belief is the guiding principle of, and fortifies, the Rationalist character and disposition. The logical consequence is that this character 'stands (he always *stands*) for independence of mind on all occasions' and that the only authority he recognizes is 'the authority of "reason"'.[235] Given his dedication and loyalty to reason, the Rationalist is 'the *enemy* of authority, of prejudice, of the

---

[234] *RP*: 6.
[235] *RP*: 5–6, original emphasis.

merely traditional, customary or habitual'.[236] Due to his belief in reason, the Rationalist is both sceptical and optimistic. He is sceptical because 'there is no opinion, no habit, no belief, nothing so firmly rooted or so widely held that he hesitates to question it and to judge it by what he calls his "reason"'.[237] He is optimistic because he 'never doubts the power of his "reason" [...] to determine the worth of a thing, the truth of an opinion or the propriety of an action'.[238] The Rationalist's belief in reason and his rejection of tradition means that he has no sense of the past which he necessarily perceives as an encumbrance.[239] For this reason, in relation to politics, the only authority he recognizes is that of reason. He believes that the 'unhindered human "reason" [...] is an infallible guide in political activity'.[240] Human reason is unhindered in so far as the mind is open and 'free from prejudice and its relic, habit'.[241] For the Rationalist, then, everything must be scrutinized by his reason. An opinion or institution cannot possess an intrinsic value merely because it exists, has existed for several generations, or is familiar. On the contrary, it can only be of value if reason has shown it to be true or rational.[242] For this reason, the Rationalist believes in argument as 'the technique and operation of "reason"'.[243] Consequently, Oakeshott argues, 'much of his political activity consists in bringing the social, political, legal and institutional inheritance of his society before the tribunal of his intellect'.[244]

Given the centrality of reason and argument to the Rationalist disposition and character, when it comes to political ideas, ideology is deemed to be superior to a tradition of ideas because it is 'self-contained'.[245] There is no question of retaining or improving a tradition of behaviour, the reason being that both retention and improvement involve submission to tradition.[246] The only acceptable option is to 'destroy' tradition. It should be noted that Oakeshott goes quite far in his use of metaphors in order to depict the aggressive and violent character of the Rationalist. Tradition is clearly threatened by the Rationalist who is determined that a tradition of ideas 'must be

---

[236] *RP*: 6, original emphasis.
[237] *Ibid.*
[238] *Ibid.*
[239] *Ibid.*
[240] *RP*: 8.
[241] *Ibid.*
[242] *Ibid.*
[243] *Ibid.*
[244] *Ibid.*
[245] *RP*: 16.
[246] *RP*: 8.

destroyed' in order for it to be replaced with an ideology which Oakeshott describes as 'the formalized abridgment of the supposed substratum of rational truth contained in the tradition'.[247] That is, ideology is a 'system of ideas abstracted from the manner in which people have been accustomed to go about the business of attending to the arrangements of their society'.[248] In other words, ideology is a system of abstract ideals or general principles derived from a tradition of political behaviour.

Hence, Oakeshott identifies the enemy of the drama: the Rationalist who is out to destroy the traditional manner of politics. Oakeshott focuses the narrative of his story on one element in the context of the emergence of the modern rationalist threat, that is, the condition of knowledge during the early seventeenth century. He argues that the state of European knowledge at the beginning of the seventeenth century was 'peculiar'.[249] Important discoveries were made and remarkable advances were achieved in the traditional manner of intellectual enquiry. In this sense, Oakeshott claims that 'the fruitfulness of the presuppositions which inspired this inquiry showed no sign of exhaustion'.[250] Yet it was deemed by 'intelligent observers' (i.e. Rationalists) that 'something of supreme importance was lacking'.[251] What was found to be lacking was not inspiration or methodical habits of enquiry, but a 'consciously formulated technique of research [...] a method whose rules had been written down'.[252] For Oakeshott, the realization of this technique or 'the project of making good this want was the occasion of the unmistakable emergence of the new intellectual character I have called the Rationalist'.[253]

However, the story of Rationalism is not only the story of its emergence as an intellectual character in the seventeenth century threatening the traditional manner of intellectual enquiry, it is also the 'the history of the invasion of every department of intellectual activity by the doctrine of the sovereignty of technique'.[254] Rationalism is the aggressor who is openly at war with traditional intellectual activity, or, alternatively, an infectious disease infecting tradition. Oakeshott claims that no activity was 'immune' from Rationalism, not literature, poetry, drama, religion, natural science, education or morality, and no society

---

[247] *RP*: 8, 9.

[248] *RP*: 51.

[249] *RP*: 18.

[250] *Ibid.*

[251] *Ibid.*

[252] *Ibid.*

[253] *Ibid.*

[254] *RP*: 22.

was 'untouched' by it.[255] The departments of intellectual activity did, however, organize a defence. The aggression was resisted to the best of their ability and some activities were able to free themselves of the Rationalist enemy. In spite of the defensive tactics, there is one field where resistance proved to be futile. That field is the activity of politics. Oakeshott asserts that of all the worlds, the world of politics 'might seem the least amenable to rationalist treatment — politics, always so deeply veined with the traditional, the circumstantial and the transitory'.[256] The traditional manner of politics proved to be no match for Rationalism. Oakeshott states that the 'greatest apparent victories of Rationalism have been in politics'.[257] The pre-eminent incarnation of politics understood as a tradition of behaviour, English politics, was unable to defeat the Rationalist invasion. Oakeshott relates that 'those traditional elements, particularly in English politics, which might have been expected to continue some resistance to the pressure of Rationalism, have now almost completely conformed to the prevailing intellectual temper, and even represent this conformity to be a sign of their vitality'.[258] That is, English identity and self-consciousness are corrupted since the English understand the fact that their politics conform to Rationalism as a sign of good health. In the case of England, the conversion of habits of behaviour into 'comparatively rigid systems of abstract ideas' began in the seventeenth century.[259] While this conversion had formerly been 'tacitly resisted and retarded by [...] the informality of English politics [...] that resistance has now itself been converted into an ideology'.[260] The significance of Rationalism's victory over the tradition of English politics should not be underestimated. Moreover, it is important to understand the extent to which English self-consciousness and identity have already been corrupted by Rationalism. That the resistance to rationalist politics has itself been converted into an ideology is an indication of the depth of the corruption. Oakeshott is adamant that 'only in a society already deeply infected with Rationalism will the conversion of the traditional resources of resistance to the tyranny of Rationalism into a self-conscious ideology be considered a strengthening of those resources'.[261]

What the English experience shows is how politics has been 'earlier and more fully engulfed by the tidal wave than any other human

---

[255] *Ibid.*
[256] *RP*: 7.
[257] *RP*: 8.
[258] *RP*: 26.
[259] *Ibid.*
[260] *Ibid.*
[261] *RP*: 27.

activity'.[262] (Here, Oakeshott uses the imagery of a tidal wave, which is the cause of death and destruction, as a metaphor for Rationalism.) This, for Oakeshott, is remarkable given the deeply traditional and customary character of political activity. However, resistance proved to be to no avail. While Oakeshott believes that Rationalism's hold upon other human activities varied in firmness over the course of the last four centuries, he claims that its hold on politics 'steadily increased and is stronger now than at any earlier time', to the point that 'all contemporary politics are deeply infected with Rationalism'.[263] That this is the case will only be denied by 'those who choose to give the infection another name'.[264] Oakeshott's concern is to consider the 'circumstances in which European politics came to surrender almost completely to the Rationalist and the results of the surrender'.[265] Again, the use of the word 'surrender' should be observed. One surrenders in a battle, a fight or a war. Oakeshott asks 'if Rationalism now reigns almost unopposed [...] What are the circumstances that promoted this state of affairs?'[266] Rationalism's 'triumph', Oakeshott argues, can be explained by political inexperience.[267] The politics of Rationalism are 'the politics of the politically inexperienced'.[268] Oakeshott claims that, during the last four centuries, European politics have 'suffered the incursion of at least three types of political inexperience — that of the new ruler, of the new ruling class, and of the new political society — to say nothing of the incursion of a new sex'.[269] The incursion of the politically inexperienced, the cause of European politics' sufferance, provoked the need for a technique of politics. The need of a man who, 'not brought up or educated to their exercise, finds himself in a position to exert political initiative and authority' will be so great that 'he will have no incentive to be sceptical about the possibility of a magic technique of politics which will remove the handicap of his lack of political education'.[270] For the new, inexperienced ruler, the offer of a technique of politics:

> will seem to him like salvation itself; to be told that the necessary knowledge is to be found, complete and self-contained, in a book, and to be told that this knowledge is of a sort that can be learned by heart quickly

---

262 *RP*: 25.
263 *Ibid.*
264 *Ibid.*
265 *Ibid.*
266 *RP*: 28.
267 *Ibid.*
268 *Ibid.*
269 *Ibid.*
270 *Ibid.*

and applied mechanically, will seem, like salvation, something almost too good to be true.[271]

The politics of the book, Oakeshott maintains, is a 'symptom of the triumph of technique which we have seen to be the root of modern Rationalism; for what the book contains is only what is possible to put into a book—rules of a technique'.[272] Each form of political inexperience has its crib writer. The new ruler has Machiavelli, the new social class Locke, Marx and Engels and the new political society, as the example of the United States shows, will rely on Locke.[273]

There is some cause to be hopeful for the fate of modern Europe's identity and self-consciousness—Oakeshott observes that there have always been 'men of genuine political education, immune from the infection of Rationalism (and this is particularly so of England, where a political education of some sort has been much more widely spread than in some other societies)'.[274] Moreover, he notes that the politically inexperienced will 'often be found throwing away his book and relying upon his general experience of the world'.[275] Nevertheless, Oakeshott holds out little hope. He asserts that 'the view I am maintaining is that the ordinary practical politics of European nations have become fixed in a vice of Rationalism [...] and that [...] we must not expect a speedy release from our predicament'.[276] He acknowledges that 'it is always depressing for a patient to be told that his disease is almost as old as himself and that consequently there is no quick cure for it', but this is the unfortunate state European identity finds itself in.[277] The threat posed by Rationalism to European self-consciousness will remain 'so long as the circumstances which promoted the emergence of rationalist politics remain'.[278] Oakeshott fears that those circumstances are here for good and that Rationalism's hold on politics will only increase and tighten over time. The patient will only get sicker. He concludes that:

> No sensible man will worry greatly because he cannot at once hit upon a cure for what he believes to be a crippling complaint; but if he sees the complaint to be of a kind which the passage of time must make more rather than less severe, he will have a more substantial cause for anxiety.

---

[271] *RP*: 28–29.
[272] *RP*: 27.
[273] *RP*: 29–33.
[274] *RP*: 35.
[275] *RP*: 35–36.
[276] *RP*: 33–34.
[277] *RP*: 34.
[278] *Ibid.*

> And this unfortunately appears to be so with the disease of Rationalism.[279]

Rationalism appears to be an incurable disease. The fate of modern Europe's self-consciousness is dire.

'Rationalism in Politics', as well as other instances where Oakeshott writes in a prescriptive mood, condemns or recommends, is a legend or a poetic construct. The story or drama Oakeshott constructs transmits a clear message. It expresses his deep and pressing concern for the fate of modern Europe which is threatened by Rationalism. The imagery of disease/infection, invasion/war and death/destruction are metaphors for the corruption of modern Europe's consciousness. It is not only the political which is diseased, but all departments of human activity, including morality. This contamination constitutes another of Rationalism's great victories. In regards to morality, Oakeshott writes that:

> there is a victory which the Rationalist has already won on another front from which recovery will be more difficult because, while the Rationalist knows it to be a victory, his opponent hardly recognizes it as a defeat. I mean the circumvention and appropriation by the rationalist disposition of mind of the whole field of morality and moral education.[280]

The extent of the corruption Oakeshott perceives is here made clear: the traditional manner of moral conduct is not even aware that it has been infected or corrupted by Rationalism, hence morality's near impossible recovery. For Oakeshott, the Rationalist character and disposition destabilize the stabilizing construct that is the legend of politics as a traditional manner of behaviour. It is this legend which endowed Western civilization with its sense of self-consciousness and identity. Thus, by destabilizing the legend, Rationalism modifies modern Europe's identity, and in particular English society's identity, beyond recognition, to the extent where it has become corrupted. In the case of England, it is the legend of political life which places the recalled artefact of Magna Carta at its centre which has become deeply infected with Rationalism. A traditional manner of politics has been converted into an ideology. The perceived Rationalist enemy, the destabilizing entity, is a counter-legend. That is, a legend in its own right.

'Rationalism in Politics' highlights Oakeshott's worry for the fate of Western civilization's identity and self-consciousness and, in particular, for that of English society. His mood is sombre and profoundly pessimistic. He does not hold out much hope that modern Europe will ever be cured of its infection. In an attempt to save the modern world from the corruption of its consciousness, Oakeshott, like Nietzsche before

---

[279] *RP*: 36–37.
[280] *RP*: 40.

him, is lead to create a story or drama about the fate of Western
civilization since poetry is the only human activity which can guard a
society's sense of self-consciousness and identity. The essay is a warning about the impending danger posed by Rationalism as well as an
effort to remind society of the myth or legend which binds the generations together: that of politics as a tradition of behaviour. Therefore,
Oakeshott is not engaged in philosophical activity, but rather in legend-
making, that is, in poetic activity. It is my position that legend belongs
to the second of three levels of political thinking between which
Oakeshott distinguishes. This kind of political thinking, which I have
termed foundational, is not radically subversive, that is, it is not philosophical.[281] The character of the political thinking present in 'Rationalism in Politics' is not subversive. Oakeshott's thought here is not 'perpetually *en voyage*'. He is not interested in considering the place of
political activity on the map of total human experience, nor does he
wish to understand ideal characters in terms of their postulates. Put
another way, his reflection upon politics in 'Rationalism in Politics'
does not attain the level of abstraction appropriate to political philosophy. Rather, Oakeshott wishes to radically guard modern Europe's
identity understood as a traditional manner of behaviour. In order to
do so, Oakeshott fully engages in the second level of reflection upon
politics. His thinking in this essay never diverges from the political
experience it springs from. His aim is to explain the fixed character of
Rationalism. This kind of reflection upon the political does not throw
off its allegiance to the political experience from which it springs
because its very aim is to establish and determine the character and
identity of the said political experience. This is achieved by the
extrapolation of the political experience's tendencies, by fixing its
elements, and by making firm its identity.[282] In short, the purpose of
political thinking at this level is to increase the knowledge of a fixed
identity. A legend of politics is knowledge of an already familiar
political world. 'Rationalism in Politics' treats two fixed characters or
identities: politics as a tradition of behaviour and Rationalism. The
former is understood by Oakeshott as being the original and legitimate
legend of political life and the latter the corrupting counter-legend. The
essay takes the form of a legend: the legend of the disease of Rationalism, a drama in which the character of Rationalism infects the character
of politics understood as a tradition of behaviour, thereby corrupting
modern Europe's identity and sense of self-consciousness. As such, it
serves as a warning regarding the fate of Western civilization. 'Ration-

---

[281] *RPML*: 148.
[282] *RPML*: 147.

alism in Politics' is Oakeshott's poetic attempt to save modern Europe from the corruption of its consciousness. In and of itself, there is nothing wrong with poetic legend-making since it is the sole human activity which can guard a society's identity and sense of self-consciousness. Oakeshott himself argues that legenda are indispensable to civilized life.[283] However, if he wishes to be engaged in political philosophy, this is not the activity he is involved in. His profound concern for the identity and sense of self-consciousness of modern Europe overtakes his thought and pushes him to overstep the boundaries of political philosophy and write in the mode of poetry. Whereas philosophy and practice do not mix, poetry and practice can and do in order to create legends of political life. This explains the perceived discrepancy in Oakeshott's thought observed by commentators. He does condemn and recommend, but when he is engaged in prescription he is not writing philosophically, but poetically.

Conclusion

The political experience of Ancient Rome generated the first and one of the greatest and most successful legends of political life. Given Oakeshott's admiration for the Roman political experience it may be concluded that it serves as the source of his own thinking on legend and myth. Oakeshott believes that the Greeks had been unable to generate such a legend due to the fact that they gave remarkably little attention to the past and were unimpressed by precedent. In other words, they did not turn to the past as a source of authority for current political conduct. The Roman legend of politics, then, serves as a model for all subsequent political legends as well as for Oakeshott's thinking on contingent foundations. To this end, it respects the criteria I identified as defining political legends. It is an imaginative construction of poets which endows the Roman people with its sense of self-consciousness; it is reflection upon politics at the foundational level, or the second level of political thinking, and it is a recalled survived artefact from the practical past which stabilizes the problematic present of Roman political life. The poetic dimension protects the Roman identity since poets, by creating and recreating the values of society, guard it against the corruption of its consciousness. Roman identity is created and recreated by exploring the intimations of the foundation. The change which is intimated is enacted and tied back to the original foundation. The legend of the foundation of Rome is thus augmented and amplified. Consequently, the Roman foundation and political identity are augmented and amplified.

---

[283] *OH*: 48.

The centrality of augmentation and amplification to the Roman political experience reveals that it is also the source of Oakeshott's conservatism. In this respect, a parallel may be drawn between the Roman understanding of politics and Oakeshott's conception of the practice of politics conceived of as the pursuit of intimations which also endeavours to guard a society's identity. Yet both the Romans and Oakeshott sense that the best political care is not sufficient to protect a society from the corruption of its consciousness since politics inevitably corrupts identity. Both find in poetry the remedy to this difficulty, a manner of protecting society's self-consciousness and its values. In other words, politics cannot be purely contingent. The threat posed to a society's identity and sense of self-consciousness establishes the need for some type of foundation. It is in this sense that legends of political life serve as contingent foundations for the political. This also holds true in modernity as the example of the English legend of political life demonstrates. Political legends stabilize the practical present, yet also allow for change. For this reason, I made the case in Chapter 4 that Oakeshott's conservatism is deeply poetic. Poetry allows a political society to assimilate change without becoming unrecognizable to itself. More than this, however, it is Oakeshott's poetic conservatism which leads me to claim that essays such as 'Rationalism in Politics' are best understood as works of poetry. Oakeshott maintains that modern Europeans have become careless of their identity, and, as a result, it is in the process of being corrupted by Rationalism. In an effort to alert European civilization to the impending crisis, we find Oakeshott writing in the poetic idiom, as it is the only idiom which can safeguard a society's self-consciousness, in an attempt to save modern Europe from the corruption of its consciousness. Thus, like Nietzsche before him, through art, Oakeshott diagnoses the crisis of our time and, since remedy lies in the diagnosis itself, removes the corrupt consciousness.

Conclusion

Legend, 'the enterprise of constructing and confirming a social identity and consciousness', is at the heart of Oakeshott's political thought.[1] This is made plain when he states that legend-making is a perennial practical necessity.[2] Commentators have noted that Oakeshott often refers to legend and myth throughout his writings, but that he never fully worked out the idea that every society requires a legend of political life if the bonds that unite *cives* to one another are to be sufficiently strong to ensure solidarity.[3] My aim has been to theorize Oakeshott's concept of legends of political life in order to resolve a tension that underlies his thought: that is, that the recognition of the authority of the rules of association as rules is insufficient to ensure human living-together. In so doing, the fundamental importance of imagination both for politics and for Oakeshott's political thought has been brought to light. He is adamant that human beings' primordial activity is to make themselves at home in the world. To this end, he affirms that it is imagination by means of an epic story of the past which allows humans to build a world of sense and meaning and, thus, feel at home in an otherwise menacing and mysterious universe. More than this, however, I claim that imagination's creations, legends of political life, by endowing a society with its identity and thereafter guarding it, serve as contingent foundations for the political. I posit that political legends are poetic constructs which tell the story of a past event and which allow societies to understand themselves in the idiom of general ideas. In sum, they stabilize a problematic practical present. It is this thesis which I explored throughout the book.

In Chapter 1, following a discussion of the problem of foundations in modernity, I adopted the theoretical framework established by John E. Seery which distinguishes between Edenic and constructed foundations. While agreeing with commentators that Edenic foundations defined as '"prior" claims about unquestionable or sacred or natural

---

1   *VMES*: 194.
2   *Ibid.*
3   T. Nardin and L. O'Sullivan 2006: 15.

premises' are not to be found in Oakeshott's thought; nevertheless, I set out to make the case that Oakeshott's concept of political legends constitute constructed foundations understood as stabilizing constructs erected or built by humans.[4] [5] Seery notes that Hannah Arendt is a leading figure of the constructivist tradition and that her primary source of inspiration is the Roman political experience. Given that legends of political life are foundational narrative constructs modelled upon the Roman political experience, I posit that Oakeshott is a weak foundationalist in the Arendtian constructivist tradition.

I then specified what I mean by constructed foundations by referring to Benedict Anderson's work on imagined communities. I follow Anderson's argument that political communities are imagined and that what is constructed is a common political imaginary which allows for solidarity amongst strangers. The idea of solidarity is central to Oakeshott's thought about the modern state. He asserts that the question of the ties that bind members of a state to one another is one of the least tangible themes of modern European political thought. In so far as Oakeshott conceives of the modern state as an historical association, I claim that the bonds which unite members of such a state comprise legends of political life, constructs of imagination, time and circumstance, which make sense of 'the long enjoyment of a common experience of living together'.[6] This is how I understand the constructed element in Oakeshott's political thought.

In order to demonstrate that Oakeshott's political thought is foundational, I determined in Chapter 3 that Oakeshott defends a form of politics which incorporates contingent and permanent elements and that this mixed form of politics therefore necessarily implies foundations. However, I showed that, for Oakeshott, contingency must dominate the mixture. This led me to argue that the foundations present in Oakeshott's thought are contingent foundations. Thus, this establishes a constitutive element of legends of political life: they combine contingency and permanence, but contingency must be the dominant element. I concluded the chapter by demonstrating that poetry corresponds to this criterion and that in poetic activity permanence and contingency are united.

In chapters 2, 3 and 4, I ascertained political legends' constitutive elements. These are foundational reflection upon the political, the practical past and poetry. First, the purpose of a legend of political life is to allow a society to understand its political experience, whether it be

---

4   J. Seery 1999: 471.
5   *Ibid.*: 472.
6   *LHPT*: 425.

actual or imaginary, in the idiom of general ideas. I argue that this sort of reflection is foundational since it is centred upon and aims to fix a political society's identity. As such, political legends are knowledge of an already familiar political world and they remain tied to the political experience from which they spring. In other words, a legend of political life seeks to determine a society's identity and deepen a society's knowledge of itself. Thus, they are a reflective enterprise centred upon politics, but of an explanatory and foundational kind.

As for the practical past, Oakeshott asserts that it is an 'indispensable ingredient of an articulate civilized life'.[7] Oakeshott could not be clearer, human living-together cannot be sustained without the practical past which is composed of symbolic persons, actions, utterances, situations and artefacts. Imagination is indispensable to civilized life, and this is the case because it is responsible for endowing individuals and associations of individuals with their identity. The practical past does this by recalling to mind a past experience in order to join a puzzling or intractable present with a known and unproblematic past so as to compose a more manageable present.[8] This is well demonstrated not only in the case of Rome where the foundation of Rome by Romulus is recalled to mind, but also in the example of England where Magna Carta is the survived artefact which forms the basis of the English political legend. In this sense, the practical past stabilizes the practical present. The virtue of such a past, which is ultimately the product of the practical imagination, Oakeshott holds, is to endow a society with an unequivocal lineage and character.[9] It is in terms of the practical past that a society comes to recognize itself and to gain its sense of self-understanding, both of which are fundamental to human living-together.

Finally, legends of political life are creations of poetry. Poetry plays a dual, perhaps contradictory, role in relation to the political since poetic activity is at once contingent and permanent. Human activity, Oakeshott argues, is poetic in so far as it is a contingent, not overly reflective habit of behaviour. I show that to this contingent understanding of the poetic character of human activity may be added a second, permanent or foundational understanding. Poetry is foundational in that it not only endows a society with its identity and sense of self-consciousness, but it founds the identity by guarding the society against the corruption of its consciousness by creating and recreating its values and ensuring that it knows itself. In other words, poetry

---

7   *OH*: 48.
8   *OH*: 18.
9   *WH*: 347.

allows for a society's identity to be amplified, but not in a manner in which change would render the society unrecognizable to itself. Poetry fulfils this foundational role by means of legends of political life, which are, in essence, poetic constructs. Political legends endow societies with their identity and guard their sense of self-consciousness from the perils of contingency. It is my position, then, that legends are a mixture of practice and poetry. It will be objected that poetry and practice cannot interact in this manner since Oakeshott staunchly defends the independence of the modes of experience. However, I argue that Oakeshott himself observes that the emancipation of poetry from the authority of practice is difficult and that it has only been uncertainly achieved in modernity. I make the case that this is because humans need creations and works which carry a meaning, transmit a message or which are symbolic. It is what allows them to build a world of sense and meaning and which tells them who they are, where they are in the world and how they came to be there. What is more, it is these creations, mixtures of practice and poetry, which allow humans and their societies to project themselves into the future. Humans cannot do without creations and constructs which are the joint realization of practice and poetry. The world would simply be unfit for human life. Imagination and practice, therefore, are intimately linked. Politically, it is through legends that imagination works to bring meaning, sense and, importantly, stability to political societies.

Together, then, the practical past, foundational reflection upon the political and poetry are what constitute legends of political life, the form taken by imagination to manifest itself politically. Consequently, political legends may be defined as poetic constructs which tell the story of a past event and which allow societies to understand their political experience in the idiom of general ideas. Legends of political life stabilize a problematic, uncertain present by endowing a political society with its sense of identity and by guarding it against the corruption of its consciousness. It is in this sense that I contend that they serve as weak foundations for the political since they found a society's identity. Political legends are weak foundations in that they combine contingency and permanence. By this I mean that a society's legend, and therefore its identity, may be at once augmented and also preserved. Thus, imagination, and more specifically legends of political life, is an indispensable ingredient of human living-together.

I argue that Oakeshott models his own conception of legends of political life upon the Roman political legend. A legend of political life is an evoked past and a work of art. As such, it has to be created, learned, cared for and cultivated. The example of Ancient Rome is illustrative of this. The Roman political legend is the creation of Roman poets. It tells the story of the foundation of Rome by Romulus which symbolizes the foundation of Roman freedom. This is precisely what Oakeshott means by an evoked past. The foundation of Rome is an event recalled to mind from the practical past and which endows Roman society with its heightened sense of political self-consciousness. Moreover, the Roman legend represents the beliefs Romans had about the sort of community they believed themselves to constitute. In other words, the Roman legend, while not philosophy, allows for the intellectual organization of political ideas. Moreover, Roman political experience provides further insight into legends by demonstrating in greater depth how they serve as weak foundations for the political. The foundation was deemed to be sacred by the Romans, but this does not mean that it was left untouched. On the contrary, the Romans augmented the original foundation and freedom by exploring its intimations and by binding all change back to the foundational legend. This practice, which allows for the Roman identity to be augmented and, yet, also preserved, is one that has been adopted by all modern political societies which are always returning to their political legend within the context of the process of its revision and enlargement. The Roman political experience exemplifies how political foundations may unite permanence and contingency.

What comes through in the discussion of the relationship between imagination and the political is Oakeshott's conservatism in both its Roman and poetic dimensions. Identity, whether a person's or a society's, is of fundamental importance to Oakeshott's political thought. The concept of the conservative disposition he develops is entirely concerned with identity. Oakeshott's objective is to find a manner in which a political society may assimilate change without becoming unrecognizable to itself. That is, without its identity being corrupted. In sum, what the Conservative seeks to preserve is a society's identity. For Oakeshott, I argue, this may be achieved in two ways. First, a society may assimilate change, if, like the Romans, it explores the intimations of its political legend and binds all change back to the narrative. Secondly, a society's identity may be preserved if its poetic character is respected. Only poetry can safeguard a society's self-consciousness from the corruption brought on by political change. Thus, I conclude that Oakeshott's conservatism is deeply poetic as well as inspired by the Roman political experience. The importance of identity to Oakeshott's political thought cannot be overstated, nor can the role played by imagination in ensuring its conservation.

Finally, given the importance Oakeshott lends to a society's or a civilization's identity and sense of self-consciousness, his writings in general, and the essay 'Rationalism in Politics' in particular, may be read in a new and different light. When the essay is read in the context of his concern for identity and self-consciousness, what becomes immediately evident is Oakeshott's profound concern for the fate of Western Europe's consciousness. While this is true of all his works, his concern is most urgently and forcefully expressed in 'Rationalism in Politics'. Within this perspective, his critique of Rationalism may be interpreted as a warning about the threat it poses for Europe's consciousness. Simply put, Rationalism threatens to corrupt European civilization's consciousness. In this essay, Oakeshott attempts to guard Europe's identity by alerting it to the immediate danger it faces. Given that only poetry can protect a civilization against the corruption of its consciousness, I claim that, in this respect, 'Rationalism in Politics' is best understood not as a work of philosophy, but as a work of poetry. The essay is Oakeshott's poetic attempt to save Europe's consciousness from corruption. He does this by ensuring that European civilization knows itself by recalling and recreating its myth of civilization. Following his interpretation of *Leviathan* as a myth, Oakeshott's aim is to enrich the dream which is European civilization. In this sense, just as he contends that Hobbes is not always engaged in philosophy, but that he is, more significantly, involved in literature, I make the same claim in regards to Oakeshott.

My aim has been to show that imagination is an 'indispensable ingredient' of Oakeshott's political thought. Oakeshott's thinking on the political cannot be properly understood without taking it into account. However, thus far, this entire sphere of his political thought has largely been ignored or overlooked by commentators, perhaps because imagination is deemed not to be a serious subject of investigation nor of philosophical consequence. As a result, when writing about Oakeshott and human living-together, commentators generally focus their attention upon the civil condition and civil association, a rule-articulated association which only requires *cives* to recognize the authority of the rules of association as rules, and conclude that his thought is devoid of foundations. While I agree that Edenic foundations are not to be found in Oakeshott's thought, I do not agree with the conclusion that his thought is altogether devoid of foundations.[10] What this interpretation neglects is imagination, a subject to which Oakeshott devotes a considerable part of his writings. Furthermore, once the role of imagination is explicated, it is possible to see the far reaching consequences it has for the political. Imagination is intimately linked to identity, a central element of Oakeshott's political thought. While a political society's rules may not require foundations, its identity does. I

---

[10] J. Seery 1999: 471.

posit that for Oakeshott it requires a particular kind of foundation, what I have called contingent foundations, which are essentially weak foundations. These foundations, which combine contingency and permanence, are the creation of imagination. I claim that legends of political life are constructed foundations which not only endow political societies with their identity, but guard them as well. A society's identity is thus founded by imagination. More is required in sustaining the bonds that unite members of a political society to one another than the mere recognition of the authority of rules. Following the dissolution of communal ties, a modern political society requires a strong sense of self-consciousness, of self-understanding and of self-knowledge which can only be provided by political legends. Legends of political life thus stabilize an otherwise problematic present by constructing a world of sense and meaning for humans to inhabit. It is the only manner in which humans can make themselves at home in the world, a primordial human activity, Oakeshott insists. Thus, if one ignores the imagination in Oakeshott's political thought, one inevitably fails to see the role it plays in founding and sustaining a political society's identity. Consequently, while it is certainly important to reflect upon Oakeshott's writings on the civil condition, this cannot be done at the cost of neglecting what he has to say about imagination and identity if his conception of human living-together is to be properly understood.

In conclusion, my objective has been to give imagination its rightful place in Oakeshott's political thought and attempt to rehabilitate it for political theory in general, as a form of weak foundationalism necessary for the self-understanding and identity of a people. To remind us of the importance of imagination and legends of political life for politics is certainly one of the important contributions Oakeshott makes to political theory. The discipline should heed his example and consider imagination to be an 'indispensable ingredient' of human life and politics worthy not only of study, but of being a central subject of investigation.

Bibliography

WORKS BY MICHAEL OAKESHOTT

OAKESHOTT, M. 1921. Shylock the Jew. *The Caian* 30, pp. 61–7.

OAKESHOTT, M. 1995. *Experience and Its Modes*. Cambridge: Cambridge University Press.

OAKESHOTT, M. and Griffith, G.T. 1936. *A Guide to the Classics, or, How to Pick the Derby Winner*. London: Faber and Faber.

OAKESHOTT, M. 1941. *The Social and Political Doctrines of Contemporary Europe*. Cambridge: Cambridge University Press.

OAKESHOTT, M. and Griffith, G.T. 1947. *A New Guide to the Derby: How to Pick the Winner*. London: Faber and Faber.

OAKESHOTT, M. 1962. Review of Hannah Arendt's *Between Past and Future*. *Political Science Quarterly* 77(1), pp. 88–90.

OAKESHOTT, M. 1991. *Rationalism in Politics and other essays: New and Expanded Edition*. Indianapolis: Liberty Fund.

OAKESHOTT, M. 1965. *Rationalism in Politics*: A Reply to Professor Raphael. *Political Studies* XIII, pp. 89–92.

OAKESHOTT, M. 1975. *On Human Conduct*. Oxford: Oxford University Press.

OAKESHOTT, M. 2000. *Hobbes on Civil Association*. Indianapolis: Liberty Fund.

OAKESHOTT, M. 1976. On Misunderstanding Human Conduct: A Reply To My Critics. *Political Theory* 4(3), pp. 353–367.

OAKESHOTT, M. 1999. *On History and Other Essays*. Indianapolis: Liberty Fund.

OAKESHOTT, M. 2001. *The Voice of Liberal Learning*. Indianapolis: Liberty Fund.

FULLER, T. ed. OAKESHOTT, M. 1993a. *Religion, Politics, and the Moral Life*. New Haven: Yale University Press.

LETWIN, S.R. ed. OAKESHOTT, M. 1993b. *Morality and Politics in Modern Europe: The Harvard Lectures*. New Haven and London: Yale University Press.

FULLER, T. ed. OAKESHOTT, M. 1996. *The Politics of Faith and the Politics of Scepticism.* New Haven and London: Yale University Press.

O'SULLIVAN, L. ed. OAKESHOTT, M. 2004. *What is History? and other essays.* Exeter: Imprint Academic.

NARDIN, T. and O'SULLIVAN, L. eds. OAKESHOTT, M. 2006. *Lectures in the History of Political Thought.* Exeter: Imprint Academic.

O'SULLIVAN, L. ed. OAKESHOTT, M. 2007. *The Concept of a Philosophical Jurisprudence: Essays and Reviews 1926–51.* Exeter: Imprint Academic.

O'SULLIVAN, L. ed. OAKESHOTT, M. 2008. *The Vocabulary of a Modern European State: Essays and Reviews 1952–88.* Exeter: Imprint Academic.

SECONDARY LITERATURE ON MICHAEL OAKESHOTT

AUSPITZ, J.L. 1976. Individuality, Civility, and Theory: The Political Imagination of Michael Oakeshott. *Political Theory* 4(3), pp. 261–294.

BLUMLER, J.G. 1964. Politics, Poetry, and Practice. *Political Studies* 12, pp. 355–361.

BOUCHER, D. 1984. The Creation of the Past: British Idealism and Michael Oakeshott's Philosophy of History. *History and Theory* 23(2), pp. 193–214.

BOUCHER, D. 1991. Politics in a Different Mode: An Appreciation of Michael Oakeshott 1901–1990. *History of Political Thought* XII(4), pp. 717–728.

BOUCHER, D. 1993. Human Conduct, History, and Social Science in the Works of R.G. Collingwood and Michael Oakeshott. *New Literary History* 24(3), pp. 697–717.

BOUCHER, D. 2005a. Oakeshott, Freedom and Republicanism. *British Journal of Politics and International Relations* 7, pp. 81–96.

BOUCHER, D. 2005b. The Rule of Law in the Modern European State: Oakeshott and the Enlargement of Europe. *European Journal of Political Theory* 4(1), pp. 89–107.

BOUCHER, D. manuscript April, 2006. Michael Oakeshott and the Study of the History of Political Thought. Copy in the possession of the author.

BOUCHER, D. 2007. Oakeshott and the History of Political Thought. *Collingwood and British Idealism Studies* 13, pp. 69–101.

CAMPBELL COREY, E. 2006. *Michael Oakeshott on Religion, Aesthetics, and Politics.* Columbia and London: University of Missouri Press.

COATS, Jr., W.J. 1985. Michael Oakeshott as Liberal Theorist. *Canadian Journal of Political Science* XVIII(4), pp. 773–787.

COATS, Jr., W.J. 2000. *Oakeshott and His Contemporaries*. Selingsgrove: Susquehanna University Press and London: Associated University Press.

COATS, Jr., W.J. 2003. *Political Theory and Practice*. Selingsgrove: Susquehanna University Press and London: Associated University Press.

COATS, Jr., W.J. 2005. Michael Oakeshott and the Poetic Character of Human Activity. In: ABEL, C. and FULLER, T. eds. *The Intellectual Legacy of Michael Oakeshott*. Exeter: Imprint Academic. pp. 306–315.

CONNELLY, J. 1998. Art, History and Science: The Contrasting Worlds of Collingwood and Oakeshott. *Collingwood Studies* 4, pp. 184–196.

DAVIS, H. 1975. Poetry and the Voice of Michael Oakeshott. *British Journal of Aesthetics* 15(1), pp. 59–68.

FRANCO, P. 1990. Michael Oakeshott as Liberal Theorist. *Political Theory* 18(3), pp. 411–436.

FRANCO, P. 2000. Foreword. In: OAKESHOTT, M. 2000. *Hobbes on Civil Association*. Indianapolis: Liberty Fund.

FRANCO, P. 2003. The Shapes of Liberal Thought: Oakeshott, Berlin, and Liberalism. *Political Theory* 31(4), pp. 484–507.

FROHNEN, B.P. 1990. Oakeshott's Hobbesian Myth: Pride, Character and the Limits of Reason. *The Western Political Quarterly* 43(4), pp. 789–809.

FULLER, T. 1991. Introduction. In: OAKESHOTT, M. 1991. *Rationalism in Politics and other essays: New and Expanded Edition*. Indianapolis: Liberty Fund.

FULLER, T. 1993. Introduction. In: FULLER, T. ed. OAKESHOTT, M. 1993a. *Religion, Politics, and the Moral Life*. New Haven: Yale University Press.

FULLER, T. 1996. Introduction. In: FULLER, T. ed. OAKESHOTT, M. 1996. *The Politics of Faith and the Politics of Scepticism*. New Haven and London: Yale University Press.

FULLER, T. 1999. Foreword. In: OAKESHOTT, M. 1999. *On History and Other Essays*. Indianapolis: Liberty Fund.

FULLER, T. 2001. Foreword and Introduction. In: OAKESHOTT, M. 2001. *The Voice of Liberal Learning*. Indianapolis: Liberty Fund.

GERENSCER, S.A. 1995. Voices in Conversation: Philosophy and Politics in the Work of Michael Oakeshott. *The Journal of Politics* 57 (3), pp. 724–742.

GERENSCER, S.A. 1999. A Democratic Oakeshott? *Political Research Quality* 52(4), pp. 845–865.

GRANT, R.A.D. 2005. Oakeshott on the Nature and Place of Aesthetic Experience: A Critique. In: ABEL, C. and FULLER, T. eds. *The Intellectual Legacy of Michael Oakeshott*. Exeter: Imprint Academic. pp. 293–305.

GREENLEAF, W.H. 1966. *Oakeshott's Philosophical Politics*. London: Longmans, Green and Co. Ltd.

HADDOCK, B. 2005. Contingency and Judgement in Oakeshott's Political Thought. *European Journal of Political Theory* 4(1), pp. 7–21.

HAVARD, W.C. 1984. Michael Oakeshott Skeptical Idealist. *The Recovery of Political Theory: Limits and Possibilities*, Baton Rouge and London: Louisiana State University Press. pp. 149–172.

HOLLIDAY, I. 1992. On Michael Oakeshott. *Government and Opposition* 27(2), pp. 131–147.

KATZOFF, C. 1992. Oakeshott and the Practice of Politics. *Journal of Philosophical Research* 17, pp. 265–277.

MAPEL, D. 1990. Civil Association and the Idea of Contingency. *Political Theory* 18(3), pp. 392–410.

MARSH, L. 2005. Constructivism and Relativism in Oakeshott. In: ABEL, C. and FULLER, T. eds. *The Intellectual Legacy of Michael Oakeshott*. Exeter: Imprint Academic. pp. 238–262.

MEWES, H. 1992. Modern Individualism: Reflections on Oakeshott, Arendt, and Strauss. *Political Science Reviewer* 21(1), pp. 116–147.

MILLER, T.H. 2001. Oakeshott's Hobbes and the Fear of Political Rationalism. *Political Theory* 29(6), pp. 806–832.

MINOGUE, K. 1993. Introduction. In: LETWIN, S.R. ed. OAKESHOTT, M. 1993b. *Morality and Politics in Modern Europe: The Harvard Lectures*. New Haven and London: Yale University Press.

MINOGUE, K. 2004. Oakeshott and Political Science. *Annual Review of Political Science* 7, pp. 227–246.

MINOGUE, K. 2005. Oakeshott's Rationalism Revisited. In: ABEL, C. and FULLER, T. eds. *The Intellectual Legacy of Michael Oakeshott*. Exeter: Imprint Academic. pp. 182–193.

MODOOD, T. 1980. Oakeshott's Conceptions of Philosophy. *History of Political Thought*, I(2), pp. 315–322.

MOUFFE, C. 2005. *The Return of the Political*. London and New York: Verso.

NARDIN, T. and O'SULLIVAN, L. 2006. Introduction. In: NARDIN, T. and O'SULLIVAN, L. eds. OAKESHOTT, M. 2006. *Lectures in the History of Political Thought*. Exeter: Imprint Academic.

NORTON, D.L. 1987. Tradition and Autonomous Individuality. *The Journal of Value Inquiry* 21, pp. 131–140.

O'SULLIVAN, L. 2000. Michael Oakeshott on European Political History. *History of Political Thought* XXI(1), pp. 132–151.

O'SULLIVAN, L. 2003. *Oakeshott on History*. Exeter: Imprint Academic.

O'SULLIVAN, L. 2004. Introduction. In: O'SULLIVAN, L. ed. OAKESHOTT, M. 2004. *What is History? and other essays*. Exeter: Imprint Academic.

O'SULLIVAN, L. 2007. Introduction. In: O'SULLIVAN, L. ed. OAKESHOTT, M. 2007. *The Concept of a Philosophical Jurisprudence: Essays and Reviews 1926–51*. Exeter: Imprint Academic.

O'SULLIVAN, L. 2008. Introduction. In: O'SULLIVAN, L. ed. OAKESHOTT, M. 2008. *The Vocabulary of a Modern European State: Essays and Reviews 1952–88*. Exeter: Imprint Academic. pp. 1–37.

O'SULLIVAN, N. 2002. Why Read Oakeshott? *Society* 39(3), pp. 71–74.

PAREKH, B. 1979. The Political Philosophy of Michael Oakeshott. *British Journal of Political Science* 9(4), pp. 481–506.

PAREKH, B. 1995. Oakeshott's Theory of Civil Association. *Ethics* 106, pp. 158–186.

PITKIN, H.F. 1976. Inhuman Conduct and Unpolitical Theory: Michael Oakeshott's *On Human Conduct*. *Political Theory* 4(3), pp. 301–320.

PITKIN, H.F. 1973. The Roots of Conservatism: Michael Oakeshott and the Denial of Politics. *Dissent* 20(4), pp. 496–525.

PODOKSIK, E. 2002. The Voice of Poetry in the Thought of Michael Oakeshott. *Journal of the History of Ideas* 63(4), pp. 717–733.

PODOKSIK, E. 2003a. *In Defence of Modernity: Vision and Philosophy in Michael Oakeshott*. Exeter: Imprint Academic.

PODOKSIK, E. 2003b. Oakeshott's Theory of Freedom as Recognized Contingency. *European Journal of Political Theory* 2(1), pp. 57–77.

PODOKSIK, E. 2005. How Oakeshott Became an Oakeshottean. *European Journal of Political Theory* 4(1), pp. 67–88.

PODOKSIK, E. 2009. Commentary on Elizabeth Corey's Interpretation of Michael Oakeshott. *Zygon* 44(1), pp. 223–226.

RAPAHEL, D.D. 1964. Professor Oakeshott's *Rationalism in Politics*. *Political Studies* XII(1), pp. 202–215.

RAPHAEL, D.D. 1965. *Rationalism in Politics*: A Note on Professor Oakeshott's Reply. *Political Studies* XIII, pp. 395–397.

RAYNER, J. 1985. The Legend of Oakeshott's Conservatism: Sceptical Philosophy and Limited Politics. *Canadian Journal of Political Science* XVIII(2), pp. 313–338.

RILEY, P. 1992. Michael Oakeshott, Philosopher of Individuality. *The Review of Politics* 54(4), pp. 649–664.

RORTY, R. 1988. The Priority of Democracy to Philosophy. In: PETERSON, M.D. and VAUGHAN, R.C. eds. *The Virginia Statute for Religious Freedom*. Cambridge: Cambridge University Press. pp. 257–282.

RORTY, R. 1989. *Contingency, Irony and Solidarity*. Cambridge: Cambridge University Press.

RUSHTON, M. 1992. Michael Oakeshott: A Review Essay. *The Review of Politics* 54(3), pp. 665–674.

SEDEYN, O. 1995. Présentation du traducteur: La philosophie politique de Michaël Oakeshott. *De La Conduite Humaine*, Paris: Presses Universitaires de France, pp.vii–xxxiv.

SMITH, T.W. 1996. Michael Oakeshott on History, Practice and Political Theory. *History of Political Thought* XVII(4), pp. 591–614.

SPITZ, D. 1976. A Rationalist *Malgré Lui*: The Perplexities of Being Michael Oakeshott. *Political Theory* 4(3), pp. 335–352.

THOMPSON, M.P. 2005. Intimations of Poetry in Practical Life. In: ABEL, C. and FULLER, T. eds. *The Intellectual Legacy of Michael Oakeshott*. Exeter: Imprint Academic. pp. 281–292.

TREGENZA, I. 1997. The Life of Hobbes in the Writings of Michael Oakeshott. *History of Political Thought* XVIII(3), pp. 531–557.

TREGENZA, I. 2002. Leviathan as Myth: Michael Oakeshott and Carl Schmitt on Hobbes and the Critique of Rationalism. *Contemporary Political Theory* 1(3), pp. 349–369.

TSENG, R. 2003. *The Sceptical Idealist*. Exeter: Imprint Academic.

VINCENT, A. 2004. *The Nature of Political Theory*. Oxford: Oxford University Press.

WALSH, W.H. 1968. The Practical and the Historical Past. In: KING, P. and PAREKH, B.C. eds. *Politics and Experience*. Cambridge: Cambridge University Press. pp. 5–18.

WATKINS, J.W.N. 1952. Political Tradition and Political Theory: An Examination of Professor Oakeshott's Political Philosophy. *The Philosophical Quarterly* 2(9), pp. 323–337.

WELLS, H. 1994. The Philosophical Michael Oakeshott. *Journal of the History of Ideas* 55(1), pp. 129–145.

WOLIN, S.S. 1976. The Politics of Self-Disclosure. *Political Theory* 4(3), pp. 321–334.

WORTHINGTON, G. 1995. Michael Oakeshott on Life: Waiting with Godot. *History of Political Thought* XVI(1), pp. 105–119.

WORTHINGTON, G. 1997. Oakeshott's Claims of Politics. *Political Studies* XLV, pp. 727–738.

WORTHINGTON, G. 2000. Michael Oakeshott and the City of God. *Political Theory* 28(3), pp. 377–398.

WORTHINGTON, G. 2002. The Voice of Poetry in Oakeshott's Moral Philosophy. *The Review of Politics* 64(2), pp. 285–310.

WORTHINGTON, G. 2005. Poetic Experience and the Good Life in the Writings of Michael Oakeshott. *European Journal of Political Theory* 4(1), pp. 57–66.

SECONDARY LITERATURE

ANDERSON, B. 1996. *Imagined Communities*. London and New York: Verso.

ARENDT, H. 1998. *The Human Condition*. Chicago and London: The University of Chicago Press.

ARENDT, H. 1993. *Between Past and Future*. London: Penguin Books.

ARENDT, H. 1963. *On Revolution*. New York: The Viking Press.

British Library. 2008. *Want to know the facts about Magna Carta?* [WWW] <URL:http://www.bl.uk/onlinegallery/themes/histtexts/magn acarta.html> [Accessed 26 March, 2008]

BUTLER, J. 1991. Contingent Foundations: Feminism and the Question of 'Postmodernism'. *Praxis International* 11(2), pp. 150–165.

COLLINGWOOD, R.G. 1945. *The Principles of Art*. Oxford: The Clarendon Press.

GOTTSCHALL, J. and SLOAN WILSON, D. eds. 2005. *The Literary Animal: Evolution and the Nature of Narrative*. Evanston: Northwestern University Press.

HAMILTON, MADISON, and JAY. 2003. *The Federalist with Letters of 'Brutus'*. Cambridge: Cambridge University Press.

KRASNOFF, L. 1999. How Kantian is Constructivism? *Kant-Studien* 90, Jahrg., S., pp. 385–409.

LABELLE, G. 1998. Le 'Préambule' à la 'Déclaration de souveraineté': penser la fondation au-delà de la 'matrice théologico-politique'? *Canadian Journal of Political Science* XXXI(4), pp. 659–681.

RORTY, R. 1988. The Priority of Democracy to Philosophy. In: PETERSON, M.D. and VAUGHAN, R.C. eds. *The Virginia Statute for Religious Freedom*. Cambridge: Cambridge University Press. pp. 257–282.

SEERY, J.E. 1999. Castles in the Air: An Essay on Political Foundations. *Political Theory* 27(4), pp. 460–490.

STROUD, D.I. 1998. *Magna Carta*. Southampton: Paul Cave Publications Ltd.

THÉRIAULT, J.Y. 2002. *Critique de l'américanité: Mémoire et démocratie au Québec*. Montréal: Éditions Québec Amérique.

Index